Already Doing It

ALREADY DOING IT

Intellectual Disability and Sexual Agency

MICHAEL GILL

University of Minnesota Press
Minneapolis / London

The University of Minnesota Press gratefully acknowledges financial assistance for the publication of this book from the Committee for Support of Faculty Scholarship at Grinnell College.

An earlier version of chapter 1 was published as "Rethinking Sexual Abuse, Questions of Consent, and Intellectual Disability," *Sexuality Research and Social Policy* 7, no. 3 (2010): 201–13; reprinted by permission of Springer. A portion of chapter 2 appeared as "Sex Education and Young Adults with Intellectual Disabilities: Crisis Response, Sexual Diversity, and Pleasure," in *The Myth of the Normal Curve,* ed. Curt Dudley-Marling and Alex Gurn, 171–86 (New York: Peter Lang, 2010); reprinted with permission of Peter Lang International Academic Publishers. An earlier version of chapter 3 was published as "Sex Can Wait, Masturbate: The Politics of Masturbation Training," *Sexualities* 15, nos. 3–4 (2012): 472–93; reprinted with permission of Sage Publications, Ltd. An earlier version of chapter 7 was published as "*The Specials* Meet the Lady Boys of Bangkok: Sexual and Gender Transgression, and Smashing Intellectual Disability," *The Review of Education, Pedagogy, and Cultural Studies* 34, nos. 3–4 (2012): 156–69; reprinted by permission of Taylor & Francis Ltd.

Published by the University of Minnesota Press
111 Third Avenue South, Suite 290
Minneapolis, MN 55401-2520
http://www.upress.umn.edu

Library of Congress Cataloging-in-Publication Data
Gill, Michael Carl.
    Already doing it : intellectual disability and sexual agency / Michael Gill.
    Includes bibliographical references and index.
    ISBN 978-0-8166-8297-3 (hc: alk. paper) — ISBN 978-0-8166-8298-0 (pb: alk. paper)
    I. Title.
    [DNLM: 1. Intellectual Disability. 2. Sexuality. 3. Education of Intellectually Disabled. 4. Sex Education. 5. Sex Offenses. WM 307.S3] RC570
    362.3—dc23

                                                                2014019915

Printed in the United States of America on acid-free paper

The University of Minnesota is an equal-opportunity educator and employer.

21 20 19 18 17 16 15   10 9 8 7 6 5 4 3 2 1

For 은정

Contents

Preface

Violations of Sexual Life

This project began out of personal experience. Early on in my graduate education in disability studies, one of my professors asked the students in her class about our earliest memory of disability. Immediately, I thought back to my then-recent work at a sheltered workshop for people with developmental and intellectual disabilities.[1] Prior to en tering graduate school, I provided vocational support in Spokane County, Washington. I replied to the professor's inquiry with a sterile and rehearsed answer, something about my experience working as a job coach and support staff member. It was not until the bus ride home after class that I recalled previous encounters with disability— encounters that escaped me only moments earlier.

When I was six or seven years old, I was at the Spokane Interstate Fair with my parents and siblings. In between the countless carnival rides and livestock animal exhibits, our family decided to take a dinner break. The fair was crowded and seating limited. After getting our meals, we decided to join another family—a mother, father, and daughter—at an open picnic table. As we sat down to eat, I was focused solely on my hot dog and fried cheese. But after a few minutes, I began to take notice of the other family. The daughter, who wasn't much older than I was, was being fed by her mother. As she ate, some of her food escaped her mouth and ran down her face and onto the bib draped around her neck. For some reason it was difficult for her to keep the entire contents of each bite of food in her mouth. My curiosity and fear were ignited; I could not keep my eyes off the family. Even my prized hot dog had lost its appeal. Sensing my fascination and abjection at what I was witnessing, my parents quickly gathered us up and left the table. Only looking back on the experience as an adult was I able to realize that my staring and othering of this girl and her parents was a result of my own learned fear of difference and disability. The girl's parents were trying to let their child enjoy the fair—the same thing that my parents wanted for me. The other experience is much more benign. As a child I had a babysitter with an intellectual disability. I did not realize this. To me, she was just my babysitter. Much like other babysitters, she assumed the role of surrogate parent when she was taking care of my siblings and me by cooking for, bathing, and disciplining us. She was a great babysitter. We played games, ate junk food, and often had impromptu dance parties. I did not perceive her as different; I had no knowledge at the time that she was disabled. I often wished my parents would go on a date so she would come over to babysit. Unlike the girl at the fair, I knew my babysitter and liked her. Disability in my home with her was natural, albeit without the label of "disability." I was in my twenties before my mom told me that our babysitter had an intellectual disability.

These experiences are quite different from each other. In one, I experienced disability as something alien; in the other, I did not realize there was disability. To this day, I am not sure why I did not share these experiences with my classmates. Perhaps I was ashamed at my response to the girl at the fair, even though I was a very young child. Maybe I thought that my experience working at a sheltered workshop was "more authentic," "relevant," and "professional" in the graduate school classroom. Irrespective of the reasoning, I chose to ignore (or forget) the earliest experiences with disability for the sake of the expected answer. Instead of finding the personal political, I depoliticized both stories in order to share my story of working in the sheltered workshop. My response to this class activity, which was set up for the students and professor to become acquainted, continues to have a profound impact on my exploration of disability. I remain committed to the exploration of disability as a *cultural process* that can be seen as marked, while also recognizing that disability is very much unmarked in other settings and circumstances. I examine intellectual disability as an embodied experience and focus on why the condition is constructed as an *impairment* that seems to require a certain degree of professionalization. As a result, the diagnostic category is often nebulous and imprecise. The nebulous nature can result in overarching authority, where those with training and graduate degrees are able to make assessments regarding competence, independence, and quality of life. This professionalization of intellectual disability management, especially in relation to sexuality, is the focus of my work.

The Nigerian writer Chimamanda Ngozi Adichie in her widely circulated TED talk discusses "the danger of the single story." Adichie conveys how her American roommate in college viewed her based on a "single story of catastrophe," where "her default position toward me, as an African, was a kind of patronizing, well-meaning pity." Accordingly, this single story didn't allow for any "possibility of Africans being similar to her in any way, no possibility of feelings more complex than pity, no possibility of a connection as human equals." This type of single story, that reinforces a position of an "other," is reflected in Western literature and popular images, where Africa becomes "a place of beautiful landscapes, beautiful animals, and incomprehensible people, fighting senseless wars, dying of poverty and AIDS, unable to speak for themselves and waiting to be saved by a kind, white foreigner."[2] While the context is different, and I think it is vital to recognize these differences, I am struck thinking if what I thought I knew about disability was based on a single story. In particular, prior to working in the sheltered workshop, I know that certain ideas about intellectual disability, especially in relation to notions of competence, self-determination, and rationality, were based on a single story—one that was daily challenged and made more complex as I interacted and became colleagues and friends with my co-workers. When discussing this project, I often encounter a response that imagines the most "severe" case. These responses, a type of single story, seek to discredit any effort to advocate for the sexual and reproductive rights of individuals with intellectual disabilities in the name of severity of disability. Intellectual disability as a category and identity is diverse. Put differently, the experiences and desires of individuals with labels of intellectual disabilities ought to be given the complexity afforded to other individuals without the label, in a way that doesn't exclude those who are configured as the most "severe." I, too, also wonder how my own life—negotiations with and experiences of gender, sexuality, and disability—is in danger of being read through a single story. As a feminist disability studies scholar, how can I inhabit the contradictions, ambiguities, and motivations of my stories?

For example, in thinking about stories, I find myself also reflecting about my relationship to the category of disability. I have at various times in the past depended on a medical model of disability to pharma-cologically treat depression. Quite possibly I might find myself seeking this type of intervention in the future. What these past (and future?) in-teractions have to do with disability identity claims are perhaps more complicated. As I write this preface, I identify as currently not dis-abled, or to turn the phrase linguistically, as marginally able-bodied. I can envision and imagine, even desire, a future disabled self. For example, I might inhabit the category of intellectual disability in the future. I also think of my own potentially fatal allergies to tree nuts. I depend on portable medical technology in the form of self-injectable epinephrine to remain safe while eating and negotiating a desire to be social and spontaneous. Personal, family, and professional histories of disability affect my scholarship and political ideology.

I am also remembering the times when my professional role re-sulted in regulating of sexual behavior. Deciding what people should do, reinforcing desirable behaviors, can be a daily occurrence in the workshop, group home, or classroom. Adichie comments, "Power is the ability not just to tell the story of another person, but to make it the definitive story of that person."[3] As a staff member in a sheltered workshop and later a job coach, I was instructed about which behav-iors to be on the lookout for, including biting, slapping, and pinch-ing; I was bestowed with professional able-bodied disciplinary power. This behavior observation and redirection can censor individual will. There were occasions in my tenure working in employment support for people with intellectual disabilities that I had to redirect individu-als from self-injury.[4] There were also times in which I attempted to regulate individual choice because I considered or was told that the behavior was inappropriate. My own disciplinary authority failed to understand or accommodate diverse motivations and realities; rather, I assumed intellectual disability meant certain things and not others, a type of single story.

Of these moments of regulation, two distinct personal experiences haunt my recollection of my time working as an employment profes-sional. These experiences within the workshop are directly related to sexuality, specifically the apparent "need" to regulate sexual ex-pression of individuals with intellectual disabilities. I share these ex-periences here as one way to open this work, as they illustrate how professionals working with individuals with intellectual disabilities become authorized to regulate sexual behaviors, even if no behaviors are present. These efforts of regulation are tangible signs of the degree of sexual repression in which individuals operate. I also participated in these efforts of regulation at the same time I was exploring my own sense of sexuality, illustrating a failure on my part to identify with my disabled contemporaries. The various registers of diversity, including aspects of sexuality, of my disabled contemporaries were covered over by a single story that individuals with intellectual disabilities ought not be sexual, while my own personal understanding of sexuality was more fluid and emerging.

I remember when the phone call came into our office. Home site staff had called to tell the workshop about some observed sexual behaviors between two of our employees.[5] These particular employees had recently been viewed holding hands and kissing in their private room at their house. Home site staff interpreted these activities as an indication of a lesbian relationship. Home site staff and the family of one of the women judged the relationship inappropriate and as a result these women were moved to separate rooms and told the behaviors were unacceptable. As a result of this information, the workshop staff decided to separate these women in any future work settings, often placing them at opposite ends of the workshop. We (the staff) were also now actively seeking out any displays of affection, intimacy, or even friendship between these two women that could be interpreted as sexual or leading to sexual actions. Effectively, although we were supposed to provide employment for these women labeled as intellectually disabled, we were now regulating behaviors not necessarily related to work efficiency. This regulation occurred because of a phone call from a home site staff member, without communicating to these women why we were regulating their behaviors, or allowing them to challenge our choices. Sexuality was a threat in the workshop. We used our authority as professionals in the workshop, in collaboration with home site staff. This example illustrates the almost automatic regulation of sexual behaviors, found so often in group homes, classrooms, and workshops. Service delivery professionals are given unbridled ability to restrain any sexual expression of individuals with intellectual disabilities.

The other personal example is more explicitly sexual and illustrative of a direct attempt to regulate sexual activity. After leaving the sheltered workshop, I took a position as a job coach providing individual employment support to a young man working in the community, Frank.[6] Frank and I were about the same age. Usually, Frank was accompanied to work by a personal assistant who assisted him in using the restroom either before or after work. On this particular day, the personal assistant did not accompany Frank, so I volunteered to assist Frank in transferring to the toilet. After transferring Frank, I left to let Frank use the restroom in private. I waited outside the restroom for almost fifteen minutes before getting worried that something had happened to Frank. Without knocking, I entered the restroom and found Frank masturbating. Immediately, I told Frank that this was not appropriate and instructed him to stop. After he did, I helped transfer him back to his wheelchair. Despite the fact that he was masturbating in a private, single-stall restroom, I thought that he should not be masturbating. I denied Frank's private activity of sexuality, exerting authority I didn't have as a temporary personal assistant. Later I would share this story with my boss and Frank's personal assistant, which led them to discuss with Frank the appropriateness of his masturbation. I denied his right to sexual activity when I told him it was inappropriate for him to be masturbating. Regardless of whether it is "appropriate" that Frank masturbated in a restroom at his work site, my intrusion into his space and choice to share this with my supervisor and others, based on my nondisabled professional authority, illustrates the exact type of professional regulation that this book argues against. Although there are active efforts to restrict or constrain sexual activities of individuals with intellectual disabilities, individuals are already sexual in these regulatory spaces.[7] Other individuals, however, because of sexual ableism, constrained choice, professional oversight, or other modes of restriction, are unable to participate in sexual activity.

In both incidents, I participated in or single-handedly orchestrated a violation of sexual rights. I violated Frank's privacy, interrupted his masturbation, and reported it, to appease my own unease at what I observed. My reaction was immediate, a type of learned reflex. For the women in the workshop, I acted as part of a team. We determined that we did not want their relationship to influence their work performance. This memory illustrates our heterosexist, ableist assumptions disguised as "naïveté." We assumed the women had just initiated this relationship and that separating them would put a swift and decisive end to it. We did not recognize that they were capable and competent actors in determining their own sexual lives. We did not realize that individuals with intellectual disabilities are capable in claiming their sexual identities. Rather, we thought it highly inappropriate that these two adult women would engage in a lesbian relationship, in the privacy of their home. Our apparent authority in the workshop extended into the women's private lives at home, despite no formal arrangement between the two organizations. This division between the public and private spheres is often unclear for disabled people and is in need of challenge. For example, can these two women be lovers in public? Additionally, we allowed the home site staff to dictate to us what we should be doing. The result in both experiences is the same. Sexual activity was policed based on assumptions about not only when and where one can be sexual, but also who can be sexual. Efforts to extend sexuality based on assumptions of capacity will inevitably exclude those assumed to be incapable. Even if the individuals attempted to counteract our efforts, we held onto our "authority" to act with quick and determined measures to desexualize individuals. Of course, Frank, much like his nondisabled coworkers, likely masturbated again since that day and the two women still found ways to be sexual with each other despite the systemic denial of the home and workshop staff. Individuals with intellectual disabilities have been practicing sexuality in the middle of oppressive regimes of desexualization through institutionalized violations, while others are unable to participate in sexual activities because of these controls.

In feminist and disability studies classes, I came to realize that these moments were violations. Feminism and disability studies theories and insights allowed me to reflectively examine these moments, and others, to contemplate what enabled my involvement and the political implications of such actions, especially as they pertain to the sexuality and reproduction of individuals labeled intellectually disabled. This book is the result of these inquiries. These two examples illustrate to what extent individual sexual agency can be restricted or repressed, subject to the danger of a single story. Individuals with intellectual disabilities are largely seen as perversely sexual, to the point of requiring some regulation to limit their sexual expressions. Despite violations of the sexuality of individuals through sterilization, segregation, invasive birth control methods (e.g., IUDs), and promotion of masturbation training as an "approved" method of sexual expression, some individuals with intellectual disabilities lead sexually active lives. These efforts to restrict sexuality, much like my own, illustrate the oppressive environment in which individuals navigate their sexuality. In what follows, I carefully advocate for an approach that not only recognizes individual agency but also a sexuality that is pleasurable. I also advocate that the reproductive desires of individuals should be respected. A sustained engagement with the claims in this work challenges the propensity to deny individual agency at the expense of protectionism. Individuals with intellectual disabilities can live sexually satisfying lives while gaining larger cultural recognition for their practices and choices.

When it comes to sexuality, the research that has been conducted specifically for this population follows two trajectories: (1) qualitative examinations of parental, teacher, social service, and general public views on sexuality for this population; and (2) studies determining the overall effectiveness of sex education for greater comprehension of how to use condoms, masturbate, and avoid sexually transmitted infections.[8] Most of the research concludes that "successful" approaches of sexuality for this population involve structure and professional oversight, and does not recognize the sexual agency of people labeled as intellectually disabled. Instead, this research focuses on developing educational initiatives for this population with the hope of increased retention of "safe" and "appropriate" sexual knowledge comprehension as well as risk reduction in relation to sexual abuse.

To date, the research focus on sexuality and intellectual disability has been quite narrow. While a tremendous amount of research has been completed, a sustained and comprehensive critical disability studies discussion about sexuality and intellectual disability has yet to be undertaken. This book begins this work, offering the field a comprehensive document that reviews the relevant research and challenges the field to move the research forward. As such, this project attempts to answer a broad set of questions regarding sexuality for intellectually disabled adults:

- What are the ways sex education materials are used to instruct and what are the methods and content of these materials?
- How does the historical construction of the sexuality of intel-

lectually disabled adults as deviant influence the current construction of sexuality for nondisabled and disabled individuals?

- How is sexuality represented in Hollywood cinema and other cultural representations and what messages of sexuality are contained in these images?
- How can consent and acceptable risk be utilized regarding sexual expression despite a preponderance of sexual abuse perpetrated against this population?
- Does a discourse of sexual pleasure facilitate a liberatory rhetoric and practice of sexuality and reproduction for people with intellectual disability?

Somewhere in the intersecting realities of lived experiences, representations, and professional programming resides an understanding of intellectual disability. Imagined as three sides of a triangle, the features studied here provide the outline of the understanding of reality. My goal is to explain what lies inside—what makes up the area of the three dimensions of intellectual disability, especially in relation to sexuality, pleasure, consent, and reproduction. The conclusions demonstrate that real and meaningful systems change is needed in the day-to-day programming of services offered to people with intellectual disabilities. My hope is that *Already Doing It* provides an intervention by remapping the terrain of disability studies with an explicit focus on intellectual disability, and by making a significant contribution to complicating discussions of which bodies are sexual and reproductive citizens in the United States.

Textual Description of Cover

The image on the front cover is a purple metallic condom package. One side of the condom package is open, with the top almost torn completely off. On the condom wrapper printed in a circle in white font is "Already Doing It" and to the right side below the condom wrapper printed in purple is "Intellectual Disability and Sexual Agency." The background of the cover is yellow and the author's name appears in purple on the upper left corner in the space between the torn portion of the condom package and the remaining package as if it is emerging from the package.

Introduction

Sexual Ableism Exposed

In January 2011, the Honorable Mr. Justice Mostyn of the Court of Protection in the United Kingdom ruled that a forty-one-year-old man, "Alan," who has an intellectual disability, was banned from participating in sexual relations, particularly with his male partner, "Kieron." In the ruling, Alan is described as having "a vigorous sex drive" that "has led to sexual relations with persons of both genders, although it is not suggested that Alan has ever had heterosexual coitus."[1] The judge remarks in his ruling that Alan and Kieron's relationship involved penetrative anal sex, mutual masturbation, and oral sex. Both Alan and Kieron live in public housing. Kieron's disability status is not disclosed in the court ruling or subsequent journalistic accounts. The local housing council that provides residential housing and support for Alan brought the suit to restrict the relationship. This judicial example reflects an ableist trend to deny the sexual agency of individuals based on assumptions of inappropriateness and incompetency. Ableism in its most broad interpretation reflects discrimination or oppression of disabled people, which can take the form of denial of rights and access and the perpetuation of stigma, hatred, and othering.

The judge based his ruling on an assessment of Alan's inability to understand the following three areas: (1) the mechanics of the act; (2) that there are health risks involved, particularly the acquisition of sexually transmitted and sexually transmissible infections; (3) that sex between a man and a woman may result in the woman becoming pregnant.[2] In the final ruling, the judge instructed the support staff at Alan's home to provide him with sex education. After a period of nine months, Alan was to return to the court for a final ruling on his ability to engage and consent to sexual activities.[3]

This case helps to illuminate the following questions regarding sexuality and intellectual disability: Why is the sexuality of those with intellectual disabilities often seen as "risky" or "inappropriate" by teachers, parents, support staff, professionals, judges, and the media as well as those with the most daily contact with them (people with intellectual disabilities)? Does having an intellectual disability generate the perception of higher "risk" than having a physical disability? Is intellectual functioning a prerequisite to sexual behaviors? Should sexual citizenship depend on IQ levels? There are individuals who would answer affirmatively to those last two questions. In their view, people with an atypical level of intelligence should not be allowed to engage in sexual activity. Despite their faith in the ability of intelligence tests to accurately diagnose and measure, this constituency might not agree on what the cutoff point should be. This is further problematized by inconsistent and ever-changing assessments of intelligence.

The court ruling raises important questions around the intersections of homophobia and ableism. For example, legal blogger Anna Raccoon remarks that "this may not be outright homophobia—but I think a general distaste for gay sex underpins the council's attitudes. The court debates issues of informed consent, wondering if any partner might be accused of raping him. Would this issue even have been raised if they were discussing a heterosexual relationship?"[4] Disability rights activist Dennis Queen brings up important points regarding privacy and professional oversight: "Landlords don't usually get the right to police our behaviour in the bedroom, but for people in supported living this is not unusual."[5] While both critics shy away from the other category at work in the case (disability for Raccoon and homosexuality for Queen), the case cannot be fully understood by considering one category and ignoring the other. Rather, it is instructive to consider how ableism and heteronormativity function to regulate Alan's sexual expression. This case is useful when considering the ways in which private decisions about sexuality are made public, particularly through judicial rulings and journalistic accounts. The case highlights how certain categories (here intellectual disability) seem to warrant explicit mention and interrogation of sexual activity in the name of denial of sexual rights. As this case illustrates, there remains a culture of sexual repression where individuals struggle to advocate for their claim to equal citizenship and right to privacy. Disabled people who participate in same-sex sexual activities in group homes are subjected to heightened surveillance. Private sexual decisions and actions are increasingly being made public.

Given the unstable nature of assessments of ability as they pertain to sexuality, as well as an understanding that not everyone needs to be or is sexual, I would like to consider why the sexuality of individuals with intellectual disabilities is seen as dangerous, or needing oversight, as illustrated in this recent court case. Considering prerequisites to become sexual, it is helpful to refer to Tobin Siebers's notion of "the ideology of ability," which he defines as "the preference for able-bodiedness" that governs sexual qualifications.[6]

To what extent is the denial of ability to be sexual (or desexualization) for individuals with intellectual disabilities connected to the idea that they (individuals with intellectual disabilities) lack the ability (as assumed by those *without* intellectual disabilities) to be sexual? Connected to the "we know what's best" paternalism is the application of able-bodied standards to adults with intellectual disabilities, who are perceived as perpetual children (as IQ is often translated into mental age), thereby erasing the embodied knowledge and unique epistemology about life and physical maturity of individuals with intellectual disabilities. The erasure of knowledge and experience, especially in relation to purposeful, meaningful, and sexual life, further illustrates the denial of disability as a worthwhile and meaningful state to occupy. Rod Michalko writes of the "difference that disability makes" and how disability is an embodied experience, one that "finds its sensibility within the ways in which a collective conceives of what it means to be human and how it makes a place for the individual in what it socially organizes as a human community. Making a place for difference, including disability, is a feature of every culture and society."[7] The judge's desire to regulate the queer sexuality between Alan and Kieron illustrates what I call sexual ableism. Sexual ableism is the system of imbuing sexuality with determinations of qualification to be sexual based on criteria of ability, intellect, morality, physicality, appearance, age, race, social acceptability, and gender conformity. Intellectual disability remains a characteristic or condition that disqualifies participation because of sexual ableism, which denies an understanding of disability as a valuable difference that yields unique perspectives of personhood, competence, sexuality, agency, and ability. In *Already Doing It,* I trace the contours of sexual ableism while exploring the ways in which certain bodies exhibit their sexuality without regulation or scrutiny, whereas others are subject to continual oversight and regulation.

In *Aberrations in Black,* Roderick Ferguson writes that "queer of color analysis presumes that liberal ideology occludes the intersecting saliency of race, gender, sexuality, and class in forming social practices. Approaching ideologies of transparency as formations that have worked to conceal those intersections means that queer of color analysis has to debunk the idea that race, class, gender, and sexuality are discrete formations, apparently insulated from one another."[8] Ferguson's answer to the myth of discreteness is to facilitate a "queer of color critique," which fosters disidentification with exclusionary representations and theoretical formations and points to "the ruptural possibilities" of "minority cultural forms."[9] Ferguson's pronunciation of the falsehood of discreteness helps me to articulate a system of sexual regulation, sexual ableism that operates through the suturing of notions of appropriateness and fitness that are in turn informed by assumptions based on identity categories. *Already Doing It* explores the intersections of notions of competency, agency, risk, and sexual citizenship to examine how individuals labeled as intellectually disabled disidentify with systems of regulation and oversight in their sexual and reproductive lives. Robert McRuer argues that systems of exclusion based on limited conceptions of heterosexuality and able-bodiedness inherently depend on each other to maintain their dominance.[10] McRuer considers that crip/queer perspectives can challenge assumptions about which bodies are able to inhabit and lay claim to normative conceptions of agency, family, and, ultimately, identity.[11] Individuals with intellectual disabilities are productively unruly bodies that challenge the sexual ableist notion that their sexual practices are naïve, deviant, immoral, or dangerous. Alan's expression of sexuality with Kieron demonstrates how systems of domination rarely operate in isolation. The notion that Alan's experience is an aberration, an isolated event, hides the potential coalitions that can challenge sexual ableism. In what follows, I explore the ways in which reproductive justice, critical disability studies, and queer theory can articulate notions of kinship not tied to ableist, sexist, racist, classist, gendered, or heterosexist qualifications of family, agency, citizenship, and ability.

One manifestation of sexual ableism is a suspicion that those whose sexuality is regulated (or denied) should also not reproduce. Michel Desjardins writes of parental negotiation in Quebec to seek sterilization of children with intellectual disabilities in order to facilitate their sexual lives. Parents created an "extraordinary sexuality" that "is neither the sexuality of the angel, or the eternal child, not that of the majority of the population (who are not prohibited from reproducing)."[12] The parents who Desjardins interviewed wanted their children to remain sexual without the "threat" of reproduction. In order to manage these seemingly conflicting desires, the parents "arrived at the same conclusion: the need to liberate their children from the threatening ability to reproduce in order that they might express genital sexuality in safety. To achieve this goal, the parents required that their child adopt permanent contraceptive devices. Thus, a new sexuality is created for the disabled adolescent or young adult: a 'special sexuality'—or, if you prefer, 'an adapted sexuality,' conceived at the scale of the individual's unfitness—that includes sexual intercourse but prohibits reproduction."[13] I am struck with the language of liberation and threat in the above quote. Parental liberation hides the agency of the individual, whereas threat transforms the act of reproduction into an action, or outcome, which requires intervention. I also find myself wondering about the implications of this "adapted sexuality" for individuals who seek intimacy without participating in sexual actions, as well as individuals who desire reproduction and would provide nurturing environments to their children. On one hand, these parents recognized that their children could be (or ought to be) sexual beings and that in order to remain sexual they sought sterilization as a way to guarantee the ability to participate in heterosexual sexuality.[14] On the other hand, the parents engage their children in a conversion process wherein "the intellectually disabled person's desire for offspring" transitions into "a desire for infertility."[15] This brief example, from Desjardins, illustrates the conflicting desires that are present when discussing aspects of sexuality and reproduction for individuals with the label of intellectual disability. Various communities connected to the individual seek expressions of sexuality that can run the gamut from active desexualization to sexual intimacy to expressions of sexual activity divorced from reproduction to a linking of sexuality with reproduction and parenthood.

Some commentators link freedom of sexuality and lack of oversight around reproduction. Reproduction, or the ability to reproduce, translates, according to Siebers, to fewer restrictions placed on sexual life and expression. Gay men and lesbians, gender queer and gender nonconforming persons, racial minority populations, poor people, and disabled people are often discouraged to reproduce for fear that they "cannot, will not, or should not contribute to the future of the human race. They will not reproduce, but if they do, the expectation is that the results will be tainted."[16] Early on, disability studies theorists argued that discussions of disability rights should also include an articulation of sexual rights.[17] When sexuality and disability are discussed, it is often in the context of medicine and rehabilitation: disability as a condition that limits sexual expression and reproductive capacity.[18] Many of the materials examined here illustrate this reality. The annals of intellectual disability and sexuality are dominated by materials authored by individuals in the medical and rehabilitative sciences.

In an effort to shift attention away from the reductive equation of sexual rights as freedom of reproduction, Siebers presents ways in which disabled people can "explore an alternative sexual culture based on the artfulness of disability" and imagines disability as a "complex embodiment that enhances sexual activities and pleasure."[19] People with intellectual disabilities certainly are already participating in the "artfulness of disability." This project explores the restrictive oversight that can exist in group homes and other residential facilities while also demonstrating that people with intellectual disabilities have an adaptive and subversive potential to remain sexual despite professional restriction. Sexual pleasure can emerge in spaces where sexual ableism operates. Public expressions of masturbation, even if considered inappropriate, can be examples of people expressing sexual desire. This work recognizes that people with intellectual disabilities are already active agents in their own sexual expression, despite compromised privacy in living arrangements and systematic intrusions and oversights. Disabled people can challenge the lack of privacy in hospital rooms, nursing homes, and group homes in order to transform these spaces into sexually viable locations.[20] By mapping out restrictive trends in sexuality for people with intellectual disabilities, we are able to recognize that people experience and express sexuality in contradictory or complex ways. I want to underscore that not everyone desires a life that incorporates sexual activity. Intimacy might be "a greater priority" for some individuals.[21] Complexity and contradictions highlight the sexual cultures of people with intellectual disabilities, and provide the theoretical impetus in this work. By disidentifying with notions of competency, citizenship, and agency, individuals with labels of intellectual disability foreground their unruly potential to challenge interlocking systems of domination.

Advocating for the sexuality of people with intellectual disabilities challenges sexual ableism insomuch as intellectual disability assumes inability to consent because of the manifestation of an intellectual impairment. Much of the discourse around intellectual disability and sexuality can be classified as "crisis responsive" or "harm reducing." For example, as I discuss in Chapter 2, sex education materials use "stranger danger" in an attempt to reduce sexual assault rates among people with intellectual disabilities. This approach gives individuals the tools to respond defensively when approached by a stranger, but the intense focus on harm reduction denies individuals sex education that recognizes their ability to actively choose sexual partners and activities. *Already Doing It* argues that the regulatory framework of sexuality operates to delegitimize sexual desire and activities of individuals with intellectual disabilities. As such, sexuality might be seen as nonexistent, despite some individuals maintaining active, diverse, and pleasurable sexual lives, regardless of the surroundings in which they live, learn, or work. In fact, the "already doing it" portion of the title takes the focus on sexuality away from a question of ability (or frequency), to an analysis of the structural and material conditions that facilitate or attempt to limit sexuality and reproduction. "Already" is about temporality and the existence of practices regardless of severity of restrictions. "Doing," as opposed to "being," emphasizes the way individuals with intellectual disabilities may express sexuality in diverse ways rather than through scripted heteronormative practices of invoking and resolving desires. Failure to recognize an individual's sexual agency might deny recognition of sexual citizenship but not sexual activity. Recognition of sexual citizenship and facilitation of sexual agency are equally compelling activities that forward the attainment of individual and group rights. I explore how the sexuality of individuals with intellectual disabilities challenges private versus public constructions of sexuality and heteronormative patriarchal society.

I am fully aware that in advocating that the sexual and reproductive rights of individuals with intellectual disabilities be respected, I run the risk of alienating various constituents. In exploring sexuality, reproduction, and intellectual disability, I acknowledge that the category of intellectual disability (and individuals that can claim membership in such a category) is marked by a diversity of experiences, desires, and practices. Specificity and context help to illuminate diverse desires, practices, and experiences. I also am aware that this book contains inconsistencies and seemingly contradictory logics and argumentation. For example, in later chapters I adopt a rights-based approach to advance an argument that an individual's reproductive desires be respected. I do so fully aware of the potential exclusionary mechanisms embedded in such a claim. Nevertheless, it seems urgent to make such a claim in the face of a sexually ableist culture that seeks to sterilize individuals and break apart families. In a later chapter, I am critical of such a rights-based claim because of the potential for exclusion. I embrace these contradictions and eagerly await challenges, complications, and expansions of my work here by others.

A Word on Terminology

Disability is an incredibly complicated term with multiple contested meanings. Context can make all the difference. Disability means different things in the courtroom, doctor's office, classroom, and sheltered workshop. Representations of disability can create diverse meanings as well. Traditionally there are two models used in disability studies to explain disability: the medical and social models. These models initiate in two different realms, the individual and the environment. The medical model of disability defines disability as a result of a "physical, cognitive, intellectual, appearance or sensory impairment, or other medical condition that limits a person's major daily activities."[22] In the medical model of disability, an individual body and the way that body functions becomes the marker of disability. Inability to walk, environmental allergies, deafness, autism, and dyslexia are tangible indicators of the presence of disability. There is a "normative" or "normal" idea of bodies; for example, bodies are assumed able to walk.[23] If a person is unable to walk because of impairment, the medical model attempts to correct the inability through medical intervention and rehabilitation. The goal is to return the impaired body to some semblance of "normal" function. Disability studies theorists have commented that this "normal body" goal of rehabilitation highlights a constructed embodiment that very few are able to achieve.[24] The medical model of disability often prioritizes medical knowledge and authority over individual autonomy and decision-making. It individualizes the experience of disability, effectively isolating an individual's differently functioning body as needing intervention and correction.[25]

Whereas the medical model of disability relies on diagnosing, treating, rehabilitating, and eliminating impairment, the social model of disability considers disablement as a social process. Michael Oliver is best known for articulating an understanding of the social model of disability. Oliver considers that "all disabled people experience disability as a social restriction, whether those restrictions occur as a consequence of inaccessible built environments, questionable notions of intelligence and social competence, the inability of the general population to use sign language, the lack of reading material in Braille or hostile public attitudes to people with non-visible disabilities."[26] In the social model of disability, a person becomes disabled not because of biological difference but rather because of the ways that biological difference is not accommodated. Impairment, here referring to the condition that results in a loss of functioning, is supposedly neutral in the social model of disability; human diversity results in a multiplicity of bodies that function in varied ways. The inability to accommodate, or actively eliminate, specific impairments becomes a manifestation of ableism.

The apparently neat separation between the medical and social models of disability, which is based on the partition of impairment and disability, has received much discussion in disability studies circles. Various theorists have advocated for a social model of impairment that takes into account the experience of living with impairment.[27] As Shelley Tremain remarks, regarding the split between impairment and disability, "Proponents of the [social] model [of disability] explicitly argue (1) disablement is not a necessary consequence of impairment; and (2) impairment is not a sufficient condition for disability. Nevertheless, an implicit premise of the model is (3) impairment is a necessary condition for disability, because proponents of the social model do not argue that people who are excluded or discriminated against on the basis of (say) skin color are by virtue of that fact disabled, nor do they argue that racism is a form of disability."[28] The notion of impairment as a prerequisite for disablement is important. For example, the Americans with Disabilities Act has a three-part definition that considers someone disabled if they have a record of an impairment, or are regarded as having an impairment. Intellectual disability is first and foremost usually a label given to someone because of an impairment that results in apparent compromised intellectual capacity. An individual's intelligence quotient can become a marker of atypical intelligence, and can result in being diagnosed as having an intellectual impairment. Levels of intelligence are not the only criteria for a diagnosis of intellectual disability. The meaning that this impairment takes can lead to an experience of disablement.

I do not define intellectual disability in this work.[29] This is an intentional and political move. There are many definitions of intellectual disability available, if the reader wants to seek these out. Some consider that individuals have intellectual disabilities when they have measurably lower intelligence than the "average" citizen. Measuring intellect using various tests can be a problematic endeavor; biases based on class, race, culture, and language, for example, are present in different standardized tests. Intelligence can also fluctuate. Historically, those with intellectual disabilities were given the label "mental retardation." The American Association of Mental Retardation, the professional organization of researchers, academics, professionals, and policy makers working in the field of intellectual disability, changed its name to the American Association on Intellectual and Developmental Disabilities. A growing number of individuals consider mental retardation an outdated and discriminatory diagnosis. Intellectual disability has become the latest acceptable term in most American circles. Mark Rapley expertly questions the utility of defining intellectual disability, and considers intellectual disability and the meaning associated with it to be a socially constructed phenomenon.[30] I agree with Rapley that the meaning behind intellectual disability is largely socially constructed. The social construction of intellectual disability is explained in this book through an exploration of sexuality. My intention in not defining intellectual disability is to highlight the artificial and problematic ways in which intellectual disability is defined. Those with intellectual disabilities are often assumed to be incompetent and unable to make meaningful decisions in their lives, let alone make and execute sexually fulfilling choices. Childlike connotations, religious–spiritual "innocence," and the concept of mental age traditionally associated with intellectual disability (such as naïveté and gullibility) can result in conflicting assumptions about individuals' capabilities, a manifestation of sexual ableism. Chapter 1 offers a sustained discussion of competence in relation to intellectual disability.

There is also a geographical consideration to intellectual disability. Terms like "learning disability," "intellectual disability," "cognitive disability," and "developmental disability" encompass different categories of people in various locations. What may be considered a learning disability in a U.S. classroom is potentially different from one in a classroom in the U.K. and other English-speaking countries. The geographical focus of this book is largely the United States. This is not to say that some of the conclusions offered are not applicable to other locations; however, it is not my intention to provide a universal account of intellectual disability across all societies. That type of academic generalization does not take into account the ways in which disability is programmed and professionalized in diverse locations.

Intellectual disability as a "thing," a diagnosis that can supposedly be discerned by certified individuals, might include certain impairments such as brain injuries, autism, or Alzheimer's. The discussion on professional oversight of masturbation practices in Chapter 3 applies to individuals in nursing homes, including those with Alzheimer's. Masturbation control in nursing homes is discussed as a way to make a comparison across impairment categories. At various moments in this work, the readers might find themselves wondering which bodies and impairments I am talking about. Does this apply to those with Down syndrome? Or individuals on the autism spectrum? Are people with intellectual disabilities capable of consenting to sexual relations? While I cannot control the curiosity or "diagnostic gaze" that might arise at these moments, withholding this type of inquiry for the sake of momentary confusion allows us to see how certain categories are not stable, preexisting entities.[31] My aim is to demonstrate that while certain characteristics or themes emerge in the study of sexuality for people with intellectual disabilities, each situation requires an examination of the context and social forces at play. I argue that the professional control and generalization about sexuality for people with intellectual disabilities capitalizes on creating rigid perceptions of intellectual disability. Supposedly, people with intellectual disability do *this* and feel *that*. This project problematizes these assumptions about sexuality and intellectual disability and seeks to analyze the mechanisms that bind them together in a sexually able-ist way.

Disability, then, in accordance with Tanya Titchkosky's assertion, is a diverse social phenomenon that highlights individuals' perceptions of what disability means, which usually contradicts disabled people's experiences of disability.[32] Disability as a process is an interaction between what is called the biological and the social. Certainly people are disabled by social processes that exclude particular bodies from participation. The bodily manifestations and experiences of these impairments are a direct result of the disablement process. The politics around language remains a site of contestation in disability studies. Categorizing disabled people as separate from people with disabilities is seen as one of the central linguistic concerns. "Disabled people" implies that people are disabled (or experience disablement) because of social oppression. "People with disabilities" pays attention to the person before the impairment.

As such, I want to explain my use of "people with intellectual disabilities" in this work as opposed to "intellectually disabled people," not because disability has to be separated from the person but because I respect the commitment of the advocacy movement to the term. The self-advocacy movement, led by people with intellectual disabilities and nondisabled people, has been quite clear on their desire to be referred to in person-first language. While I argue that intellectual disability is an inconsistent and inexact impairment and that personhood as neutral has to be problematized, I use mostly self-advocacy language out of deference for the movement. However, I do at times highlight the problematic and constructed nature of the impairment and resulting social meanings.

Intellectual Disability and Sexuality

Since 2002 there has been increased journalistic coverage in such places as the *New York Times* of individuals with intellectual disabilities doing a multiplicity of common tasks: obtaining gainful employment, living independently, or competing in the Special Olympics.[33] In April 2006, the *New York Times* ran an article that addressed teaching individuals with intellectual disabilities sex education in hopes of facilitating "fuller lives." The article described two sets of partnerships and their discussions of sex. One couple, Mary Kate Graham and Gary Ruvolo, are being "coach[ed] in dating, romance and physical intimacy by a social service agency at the cutting edge of a new movement to promote healthy sexuality for the seven million Americans with mental retardation and related disabilities."[34] For the last several decades, the general public's perception of intellectual disability has been largely dependent on journalistic accounts and other representations in popular culture: actors Chris Burke in the television show *Life Goes On* and Lauren Potter in *Glee,* Special Olympians, the greeter at Wal-Mart, the Kennedy family, the special interest piece on a television news program, a video circulated through social media of an individual going to prom or playing on a sports team, the popular image of the kids on the "special bus."

Simultaneously, media references around sexuality within the United States have been changing from primarily heterosexual affairs to a multiplicity of sexual and gender identities and various methods of reproduction. Couples, married or not; individuals, gay, straight, bisexual, queer, asexual, and otherwise, can utilize adoption, surrogacy, or in vitro fertilization and other assistive reproductive technologies to create families. Many of these technologies are restricted to (white) wealthier individuals and those from geographic locations where private insurance covers these services. Ability to adopt is also restricted based on able-bodied heteronormative assumptions of parental fitness that can exclude gay, lesbian, single, transgender, or disabled parents. Gay marriage has polarized municipalities and communities throughout the United States. Social media sites such as Facebook allow users to publicly display their sexual identity for other users to see, albeit using a medium that allows for self-fashioned identities. Within the United States, sexual behaviors and their purposes are all subject to public inquiry, particularly on the Internet. As Altman argues, in this age of globalization, or "Americanization," technology is being utilized to allow for a diversity of sexual identities and opportunities for sexual expression.[35]

Individuals with intellectual disabilities might not be given access to technologies such as the Internet, which can facilitate exposure to these representations of sexuality. A lack of financial resources, as well as the structure of a group home, might result in limited exposure to television and films that represent sexuality. The presence of popular cultural representations about the sexuality of intellectually disabled individuals is also not reflected in similar stories involving other segments of the population.

Simultaneously, however, professionals are expending a tremendous amount of research dollars studying and educating individuals with intellectual disabilities about their sexuality. This increase in professional discourse of sexuality has its roots in a historical management and treatment for a host of individuals labeled as sexual deviants in relation to reproduction of disability. Within the United States, individuals with intellectual disabilities have historically been subject to eugenic practices of sterilization and subsequent institutionalization in order to control the numbers of disabled people. Sharon Snyder and David Mitchell argue that this is a type of transatlantic eugenic exchange of information and policies aimed at regulating the sexuality of individuals with disabilities, a precursor to the contemporary global exchange of sexuality.[36] According to Winifred Kempton and Emily Kahn, "Their [individuals with intellectual disabilities'] sexual needs were ignored; their sexual behavior was punished; they were randomly sterilized; they were closeted in their homes or isolated in large institutions, segregated by sex to prevent them from reproducing. In fact, they were actually oppressed largely *because of their sexuality*."[37] This regulation of sexuality through institutionalization, sterilization, and residential patterns to limit reproduction resulted in the oppression of entire generations of individuals with intellectual disabilities within the United States. These activities to regulate sexuality are slowly being acknowledged. For example, in 2002 and 2003, Oregon and California apologized for sterilizations performed on individuals with intellectual disabilities.[38] More recently, legislators in North Carolina decided to authorize compensation payments for people sterilized under the state's eugenic sterilization program. The number of eugenic sterilizations point to influential historical ideas about the sexuality of individuals with disabilities in dominant U.S. discourse.[39] Eugenic sterilizations were also practiced on ethnic and racial minorities in the United States; Nelson and Gutiérrez document the ways in which sterilization abuses were inflicted on women of color well into the 1970s.[40] Although these sterilization procedures are no longer a dominant practice, entire generations of disabled people, mostly women, have been forcibly sterilized. Countless women of color have also been coerced into sterilization. Many of the sterilized individuals with intellectual disabilities are still living and working in professionally controlled locations. These sterilized bodies serve as signifiers of the degree of regulation that occurs on disabled people's reproduction and, further, their sexuality in general.

The historical control and management of the sexuality of disabled bodies, including individuals with intellectual disabilities in the United States, informs this project, which explores the historical process of constructing the sexuality of intellectually disabled people as needing professional oversight. It would be misleading, however, to focus exclusively on historical or professional literature, as professional literature and historical regulations of sexuality are in conversation with more popular cultural representations of contemporary times. This book analyzes these components of disabled sexuality by examining contemporary popular films depicting the sexuality of individuals with intellectual disabilities and professional visual images, including sex education videos that are used to train professionals, within the contexts of a historical examination of sexuality discourse. The triangulation of professional literature, historical practices, and cultural representations creates a more comprehensive understanding of how the sexuality of individuals with the label of intellectual disability is imagined, represented, and subsequently controlled. The analyses focus on the assumptions and normalcy of sexuality and the sites of sexual oppression of people with intellectual disabilities. This sexual oppression reveals the necessity for libratory action in the form of a sexualized revolution for individuals with intellectual disabilities. In the interstitial space among the historical practices, cultural representations, and professional knowledge-making, an understanding of intellectual disability can be found as constituting parts of the sexual oppression of disabled people. In other words, this study aims to explain and understand the dynamics of the historical, professional, and cultural *processes* of constructing, managing, representing, and imagining the sexuality of adults with intellectual disabilities in the United States.

Professional Oversight

People with intellectual disabilities typically interact with multiple programming efforts in their lives, starting in special education classes and continuing through some sort of vocational activities and, most likely, residential settings. Even if intellectually disabled adults live with their parents or other family members, they will have some sort of day programming whether it is vocational or recreational. In each of these locations, professionals determine which training and educational initiatives are most appropriate for the clientele in these settings.[41] While working in a sheltered workshop in the northwest United States, I learned that the county board of developmental disabilities determined most of the programming and subsequently the ideas about what constituted "work." For example, if our workshop wanted to transition from sheltered employment into more individualized vocational settings, the board of directors would have to petition the county for approval. This expert-controlled programming ensures that individuals have very little agency in determining their educational, residential, and vocational choices.[42] Disability remains highly medicalized in these locations. Medical authorities diagnose impairment, and these diagnoses determine qualification for services. In addition, the medical conception of impairment helps to formulate assumptions about these individuals' abilities and potentials. These assessments can become the basis for the services offered in professionally controlled locations. Jack Levinson traces histories of professional management of intellectual disability, including various efforts to facilitate community integration.[43] Levinson's in-depth analysis of Driggs House, a group home in New York State, illustrates the productive tensions between notions of professional authority, freedom, and individual choice.

In response to this professionally controlled programming, many different stakeholders in the field, from professionals and academics to family members and intellectually disabled persons, argue for more control over what type of services are offered. These stakeholder groups try to influence this programming, often through participation on consumer or parent advisory boards and councils. The motivation for this springs from different philosophies about which life situation is most appropriate for individuals labeled as intellectually disabled.[44] Although programming attempts which allow for increased self-determination exist in each of the locations, many service options are under direction of professionals at all levels. In reality, there are not many people with intellectual disabilities who do not interact with some sort of professionally run organization. Often at least one major feature of daily living, including vocational activities and housing settings, is administered by professionals. Therefore it is important that professionals and people with disabilities work together toward common goals of greater autonomy and increased rights. A large number of Americans with intellectual disabilities pass through these locations, which are suggested as ideal settings for work, home, play, and socialization. Their experiences can be represented and understood by cultural discourse, which shapes certain images of their lives.

A Need to Be Sexual?

There are, perhaps, very few categories of adult citizens who are expected to be celibate. Those who vow celibacy for religious reasons, including nuns, priests, and monks, are expected to live with the anticipation that sexual relations will not become central to their lives. Convicted sex offenders are another group of individuals that are expected to largely remain celibate, and multiple laws and regulations attempt to control their interaction with populations at risk of sexual assault. While the elderly are not always considered as having fulfilling sexual lives, their sexuality is not necessarily frowned upon or expected to be absent.

Some individuals consider disabled people to be the exception when it comes to sexuality. The "myth of asexuality" is common for disabled people. Anne Finger remarks that sexual oppression can be a source of deep pain for disabled people and individuals, stating that "sexuality is often the source of our deepest oppression; it is also often the source of our deepest pain. It's easier for us to talk about—and formulate strategies for changing—discrimination in employment, education, and housing than to talk about our exclusion from sexuality and reproduction."[45] Desexualization and assessments of asexuality can warrant interventions, including requests for government-subsidized sexual services and a loosening of sex work monitoring. Being sexual is not central to being human; certainly many people live satisfying lives without sexual activity. Eunjung Kim discusses the intersectional ramifications of recognizing that asexuality is a valid sexual orientation for both disabled and nondisabled people.[46] Notions about the ability to be sexual are intertwined with gendered, classed, and racialized assessments of fitness. Some bodies are able to be sexual, without oversight and intervention. Others appear to need regulation or oversight. Children under the age of sixteen (or eighteen, depending on the location) are assumed not legally able to consent to sexual activity; adults participating in sexual activities with minors are rendered criminal partially because of an assessment that the minor lacks the ability to consent to and understand the ramifications of the sexual act. One of the lasting contributions to discussions of sexuality that feminists have offered include a reminder that sexual relations can be as much about power and control as they are about pleasure and desire.

In discussing the sexuality of men and teenage boys with significant and moderate intellectual disabilities, Nathan Wilson and colleagues forward a notion of "conditionally sexual," "that the developmental capacity of the individual was central to the construction of one's sexuality, together with the perspective and influence of paid disability support workers. That is, variations, and staff perceptions of these variations, in cognitive, emotional, physical, anatomical, hormonal, functional and social development were central to how one's masculine sexuality was constructed and to the gate-keeping role of staff in overseeing sexual behaviour."[47] The authors discuss how staff in group homes interpreted activities as sexual or helped facilitate sexual activity (e.g., allowing privacy to masturbate) based on assessments of self-discovery, hormones, pleasure, personal beliefs, a sense of duty to care, and ability to act as gatekeepers.[48] Describing sexual actions as "conditional" illustrates how disability, assessments of capacity, and capability combine with morality and decorum, as perceived by staff members, to create a situation in which individuals with intellectual disabilities act out their sexuality. Wilson and colleagues note that being conditionally sexual results in a "life that is reduced to a penis/body-centric experience. Furthermore, the focus on these men and teenage boys' masculine sexuality is not geared toward what is developmentally normative, what feels nice and what is fun. Instead, their sexuality is problem-led within a service-centric risk-hierarchy that renders to a secondary consideration the 'right' to develop a healthy masculine sexuality. Their lives, and their masculine sexualities, are circumscribed by an environment whose prime purpose is led by their day-to-day high 'physical' support needs at the expense of supporting an individual within a broader socio-cultural 'sexually healthy' framework."[49]

Normative sexual experiences, according to Wilson and co-authors, are sacrificed in this "management" of sexuality. If sexual experiences are largely reduced to regulation of masturbation, especially for men with intellectual disabilities, it is little wonder that individuals can be ill equipped to navigate their sexual lives with limited sex education and increased professional oversight of their sexual activities. Women's sexual lives are largely constructed around the twin poles of "regulation of pregnancy/reproduction" and "protection from sexual abuse and assault." It can be extremely rare for women with intellectual disabilities to be recognized as competent sexual agents. Later chapters address how sex education materials as well as masturbation training work not to proffer sexual knowledge to achieve agency but rather to construct sex as risky and masturbation as primarily about the reduction of behavioral issues. There is a long history of trying to regulate the reproductive potential of individuals with intellectual disabilities, primarily women, through prescriptions of invasive birth control measures and eugenic sterilizations. Women with intellectual disabilities share this common history with other disenfranchised women, including poor women and women of color, and women from multiple identity groups.

Sexual expression for individuals with intellectual disabilities, regardless of knowledge and desire, becomes almost too risky a proposition to undertake. In addition to forbidding sexual expression, such as the court case between Alan and Kieron, constructing masturbation as the only sanctioned type of sexuality becomes another mode of sexually ableist intervention. Even benign courting is the subject of much debate in group homes and families, the assumption being that dating can immediately lead to sex. Even if one affirms the sexual rights of people with intellectual disabilities, it is often conditional: only *if* there is no risk of pregnancy or sexually transmitted infection. We saw this in the judge's ruling. Other qualifiers might include only *if* the individual is sexual with another person with an intellectual disability or only *if* the individual has "mild" intellectual disabilities. Other populations such as women in poverty, in prison, or in institutions whose reproductive rights are historically curtailed, are also subjected to a similar "only *if*" clause. By no means are individuals with intellectual disabilities the only population whose sexual rights are infringed upon. Even so, adding "only *if*" to the above question illustrates how individuals with intellectual disabilities are largely denied the right to express their sexuality. As U.S. society continues to debate the boundaries of sexual citizenship, the sexuality of individuals with intellectual disabilities challenges us to reconsider sexual agency and competency. It seems that the sexual and reproductive rights of individuals with intellectual disabilities have yet to capture the imagination of the U.S. public. The system of sexual ableism continues to be tenuously upheld through proscriptions of deviancy, incompetence, and a redirecting of sexual desire and activities.

I conclude this introduction with five theoretical case studies. This presentation is patterned after Cynthia Enloe's efforts in *Globalization and Militarism: Feminists Make the Link* to invite the reader to consider the diversity of people whose experiences might fall under purview of this work.[50] My goal is to expand the reader's understanding of what intellectual disability means and to challenge what is often associated with the diagnosis. Challenging the accepted meaning of intellectual disability through our exploration of sexuality begins to upset the "naturalness" associated with the diagnosis. Constructs such as competence begin to be exposed as fictions. Context and individual will help to challenge sexually ableist blanket assessments of people with intellectual disabilities as in need of oversight, unable to participate in sexual relationships free of abuse and coercion.

Susan is a twenty-year-old African American woman with an intellectual disability from the north side of Chicago. She is the youngest of five siblings and recently graduated from a Chicago public school. Susan wanted to attend college, but her parents decided that she should try to get a job and live in a group home in the community. At the group home, Susan shares a room with June, another young woman with an intellectual disability. Shortly after moving in, June and Susan started a sexual relationship. One night while they were engaged in sexual activity, a staff member entered the room without knocking. There is a meeting scheduled next week to discuss June and Susan's relationship. Susan's parents are planning on attending and want to move their daughter out of the group home and back to her childhood residence. June and Susan are not invited to the meeting. Will June and Susan's wishes be respected or even considered at this meeting?

John is forty-five, a white man living on a combination of food stamps and disability benefits in a one-room apartment in Atlanta.

John grew up in poverty and remains there. Unemployed and without any family, John frequently takes art classes at the local community center, funded through the county board of intellectual and developmental disabilities. One day while John was at the center before class, he saw a seven-year-old boy walking outside by himself. Without pause, John goes to check on the boy. At the exact moment John reaches the boy to check on him, the child's mother shows up and accuses John of trying to sexually molest her son. John has never received any sort of sex education class and likewise does not know what is meant by the terms "molest" and "pervert." The police are called. What will happen to John? Who will believe him?

Tony never knew his parents. He grew up in a state institution in Maryland. When the institution closed because of a reduction in state funding and pressure from disability activists, Tony moved into the community and started attending a day center, where he met Grace. After getting to know each other, Tony and Grace decide that they want to date. After a few months pass, Tony and Grace decide that they want to become sexually active with each other. Neither individual has ever received any sort of sex education. When Tony and Grace approach a staff member at the day center asking if they can receive some sort of sex education, the staff member decides that there is a need for this service. The staff member advertises the upcoming sex education class and within weeks thirty adults with intellectual disabilities are enrolled in the class. Although some staff members complain that "these people" should not be taught about sex, the classes continue. Can Tony and Grace become parents? If they want to have children, will they retain custody? Or will the state take their children away?

Sara is sixty-five and living in a nursing home. Although she has siblings, they live out-of-state and would rather their sister be looked after by those who are better trained to meet her needs. At night a male nurse enters Sara's room and sexually molests her. The assault is a nightly occurrence. Even though Sara, who is largely nonverbal, tries to communicate with the staff members at the nursing home, nobody listens to her. No one takes the time to understand Sara's concerns. With no one to listen to her and her family not in the picture, what will happen to Sara? Will the assault continue? How can the nurse committing the assault be caught? And when he is caught, what is the most effective response that demands justice but does not pity Sara?

Finally, Jose is eighteen and beginning to take a sexual interest in his peers. Although his parents gave him the "birds and the bees" discussion, Jose still feels unsure about sexuality and is questioning his sexual identity. He thinks he might be gay, but something about this label makes him feel ashamed and embarrassed. Jose wants to explore his sexual inclinations but is unsure how he can do so without fearing reprisal or public identification of his sexual identity. Jose decides to obtain a gay pornographic magazine from the adult bookstore down the street from his house. While at the bookstore, an adult man, who is twice Jose's age, approaches Jose and leads him to a private room. Jose and the man masturbate in front of each other. When the encounter is over, Jose leaves the bookstore not feeling any guilt or remorse over what just transpired. Was the encounter sexual abuse, even though Jose enjoyed it? Is it significant that the two men only masturbated? Will Jose later regret this encounter? Did the other man know Jose was an individual with an intellectual disability? Does it matter?

These are all complex and difficult questions. Each vignette provides a different vantage point from which we can explore the issues around intellectual disability and sexuality. The reader might think that not enough details are provided to adequately gauge whether the individuals should be sexual or whether they experienced abuse. These stories illustrate that any conversation about intellectual disability and sexuality is not monolithic—diverse people, motivations, practices, and situations require more nuanced conversations. The issues raised should provoke discussion about what we think about intellectual disability, what it means to be sexual, and how all types of individuals can express their sexuality without fear of reprisal and oversight. This work addresses intellectual disability and sexuality, but also attends to larger issues around sexuality for all individuals, regardless of intellectual ability or diagnosis. Sexual ableism as a theory articulates how different types of bodies, regardless of labels of intellectual disability, experience oversight and regulation of sexual and reproductive behaviors. Remember the stories of Jose, Tony, Grace, Sara, June, Susan, and John as we examine what it means to be sexual and how competence, citizenship, and intellectual capacity intersect with sexuality.

1 Questions of Consent

Rethinking Competence and Sexual Abuse

In *Looking White People in the Eye,* Sherene Razack wonders how feminists can "talk about the social context of women with disabilities without reifying the othering that marks this context in the first place."[1] More explicitly, Razack asks us how we can discuss sexual assault and abuse without recognizing that the very labels and management of disability make this abuse more likely. In discussing cases of abuse involving women labeled with intellectual disabilities, Razack outlines how to recognize the social circumstances surrounding sexual abuse, even when commentators frame the victim as "enjoying the experience of sexual abuse," thereby perhaps denying the occurrence of abuse.[2] Similar to Anne Fausto-Sterling's discussion on the medical and resulting social meanings mapped onto sexuality, Razack's work describes how nondisabled (primarily feminist) thinkers imagine situations of abuse for developmentally disabled individuals, especially in situations in which gender and disability categories collide with notions of pity, "othering," and a sense of special circumstances.[3] Additionally, Razack questions how the predominance of sexual abuse for women with intellectual disabilities can be addressed without making the victims symbols of humiliation.[4] Acknowledging social forces such as ableism, racism, classism, and sexism that portray women with intellectual disabilities as warranting special treatment is the first step in understanding the interplay between these same systems in order to dismantle them.[5]

This chapter explores how to reimagine and reframe legal and journalistic narratives of sexual abuse of women with intellectual disabilities[6] by using crip theories that reveal gendered, heteronormative, and ableist assumptions about sexuality and pleasure. I examine the American case of Kalie McArthur, a young white woman with an intellectual disability who was sexually abused by her white male peer-educator, in order to consider how stories about "victims" in cases like this can expose and dismantle interlocking systems of oppression existing in situations that result in abuse and assault.[7] McArthur's case and the discourse around it are instructive because of the ways in which notions of pleasure, competence, morality, and disability are used to frame the woman as a vulnerable victim and the peer educator as a predator. I argue that expressions of pity, largely unproblematized in feminism, limit the necessary respect for disabled women in abuse cases.[8] The utility of assessing competency based on intellect is also discussed in order to deepen feminist disability studies analyses of the interplay between categories of gender, disability, race, and sexuality. Finally, this chapter discusses possible ways to theorize sexuality for people with intellectual disabilities, being mindful of (but not restrained by) the high prevalence of sexual abuse and complicated notions of consent.

The Case of Kalie McArthur

On June 30, 2006, conservative radio and talk show host Glenn Beck introduced a segment on his CNN program the following way: "My faith teaches me that the handicapped are the most valiant among us. My gut tells me, after I volunteered for Special Olympics, that when we get to the end, when we go see God face to face, we're going to realize that we're the retarded ones, not those who are fighting with mental disabilities."[9] Beck, who has a daughter, in his words, with "special needs," took it upon himself to lead a crusade so that what happened to Kalie McArthur would not happen to other disabled children. Beck's outdated and problematic language reflects a charitable approach to disability, where agency can be covered by a discourse of "bravery" and "inspiration." For Beck and many others, abuse enacted against disabled individuals has to be countered and eliminated. Later in the same show, Beck said to a guest that "there is nothing that will put you at the gates of Hell faster than raping a child or raping a handicapped person."[10] In Beck's moralization of disability, the "us"/"them" dichotomy is established with disabled individuals who are unconditionally moral, innocent, and childlike needing to be protected from sexual assault. Beck's use of "special needs" and "retarded" also further creates differential power dynamics that seem to warrant a reinforcement of protectionism and sexual ableism. It is precisely Beck's moralization and simplification of situations such as Kalie McArthur's that make a more nuanced reading of cases of assault for intellectually disabled individuals difficult; in this chapter I will attempt one such nuanced reading.

Kalie McArthur was eighteen years old in 2004. She was in a special education class at Rampart High School in Colorado Springs. As part of the policies of School District 20 (D-20), students in special education classes are given the option of being assigned a peer-trainer. During the 2004–2005 school year, McArthur was assigned to a fifteen-year-old freshman peer-trainer, Robert Harris, to assist her in various janitorial tasks at the school. While not the focus of this chapter, the quality of McArthur's education is suggested by her assignment to janitorial work in the school. Instead of learning what her peers were learning, she was cleaning the school.[11] On September 14, 2004, the football coach at Rampart, Charles Yost, discovered McArthur and Harris interlocked in a position, McArthur on top of Harris moving back and forth. Both Harris and McArthur's pants were pulled down and Harris was wearing his boxer shorts. At the time of the incident, McArthur was supposed to be cleaning dirt off the floors at the school, but instead she was in the stairwell with Harris.[12] McArthur and Harris were left alone without adult supervision, even though McArthur's Individual Education Plan called for adult supervision at all times.[13] Yost immediately took both McArthur and Harris to the principal, Gil Bierman. Yost considered their activity to be sexual and that Harris was abusing McArthur, and Harris was charged with having unlawful sexual relations with a minor, although he was minor himself and younger than McArthur. During the court case against Harris, it was determined that Harris did not rape McArthur, but rather sexually assaulted her.[14] Sexual assault refers broadly to unwanted sexual contact whereas rape refers to forceful vaginal, anal, or oral penetration. Harris pleaded guilty to the charge of unlawful sexual contact and served fourteen days in juvenile detention. He also was required to register as a sex offender and undergo behavioral therapy.[15]

Following Harris's criminal trial, McArthur's parents sued D-20 and McArthur's teacher for negligence in a civil case. The suit was settled in 2007 for an initial payment of $1.2 million. The initial payment covered the family's legal fees and set up a trust fund that provides a monthly payment for McArthur's personal assistance services and other living expenses. The monthly payment is guaranteed for McArthur's lifetime, resulting in a total settlement estimated at $4.3 million. During the negotiations for this civil case, a professional for the school district claimed that the experience for McArthur was "pleasurable, not traumatic" and that it "ignited her female desires."[16] While not denying that the teacher was negligent for leaving McArthur alone with Harris unsupervised, the school district attorneys argued that the incident between Harris and McArthur was not sexual abuse but rather a gender-reaffirming event that satisfied her sexual desires.

The claim that this abuse reaffirmed her "female desires" illustrates how patriarchy depends on seeing masculine aggression as a "gift" that awakens female sexuality. Razack discusses how histories of sexual violence must be overcome before women with intellectual disabilities can be seen as vulnerable; their sexual virtue has to be established in the face of sexual violation.[17] Razack's observations are important to consider because women with intellectual disabilities are often subjected not only to experiences of sexual abuse and assault, but simultaneously rendered incompetent to participate in sexual relations. By extension all (or almost all) sexual activities are automatically assumed to be assault—they have to be proven otherwise in criminal and legal mechanisms, as such sexual "virtue" has to be claimed. D-20 and the experts it hired chose to say that this experience with Harris incited her female instincts and that she transformed from a girl to a woman in the stairwell. In an interview given by Harris and his grandmother, it is suggested that McArthur asked for and/or enjoyed the sexual activity, or even that she assaulted Harris.[18] It seems illogical that McArthur, the same young woman presented as having the "mind of a child," would not only become a predator but also enjoy the experience with Harris. Regardless, we need to be clear that *even if* McArthur enjoyed the experience, it does not mitigate the unequal power dynamics and assault that she also may have experienced.

What interests me most in this case are the ways media representations and court documents describe both McArthur and Harris. Rather than determining who is at fault and who is a "victim," I am analyzing how various discourses of competence, gender, sexuality, consent, and labels of disability are presented in the case. For example, Harris is described as having been suspended multiple times, being absent eighty times during the school year, and having a 0.0 grade point average prior to 2004.[19] Additionally, McArthur's lawyers describe the boy as having been arrested for shoplifting, not "exercising good judgment," and as a "hormone-filled teenage boy."[20] In an interview with *The Gazette,* Harris said that after being convicted as a sexual offender, he was "bitter and depressed."[21] Harris contends that he was merely a "curious adolescent" who had a momentary "lapse in judgment" but ultimately did nothing wrong that day at Rampart High School. At the time of the incident Harris says he was "going through depression," and he is now on antidepressants, according to his grandmother.[22] Harris implies that he is as much a victim as McArthur in this situation, punished for his sexual curiosity and unstable mental health.

In the same interview with the *Gazette,* Harris provides a revealing look into his psyche and perception of the events with McArthur. Many of the statements by Harris in this interview are typically repeated by those convicted of sexual assault and do not garner him much sympathy from readers. For example, at one point in the interview Harris remarks that he "made her [McArthur] feel like a queen" and that he "did nothing but good to her."[23] He continues, "Me and Kalie know exactly what happened. I cared about Kalie, and I'm more than sure she cared about me."[24] Despite the other representations of Harris as a poor student and predator, he contends in this interview that their relationship (as peer-trainer and otherwise) was based on mutual feelings, and that nothing inappropriate or illegal happened between the two of them. In fact Harris's grandmother makes the most provocative comment in this interview by saying that "he [Harris] was a child just as much as she [McArthur] was a child. To me, she could've been the one raping Robert."[25] Harris's disability is not meaningfully discussed in any of the media representations. Instead, he is presented largely as a hormone-filled predator, seeming to confirm gendered assumptions of (white) teenage boys. The contention that McArthur raped Harris might upset the sensibilities of many commentators, but in this case, Harris's age and gender come into direct conflict with McArthur's competence and disability status. McArthur's disability status interacts with her gender identity while his impairment seems a leftover addendum to the event, not central to the act, largely because of the representations of his gender and McArthur's disability status.

Kalie McArthur and her family are the subjects of a series of articles in *The Gazette* from January 12 to January 15, 2008. The three articles trace the family's move to Alaska, describing what life is like for McArthur since Harris sexually assaulted her. The first article in the series, "Innocence Undone," states that experts think "her [McArthur's] childlike mind has since descended into a dark place from which it may never emerge."[26] The articles explore the behavioral and personality changes that McArthur has undergone since 2004. In all the articles, interviews, and court documents, McArthur's voice or experiences are often interpreted or expressed by other people: her family, lawyers, Harris, and cable news reporters. In this series of articles, McArthur is not directly interviewed, but the author, Brian Newsome, says that almost four years after the incident McArthur frequently asks, "Do I have to take my clothes off?" and repeats, "I'm afraid, I'm afraid, I'm afraid."[27] The representational contrast between McArthur's mitigated voice and Harris's interview is striking. The comprehensive picture painted by these articles and the additional media representations describe McArthur as the stereotypical child-like adult with an intellectual disability, unable to live, work, or function independently. McArthur is rendered completely vulnerable and dependent, incapable of consenting to sexual relations with Harris. As much as Harris is vilified, she is pitied. She is not given the opportunity to speak about her experience in either the trials or the journalistic accounts of the events.

Both McArthur and Harris are selectively referred to as adults and children throughout the pieces—McArthur is an adult when the experience of abuse was supposedly "enjoyable," but childlike in her actions, comprehension, and life since the event in the stairwell. McArthur is chronologically older than Harris. Theoretically she could be charged with unlawful sexual contact with a minor. Even though her chronological age makes her an adult, her disability supersedes adulthood.[28] Her disability positions her as "cognitively younger," illustrating the infantilizing mechanism in this discussion. Harris is an adult insomuch as he is found guilty of the assault, but simultaneously childlike by representations of vulnerability by his grandmother and his own statements to reporters. The man–boy and woman–girl shift in language helps to illustrate that these two individuals are as much actors as well as pawns in the representations and ensuing controversy around this case.

McArthur's lawyers describe the situation between Harris and

McArthur as "akin to placing a wolf in charge of a defenseless lamb and leaving the two alone."[29] The wolf (Harris) in this metaphor is the actor while the lamb (McArthur) is the recipient of the action. Although as observers we will never quite know what happened in the stairwell, there remains some question about McArthur's exact role in the situation. Unlike the Glen Ridge case, in which high school athletes raped and assaulted a girl with an intellectual disability multiple times using baseball bats, broomsticks, and other sticks while being cheered on by their friends, McArthur's story is not as definitive. The Glen Ridge case was framed with consent as the central legal question. The prosecution contended that the victim could not consent because of her disability, while the defense argued that the girl's prior sexual history was evidence that she was a willing participant.[30] We know that Harris was convicted of unlawful sexual contact with a helpless victim. We also know that Harris held power over McArthur because of his gender and role as peer-educator, even if he does not think so. And we know that McArthur's daily behaviors have changed since the event and its aftermath. We also know that Harris was diagnosed with a mental impairment, depression, at the time of the incident. McArthur's impairments have been used to explain her vulnerability, but Harris's impairment has not received the same attention, other than to imply that Harris would have to be "sick in the head" to assault McArthur. While Harris's depression does not excuse or vindicate his actions, I would argue that recognizing his impairment might do more to explain his reasoning than does defining him simply as a hormone-filled boy.

In the court brief filed by McArthur's parents, she is described as "loving like a toddler without a sense of boundaries" and as "functioning at the level of approximately a 3 or 4 year old."[31] Likewise, McArthur's father has been quoted as saying that his daughter "used to be passive and affectionate, [but] now she's aggressive, especially toward males. She could end up hurting someone, maybe a little boy."[32] This threat of future violence is not commented on in the coverage of the case. It only serves as a marker of the gravity of the situation and a consequence of victimization, one that might be replicated at the hands of McArthur on a younger boy victim. For McArthur, her IQ and supposed levels of functioning are all widely reported on as well as her supposed inability to act in rational ways.[33] It seems that a successful prosecution of both Harris in the criminal case and D-20 in the civil case is dependent on making McArthur appear consistently vulnerable to unwanted sexual advances and that her innocent nature has been lost because of this experience. Almost all the public discourse about this incident has framed McArthur as the defenseless victim and Harris as the culpable predator.

Nonetheless, McArthur and assumptions about her sexuality remain central to the failed defense of D-20 and Harris. Robert McRuer argues that heterosexuality and able-bodiedness are linked, which in effect limits the recognition of the sexuality of individuals with disabilities.[34] McArthur is seen as childlike insomuch as this framing portrays her as not sexually competent or able to act on her sexual desires.[35] Recognition of sexuality can challenge the assumption that individuals with intellectual disabilities always need protection from sexual abuse by actively denying their sexual lives. To be clear, I am not arguing that what she experienced was or was not sexual violence. The emphasis on virginal and innocent status to justify victimhood is my focus in this case, primarily because such an emphasis seems to lead to pity and unequal power dynamics.

There is also a stereotype that individuals with intellectual disabilities are uncontrollably and inappropriately sexual, for example masturbating in public locations. Eugenic practices in the United States and elsewhere actively sought the sterilization of women with intellectual disabilities because of beliefs about their fecundity and insatiable desire for sex.[36] The virgin/whore dichotomy is at play in many discourses about violence against women around the world, and women with intellectual disabilities are also subject to such a framing.[37] The implication is that if someone who experiences abuse and assault is also sexually active or has multiple sexual partners, then the actual experience of abuse is mitigated. The sexual history of many women who are raped is used as a defense by the predators and their legal teams, despite rape shield laws. The virgin/whore dichotomy likewise places most intellectually disabled women in positions in which their sexual experiences become public knowledge and previous sexual experiences supposedly negate the ability to be sexually abused.[38] Kalie McArthur's case places her within this dichotomy, her parents and the media pointing to her "childlike innocence," while others see her as sexual primarily because of her gender.[39] The defense team argued that her sexuality and gender were inseparably affirmed through the experience of sexual abuse. Consistently lost and ignored in this equation are McArthur's thoughts about the experience. Instead, those around her continue to interpret her knowledge and feelings about the encounter by describing her as a victim, thus robbing "the individual from any notion of agency and subjectivity and to ideologically locate the . . . person as helpless and pitiful."[40]

While McArthur's case ended in a successful prosecution of Harris and a financial settlement, I cannot help but wonder what the ramifications are for McArthur and other individuals in similar situations when they are not allowed or given the opportunity to testify in court or through other means such as videotaping or drawings. Jurors consider individuals with intellectual disabilities as credible witnesses, which results in higher rates of successful prosecution for the offenders.[41] Structured questioning by the prosecution can facilitate clear testimony by individuals with intellectual disabilities.[42] Even so, many individuals who experience sexual assault are not given the opportunity to testify and give voice to their experiences. Individuals often express a desire to have a moment in which they can share their story as one way to deal with the experience. McArthur was denied this opportunity.

Abuse against individuals with intellectual disabilities can become especially heinous, considering the ways in which intellectual disability is defined as a significant limitation in intellectual functioning and adaptive behavior. If professionals, as well as a portion of the general public, consider intellectual disability to be equated with a lack of consent and the ability to act in "conceptual" and "adaptive" manners, then how can discussions that occur around these incidents demand justice without reifying the individual as pitiful and defenseless? The professionalization of intellectual disability, as well as the social and cultural meaning of intellectual disability, works to deny individuals the ability to consent to sexual activity. Those that experience sexual abuse remain pitied and are constructed as vulnerable. There is the potential to cover up these crimes in various group homes and institutions, which creates a "culture of silence" in these settings.[43] Staff members can actively protect their colleagues by not reporting sexual abuse and assault. When residents sexually abuse other residents, staff members might also not report this to authorities for fear of creating organizational problems or concern. Reporting sexual abuse requires a change to the status quo. It is easier to deny the experience or consider it an isolated event.

The response around sexual assault points to a larger approach around "crisis response." When sexual assault is discovered or found, sexuality is openly discussed. However, prior to a report of sexual assault, individuals in different settings are silenced from expressing or discussing sexuality. Sexuality can be individualized and shamed, which are precisely the kinds of feelings that people report after victimization. The sexual culture of the group home or institution might be such that sexuality is actively ignored and discouraged.

Sexual Abuse and Notions of Consent

Sexual abuse invokes strong responses. Feminist theorists have long examined how sexual abuse reifies constructions of gender because sexual abuse is often about men exerting power and domination over women.[44] While sexuality remains a source of repression and danger, it is also a site of pleasure and agency. Any discussion of sexuality ought to balance these two seemingly competing trajectories.[45] There is a complicated relationship between sexual pleasure and danger; sex can bring gratification as well as oppression. Some radical feminist theorists caution that all sexual exchanges, especially between men and women, reinforce damaging and oppressive power dynamics based on an unequal gender system: "So long as male supremacy exists and is sexual, male identification will exist and be sexual also, and sexuality will be gendered and unequal."[46] This position elicited much criticism among feminists because of the sustained focus on sexuality as a means of oppression. While not everyone might agree that all sexual exchanges fall into an unequal gender system where men are dominant and women are subjected to that domination, it is instructive to think about these sexual exchanges as being located on a continuum where sexual pleasure and oppression/domination lie along the multidimensional, nonlinear continuum. The use of continuum is intentional here because on a continuum separate categories or groupings such as stylized sex and fantasy blend into each other, sometimes making it very difficult to determine to which category one event might belong, if any. When determining whether sexual encounters warrant claims of abuse, multiple factors—including age of consent, knowledge of the activity, and ability to consent—are examined. The social context of the event—including the environment in which it occurs—can also be an important power dynamic. Sexual exchanges between individuals with intellectual disabilities might be placed at a different spot on the continuum from those between people without intellectual disabilities, based on sexually ableist notions of ability to consent and understandings of sexuality, whereas sexual actions between an individual with an intellectual disability and a nondisabled person might raise more concerns when it comes to sexual abuse because of their different ability status.

There have been multiple political, theoretical, and legislative efforts to define what constitutes sexual abuse for individuals with intellectual disabilities. Michelle McCarthy and David Thompson summarize various definitional attempts.[47] These summarized definitions include the distinctions that sexual abuse happens "where sexual acts are performed on or with someone who is unwilling or unable to consent to those acts,"[48] where "any sexual contact which is unwanted and/or unenjoyed by one partner and is for the sexual gratification of the other"[49] and "where that person's apparent willingness is unacceptably exploited."[50] These definitions of abuse rely on the lack of consent or willingness to engage in sexual activity, but also focus on the presence of exploitation. McCarthy and Thompson comment that H. Matthews's definition based on the presence of exploitation is most "helpful because it moves away from the albeit crucial issue of consent and indicates that although a person with learning disabilities may have been willing to engage in sexual contact, they may still have been abused, because of the position or motivation of the other person."[51]

Safety is also an important consideration in discussions of consent. Having individual choices respected and feeling safe in expression of these choices is an important implicit consideration in a determination of consent. Perpetrators can sexually abuse and assault individuals with intellectual disabilities, even if the individual expressed willingness to participate in the sexual action. Unequal power dynamics, instead of willingness, becomes one of the determinants of abuse. Sobsey argues that individuals with intellectual disabilities are four to ten times more likely to be sexually assaulted than are nondisabled individuals.[52] Research also reveals incidents of abuse being committed by trusted individuals like family members and in-home caregivers.[53]

Also, individuals with intellectual disabilities may abuse other individuals with intellectual disabilities.[54] Defining sexual abuse as an issue of power and exploitation rather than an issue of consent underscores that those who experience sexual violence do so not because of a "lack" of intelligence but rather because of unequal power dynamics that might favor professionals, family members, and staff. Unequal power dynamics point to wider social inequalities around disability as well as a reinforcement of male-dominant culture. Men with intellectual disabilities who commit sexual abuses may benefit from unequal power dynamics vis-à-vis their female counterparts. Issues of intellectual capacity are not sufficient to explain why some individuals encounter abuse. Experiences of privilege and discrimination, circumstantial power dynamics (e.g., between a boss and an employee), and a social atmosphere that condones sexual violence affect which individuals may experience or perpetuate sexual assault.

The relatively high frequency of sexual abuse has spurred researchers to conduct a significant amount of research focusing on those who experience and participate in the abuse. The research broadly falls into three categories: (1) research about those who sexually offend, (2) research about those who are abused sexually, and (3) perceptions and observations of sexual abuse by service providers, criminal justice officials, and potential jurors in abuse cases. More specifically the topics range from relapse prevention for those who offend;[55] effectiveness of group treatment for both those who sexually offend and those who experience abuse;[56] and the chronic nightmares and other symptoms of posttraumatic stress disorder of those who experienced sexual assault[57] to issues related to sexual abuse for children and adolescents with intellectual disabilities, victims and offenders alike.[58]

The research about those who sexually offend mostly tries to explain the abuse pattern and why certain individuals (e.g., men with intellectual disabilities) abuse women with similar disabilities. Since the majority of large residential facilities, and even some smaller group homes, are not sex-segregated, men with intellectual disabilities can be given unrestricted access to female residents, facilitating abuse. McCarthy and Thompson consider that women-only services might ensure the safety of women with intellectual disabilities.[59] In short, gender-mixed housing can place individuals with histories of sexual abuse in residential facilities. The institutional preference to house people in gender-mixed settings creates higher vulnerability to sexual abuse for individuals with intellectual disabilities, not because of an impairment, but rather because of external forces, such as having no control over the selection of their roommates or the staff on duty.[60] The literature on social role valorization critiques the tendency to devalue individual choice, including decisions related to living arrangements.[61] Female-only spaces could mitigate sexual abuse between men and women with intellectual disabilities, but not necessarily with male staff or family members. Group homes can be "mini-institutions" where individuals have no control over their living arrangements, reflecting a broader disavowal of choice. The structure of the institution that limits individual choice and autonomy needs to be challenged in order to lessen sexual abuse. Furthermore, restructuring housing based on a single-sex model can obfuscate the reality that sexual assault still happens inside gender and sex categories, especially between men with intellectual disabilities.

Marklyn Champagne contends that "when sexual assault is understood as an issue of power and control, the particular vulnerability of the person with an intellectual disability becomes more apparent" because "perpetrators often choose their victims because of the victim's intellectual disability, figuring that detection is unlikely."[62] While Champagne does not mention differences in the rate and type of abuse experienced along gender identities, her comment brings up important issues surrounding the frequency and duration of sexual abuse, as well as the potential for perpetrators to seek out individuals because of their apparent passivity, vulnerability, and lack of believability and cognitive ability. Judgments are made about what an intellectual disability means and how individuals with intellectual disabilities are supposedly unable to resist unwanted sexual advances. Essentially, the concept of intellectual disability assumes that people are unable to adequately advocate for themselves and need constant supervision and support. Individuals are assumed vulnerable to sexual abuse and exploitation. In addition, intellectually disabled individuals are also generally not assumed sexually attractive or desirable partners, especially by those without intellectual disabilities. As such it is assumed that their sexual rights should be protected while their sexual expression should be shunned and silenced. These assessments and assumptions are defining characteristics in how the system of sexual ableism operates. Individuals are restricted from certain sexual actions through narrow conceptions of competency and agency, as interpreted through able-bodied standards. The self-advocacy movement, however, illustrates that many individuals with intellectual disabilities are capable of self-determination and are able to advocate for themselves and their rights. Individuals are demanding and reclaiming their rights. However, this is not a universal occurrence. The methods in which services are delivered and designed feed into a higher rate of sexual abuse and assault. Individuals are told what to do, where to live, whom to love, and how much. An individual's ability to consent to sexual activity is important to consider, but so is an examination of various residential settings that place individuals in situations that facilitate abuse, regardless of impairment diagnoses. Furthermore, Mark Sherry makes an important point that crimes against disabled individuals be recognized as crimes and not referred to generically as "abuse."[63]

When individuals with intellectual disabilities experience sexual assault, how can activists, academics, the individual, and others address and confront the assault without further reifying the individuals who experience the assault and responding in pity? And to further complicate this issue, how can sexual encounters of individuals with intellectual disabilities be found pleasurable and not harmful amid predominant violence and the assessment of their incompetence based on their impairment diagnosis? A discussion about intellectual disability in general can begin to allow us to rethink issues of competency to imagine pleasure and intellectual disability together.

The U.S.-based definition of developmental disability which encompasses intellectual disability is primarily based on limitations as evidence of impairment. The focus on "substantial functional limitations" communicates the idea that an individual diagnosed with an intellectual disability or some other developmental disability is naturally dependent on the assistance of others and relies on "special" services: educational, vocational, recreational, and residential, often paid in part or in full by the government. If in order to receive these services individuals have to prove that they are unable to perform daily living tasks, then incompetence becomes a necessary qualification to receive these services and claim membership in the category. Being labeled "incompetent" in their ability to learn and live independently positions individuals with disabilities as not able to participate as full citizens, because their measurably low level of intelligence (or physical limitation as it relates broadly to developmental disability) apparently "proves" their incompetence.

As Mark Rapley has put it, referencing Michel Foucault's *Madness and Civilization*,[64] "In much the same way then that 'madness' can be the 'absence of work' (Foucault, 1965), it appears that people who will not, or can not, meet societal expectations about self-sufficiency, employment and normative expectations about the discharge of social responsibilities—of proper conduct—can, potentially, be diagnosable as intellectually disabled."[65] The "inability" (or unwillingness) to meet Western societal expectations of "self-sufficiency" places an individual at risk to be labeled as intellectually disabled and by extension incapable of living a normative life.[66] The "cloak of competence," in Robert Edgerton's terms, refers to placing individuals in situations in which circumstances (usually positioned on them by external forces) help to shape their place as incompetent in society.[67] Despite expressions of self-determination of individuals labeled as intellectually disabled, there are definite social and cultural factors that construct the individuals as inherently "less than" based on normative assessments of intelligence and behavioral skills. Licia Carlson refers to this structuring of individuals as cognitive ableism, "prejudice or attitude of bias in favor of the interests of individuals who possess certain cognitive abilities (or the *potential* for them) against those who are believed not to actually or potentially possess them."[68] Assumptions of naïveté and acquiescence seem to warrant sexually ableist interventions.

Laws in the United States, Canada, Australia, New Zealand, and Western Europe do not automatically assume that individuals with intellectual disabilities are unable to consent to any sexual activity.[69] The lack of consistent criteria to determine consent across jurisdictions results in assessing consent on a case-by-case basis.[70] One study suggests that individuals with intellectual disabilities generally do not know the various laws that relate to sexuality.[71] Guardians are encouraged to know the laws of their jurisdiction in order to advocate effectively for individuals in their care.[72] Some researchers advocate that sex education should address laws related to sexuality and consent in order to facilitate this education.[73] Knowledge of legal issues as well as the social, biological, and moral meanings and consequences of sexual activities are needed for determining consent. Knowing the age of consent for sexual activity becomes one of the benchmarks for determining consent. However, the rules including age of consent vary by location. Clare Graydon and colleagues discuss how the issues related to consent in Australia vary by states attempting to facilitate "protection from sexual exploitation," but this often results in "undue interference with their [individuals with intellectual disabilities'] right to sexual expression."[74] Moreover, what constitutes sexual abuse and exploitation in one jurisdiction is not consistent throughout all jurisdictions.[75] The complicated mechanism of ensuring consent can work to deny the ability to consent and pose barriers to educating and facilitating sexual agency. The determination of consent process is legally complex and often relies on physical, chronological age instead of "mental" or "intellectual age." A medically determined "mental age" can take legal precedence over physical age of consent. In these moments, the diagnosis of "mental age" is held up as "evidence" of intellectual disability, even though a diagnosis of intellectual disability is given prior to entrance into the courtroom. Mental age is an ableist notion that can actively discredit individual choice and perpetuate assumptions about incompetence, childhood, and necessity for protection by prioritizing professional medical authority at the expense of individual desire and epistemology.

Efforts to Determine Consent

Various sexual knowledge assessment scales have been proposed to determine ability to consent.[76] Martin Lyden, for example, argues that there are three areas that need to be assessed to determine ability to consent: rationality, knowledge, and voluntariness.[77] According to Lyden, not only does an individual need to know the various repercussions involved in the sexual act, such as pregnancy or disease infection, but also needs to comprehend the illegality involving coercion. With these understandings, individuals should actively choose to engage in the sexual activity.

Paul Stavis and Leslie Walker-Hirsch advocate for a selective assessment of competence based on levels of risk and type of sexual activity.[78] For example, they argue that individuals who participate in low-risk activities, such as solo masturbation, which generally are not regulated by the state, do not need to be assessed for ability to consent.[79] Sexual activities that involve the exchange of genital fluids, considered high risk, and can result in unintended consequences, they argue, require formal assessments of consent.[80] Therefore, most sexual activities involving a partner require a determination of consent in this framework.

When individuals reside in some sort of congregate housing, such as a group home, the responsibility rests with the home supervisor to determine consent. In the United States the consent process usually begins when individuals are observed engaging in sexual relations or express their desire to enter into a sexual relationship with another individual. Most often this consent process starts with assembling those staff members familiar with the individual. Guardians and/or family members are also invited to participate. As such, the person is queried to determine individual understanding of sexuality.[81] After the assessment of sexual knowledge, the assembled committee determines if the individual is able to consent to sexual activity or if active steps including sex education classes are needed to facilitate increased knowledge that will hopefully lead to the ability to consent. Much of this process is really about granting permission to engage in sexual activities. Usually each group home or residential institution has its own set of protocols to follow when a determination of consent is made. These protocols might not be implemented, and the moral standards, beliefs, or religious doctrines of an individual home supervisor can influence the execution of these policies.

Unfortunately, some homes make a blanket determination that all individuals with intellectual disabilities are unable to provide consent. Group home and institutional staff members can be given license to stop the consent determination process before it begins based on their own biases, and staff members may try to "manage" the sexuality of individuals by denying them the recognition of consent even when they understand and can appreciate the risks and potential consequences of the activity. Recognizing the capacity of consent in individuals allows for individuals to be active participants in their sexual development.[82] Assessments of consent are not static but rather situational and largely dependent on increased sexual knowledge and ability to act with intention.

Given the potential for inconsistent assessments of competence, how can disability studies theorists attempt to analyze cases of abuse and assault in such a way that recognizes the inherent power dynamics and oppressive forces at work without further "othering" those individuals labeled as intellectually disabled? How do we determine which activities constitute assault when individuals with intellectual disabilities engage in sexual activities? Identifying assault, while also critiquing and dismantling unequal power dynamics determining consent and violence, is imperative when answering these questions.

Some scholars assert the tendency of people with intellectual disabilities toward acquiescence.[83] This discourse suggests that individuals with intellectual disabilities are from the very beginning vulnerable to abuse. And if being labeled with an intellectual disability makes an individual predisposed to abuse, then logic would suggest that the category (or impairment) itself, regardless of ability to function, can aid in making an individual vulnerable. This circular logic between the meaning and the management of the impairment continues to enforce vulnerability for individuals with intellectual disabilities. Impairment diagnosis and the meanings attached to the diagnosis affect how individuals are seen as vulnerable or incompetent by potential predators.

Competence and vulnerability are extremely important concepts to unpack. As Mark Rapley puts it, "Competence is *very much* a relative concept, and moreover one which is, in actual social practices, actively negotiated."[84] In the McArthur case, McArthur is portrayed, almost exclusively, as vulnerable to sexual abuse and unable to consent, while her counterpart is represented as taking advantage of her vulnerability and lack of competence. Additionally, she is pitied because of her experience. I argue that the response of pity jeopardizes respect.

Crip Theorization about Sexuality

How can we talk about the experiences of Kalie McArthur and other individuals with intellectual disabilities without treating them as objects deserving our pity? Most disability rights activists would argue that any restrictions on the sexual lives of individuals with intellectual disabilities are not justifiable.[85] However, people with intellectual disabilities in certain settings such as group homes and special education classrooms are seen as special exceptions, deserving a different approach, primarily because of their impairment label.[86] This exceptional approach is a manifestation of sexual ableism. Focusing on special services or approaches can further isolate individuals with intellectual disabilities, as well as those with brain injuries and cognitive disabilities, from greater participation with their nondisabled peers and reinforce their positioning as an "other." In order to escape discussion of "special sexual education" aimed at this "special" population, disability studies can further engage in discussions about diverse sexual practices of intellectually disabled adults. Davina Cooper notes that "'special needs' are depicted as non-social facts that should be dealt with, where possible, through remuneration, not by changing (or diversifying) the normative assumptions of embodiment that anchor and underpin the social."[87] Cooper is criticizing the trend to address disability through monetary compensation without addressing the social management of disability. Intellectual disability upsets normative assumptions about embodiment and cognition; those with intellectual disabilities are seen as essentially different and not possessing the prerequisite intelligence for sexuality, rather than having diverse sexual lives. Those with intellectual disabilities are sexually *disabled* because of these assessments of intelligence. As a result, the focus becomes excluding those with intellectual disabilities. As Cooper maintains, instead of promoting "special needs," disability studies can continue to examine the social circumstances and disadvantages that oppress and disempower individuals with intellectual disabilities.

There is potential to repress sexual expressions and ability to consent because of disability status. Robert McRuer in his book *Crip Theory* notes that "little notice has been taken of the connection between heterosexuality and able-bodied identity. Able-bodiedness, even more than heterosexuality, still largely masquerades as a nonidentity, as the natural order of things."[88] The association of heteronormativity with able-bodiedness not only limits sexual expression of disabled individuals but also severely limits the recognition of the sexuality of individuals with intellectual disabilities. Both heteronormativity and able-bodiedness as systems of embodied regulation depend "on a queer/disabled existence that can never quite be contained."[89] The lack of containment brings forth the possibility of collapse and change. Recognizing the sexual potential for all embodiments, including those with intellectual disabilities, facilitates recognition of sexual subjectivity beyond the boundaries of able-bodiedness and heterosexuality.[90] The tremendous focus on limitations associated with intellectual disability erases the sexual diversity of those with intellectual disabilities.

Sexuality becomes off-limits. Those without disabilities are assumed to be (hetero)sexual by default, while those with disabilities often have to advocate for their own sexuality.

When it comes to approaching the sexuality of intellectually disabled adults, a crip theorization can potentially bring discussions of sexuality beyond pity and abuse and into discussions of the ability to consent and freedom of expression. As Mark Sherry suggests, "The lesson for disability studies is that rather than looking for a binary disabled/nondisabled social relation, it is necessary to recognize the multiple, fluid and contradictory social relations that underpin shifting identities and conceptions of citizenship."[91] Striving for citizenship also encompasses the right to be sexual. An element of Sherry's call to recognize what constitutes citizenship is to examine why intellectually disabled adults are usually deemed to be not competent, not only in choices of living and working situations but also in terms of sexuality. Regulation of sexual expression jeopardizes attaining sexual citizenship while simultaneously reinforcing qualifications for sexuality and able-bodied heterosexuality, a marker of sexual ableism.[92]

Being more vulnerable to sexual abuse ought not to justify the denial of sexual expressions and activities. If individuals are subjected to higher levels of abuse than those without a certain impairment label (intellectual disability, for example), how can disability studies further theoretical claims that recognize the abuse without further "othering" the population with talk of special programs, special circumstances, and special protection to facilitate decision-making motivated by compassion and pity? Carrie Sandahl notes that "compassion is only a step away from pity, and it is impossible to be equal to someone who pities you. *Pity* implies not only compassion but contempt for the object, who is seen as weak or inferior. Pity is no remedy for hate. People with disabilities know that playing the 'supplicant' does not win civil rights or even common respect."[93] While pity does not always necessarily result in contempt, the potential for respect is mitigated when one is pitied. When pity is expressed primarily because the abuse is perceived to be the result of a position of vulnerability, here disability, the potential remains to not recognize the conditions that perpetuate the abuse.[94] Expressing pity, as opposed to demanding respect and justice, shores up separation between those who experience abuse and those who prosecute, write, and raise awareness about the abuse. "Privileging non-disabled norms" partially occurs by creating separation, while differentiating the meaning behind impairment.[95] What seems most pressing is how to recognize citizenship (in Sherry's terms) without facilitating pity (in Sandahl's terms) in order to cultivate respect.

The response to McArthur's case (such as Glenn Beck's moralization resulting in pitying—"there is nothing that will put you at the gates of Hell faster than raping a child or raping a handicapped person") may well have been different were McArthur an able-bodied woman. It seems that when someone of a "vulnerable" population is sexually assaulted, that assault generates additional emotional responses in commentators, here pity. While we can never say for certain whether the McArthur case would have been reported on were she not disabled, the discourse of pity surrounding the event does not challenge the larger educational and service delivery system that can frame individuals with intellectual disabilities as susceptible to experiencing sexual assault and abuse. McArthur's disability, racial status, and gender intersected with the social meaning of those categories. Recognizing how McArthur was treated differently from other non-disabled women who experience sexual abuse can not only allow for an examination of how systems of domination influence the court proceedings, but also why women with intellectual disabilities continue to experience sexual abuse and assault in different and similar ways from other women. McArthur is a white woman, and her whiteness is not remarked on in discussion of the case. Rather, her whiteness acts to mark her as the quintessential virginal white woman. Her whiteness makes the abuse even more "horrific," the perception that a sexually abused woman of color might not generate.

American society programs offer assistance for education, living, and other life processes in a way that places people with intellectual disabilities in the exact situation that puts them most at risk of sexual abuse. Structural violence—historical and cultural processes that constrain agency and choice—not the manifestation of impairment, renders people with intellectual disabilities more likely to experience abuse.[96] Rethinking and changing various support systems, including community-based residential options for people with intellectual disabilities, can help to bring about a reduction in sexual abuse and ultimately can lead to a rethinking of conceptualizations of competency and choice. Respecting the self-determination of individuals with intellectual disabilities over their residential lives is one concrete example that can facilitate a reduction in abuse.

Studies of the frequency of sexual abuse or the behavioral outcomes associated with sexual abuse are helpful to determine the impact and scope of the problem. However, system change that recognizes the sexual lives of individuals refocuses how individuals with intellectual disabilities are competent and active agents. By extension, individuals can be responsible for the outcome of their life choices. Sexual abuse and assault may still occur even if individuals are fully integrated in school settings, but individuals can participate in demanding justice and respect. When McArthur was pitied, victim-orientated restorative justice and respect were subsequently denied. Certainly punitive justice in the traditional sense was obtained with both Harris's conviction and the settlement against the school district. Winning both of these cases guaranteed justice. A true sense of justice would allow McArthur the opportunity to discuss the experience and resulting impact of the event on her life, either inside or outside the courtroom. Attorneys assess whether it would be strategically appropriate for a client to testify. My intention is not to critique McArthur's legal representation, but rather to call attention to the importance of the venues for McArthur and others to speak about the experience of sexual abuse and the right to be heard. Respect for McArthur does not allow for her to be seen as either an innocent child or a seductive temptress robbing Harris of his virtue. A critical crip-oriented approach to McArthur's story would reframe Glenn Beck's moralization this way: "There is nothing worse than denying individuals the opportunity to make meaningful decisions about their lives and bestowing on them an overwhelming sense of pity." And by extension, "the presence of impairment does not negate the opportunity for individuals to choose to be sexual and demand justice if they are sexually abused."

New alliances in disability studies between scholars in law, humanities, psychology, rehabilitation, and other fields can begin to reframe situations where abuse results in pity or justification within the dichotomy of powerless victim or hypersexual temptress. Pity is generated when the crime is thought of as originating from the affected person because disability itself is seen as a cause of crime. It is considered pitiful that the person has a disability, instead of the fact that he or she was subject to degrading treatment. There is a difference between expressing pity for a person with an intellectual disability who was sexually abused and demanding justice through an expression of anger. Pity interrupts respect, because behind an expression of pity is a recognition of power. When one is pitied, it is difficult to advocate for oneself. This power differential is best seen in an ableist quote by Myra Terry, the New Jersey chapter president for the National Organization for Women, when discussing the Glen Ridge case: "This is a pathetic eight-year-old in a woman's body. How could she consent?"[97] It becomes hard to imagine how a "pathetic" individual with an intellectual disability can be respected in that situation, while recognizing the harm done. Discussions can occur about how different systems interact in relation to different bodies, marked by race, gender, disability, impairment, nationality, and other identities around the emotions of pity, inability to consent, external labels of asexuality or hypersexuality, as well as the assumptions of inappropriateness of reproduction. These discussions can expose how interlocking systems are reliant on maintaining oppression and upholding sexual ableism as well as how these new alliances, across impairments and disability identities, can begin to foster a crip theory that "demand[s] that . . . another world is possible, or that—put differently—an accessible world is possible."[98] Only then can sexuality for intellectually disabled adults, as well as other disabled people, be reframed to promote desires and expressions without discussions of pity and special circumstances in such a way that the possibility of victimization does not preempt all sexualities.

This chapter argues that assessments of competence and precondition of consent can work to deny adults with intellectual disabilities the right to be recognized as sexual; as such, institutions and group homes regulate individual sexuality. When sexual abuse and assault are discovered, the discourse of pity and moralization prevents an individual from being treated with respect. Discourses of pity interrupt equality. Able-bodiedness, heterosexuality, and normative assumptions about intelligence seek to reinforce an approach to intellectual disability that sustains professionalization. This professionalization of every life aspect of people with intellectual disability has to be challenged so that the restrictions placed on sexuality are removed, allowing individuals the opportunity to be active agents in their sexual lives.

2 Pleasure Principles

From Harm Reduction to Diversity in Sex Education

Stephen Lance's 2007 Australian short film *Yolk* narrates the experience of Lena (Audrey O'Connor), a teenager with an intellectual disability, who steals a copy of *The Joy of Sex* from her local library at the moment her sexual knowledge and curiosity are awakened.[1] Lena also carries around a chicken egg that she calls her baby. Lance juxtaposes signs of reproduction, fertility, love, and sexuality in his film, highlighting Lena's understanding of self as a sexual being. Her interest in sexuality and the technicalities of sex is marked in the film by her question to her mother on the mechanics of having a baby, as well as her secretive meeting with the neighbor boy, Daniel (Hamish Irvine), in the woods, and most vividly, the secretive glances of the stolen book from the library.

After Lena takes the book from the library shelf, she returns home to place it in a briefcase below her bed along with a crude drawing of a penis that Daniel and his friend Ian (Angus Robertson) previously passed to her on the school bus. The location under the bed is significant because it is a place where she can hide things from her mother.[2] Her mother later discovers the book and confronts Lena, ultimately making her return the book to the library. When confronted by her mother, Lena squeezes the chicken egg she is carrying. The egg breaks and yolk runs down her hands. Her mother offers a replacement egg but Lena's attention has shifted from parenting the egg to learning more about sexuality and fantasizing about her neighbor, Daniel. Of note, Lena expresses her agency and desire to learn more about sexuality by only pretending to return the book to the library. In the library, she slips the book under her overalls and returns to her mother's car to dream about cuddling with Daniel in the woods. Her fantasy with Daniel is filmed in vivid colors, which stands in stark contrast with the muted landscape of the rest of the film. In the dream, they are lying down on a bed of mossy greenery, surrounded by bright red flowers. They are both wearing their school uniforms. Daniel is asleep while Lena is resting her head on his stomach, looking up at the sky. The film ends with Lena smiling looking up at the sky, her head outside the car and the stolen book clutched underneath her overalls. Her fantasy with Daniel is a perfect imagination of a traditional heterosexual love story.

Prior to her mother's discovery of the book, late at night, Lena takes the book into the bathroom in her house.[3] As she sits on the toilet, she opens *The Joy of Sex* to a line drawing of a naked man and woman engaging in sexual intercourse. Lena begins to trace the outline of the woman's breast with her finger. As her finger redraws the outline of the breast, Lena begins to mark out her own breast on top of her nightgown. We are seeing Lena explore her own physical self with the aid of the drawing in the book. The scene quickly ends as the camera fades to black.

While the image in the library book is strictly heterosexual, the scene itself is quite queer. Lena is using the woman's drawing to find her own sense of pleasure. The scene ends without an explicit indication that she will continue to explore her body, perhaps leading to masturbation. The implication that she is seeking pleasure on her own terms is quite clear as the camera dissolves on her face marked with a smile. Lena's late night solitary exploration could be read as a necessary step before her later fantasy of union with Daniel in the forest, or alternately, as a valuable moment of self-discovery and pleasure.[4] The fact that she retains the book at the end of the film, however, points to the potential for more solitary late-night explorations in the bathroom. These two scenes situate the delivery of sex education for individuals with intellectual disabilities. Lena exercises her will to obtain the relevant sexual information and uses this information to actualize her sexual self. I begin the chapter with this film because the content marks a new mode of representation around sex education, a representation that highlights the agentive potential of individuals with intellectual disabilities in becoming sexual beings. Additionally, the imaginative pairing of Daniel and Lena shifts traditional pairings of individuals with intellectual disabilities to illustrate the transgressive pairing of a disabled woman with her nondisabled neighbor.[5] While it appears the film is ambivalent about this pairing, Daniel is at the very least interested in Lena as he follows her into the woods for a brief conversation. The film focuses on Lena's agency, despite her restrictive living situation, to obtain the sex education and begin the process of sexual actualization.

In this chapter, I examine sex education for individuals with intellectual disabilities in the United States. I discuss historical changes, content, and overall messages about appropriate sexuality within sex education.[6] Generally, battles around providing comprehensive sex education for school-age children and adolescents illustrate ideological divisions in the United States, stemming from different viewpoints regarding appropriate (normal) expressions of sexuality. The Christian Right, comprising conservative Catholics and Christian evangelicals, has rallied against comprehensive sex education during its rise to political power in the United States over the last forty years.[7] In contrast, since the 1960s the Sex Information and Education Council of the United States (SIECUS) has argued for more comprehensive sex education, including a discussion of sex as pleasurable and not merely reproductive.[8] In towns and municipalities across the country, which aspects of sexuality should be taught to teenage school-age children remain a subject of much debate. This chapter takes up the historical debate about sex education as the background to discuss sex education for people with intellectual disabilities. While at times the content of sex education for individuals with intellectual disabilities can look quite different from education aimed at a nondisabled cohort, a comparison between sex educations for both populations of individuals allows for a nuanced understanding of sexuality for people with intellectual disabilities. Abstinence-only (or abstinence-plus) education has become the most widely used approach for nondisabled and disabled students in classrooms across the United States.[9] Sex education that meaningfully incorporates a discussion of homosexuality, asexuality, and bisexuality is rare, especially in special education classrooms. Sex education remains a location in which morality, religion, notions of normality and abnormality, and ableism work to endorse and reinforce nonreproductive heterosexual expressions while distancing discussions about sex away from various notions of pleasure and self-awareness.

This chapter comprises three distinct but related sections to identify the conflicts around sex education and the efforts to minimize discomfort about sexual expression for people with intellectual disabilities:

1. I review and draw out the major themes of the professional literature pertaining to sex education. These studies in general advocate for the need for sex education for people with intellectual disabilities as well as to assess the overall knowledge of individuals with intellectual disabilities when it comes to issues relating to sexuality. A comparison is made to sex education efforts for those outside of special education classrooms and group homes. As we look at the types of education offered for those with and without disabilities, we can begin to understand how national discussions regarding sexuality can enforce a restrictive view of sexuality while alternate options, including a feminist approach on teaching pleasure, have been utilized to escape the moral discourse around sexuality.[10]

2. Major features of sex education for individuals with intellectual disabilities entail educating individuals about anatomy, often using explicit images of genitalia and naked bodies as well as teaching staff and individuals with intellectual disabilities about the appropriate and "street" terms for these various body parts and sexual activities. Street language and more colloquial terms for sex and sexual organs often reference a history of oppression and discrimination. The language used in classrooms can reinforce a silencing in these spaces where women and queer individuals become sexual deviants.

3. Perhaps the most widely taught sex educational materials are the CIRCLES® series by James Stanfield Publishing Company.[11] The CIRCLES® sex education materials focus on appropriate and inappropriate ways of relating to and interacting with people based off an approach in which there are a range of circles, from stranger circle to private circle. In this section, I discuss the themes and approaches advocated in the CIRCLES® series as illustrative of a kind of rigid view of sexuality for people with intellectual disabilities that only occur in committed heterosexual relationships. The almost exclusive attention on heterosexuality in sex education denies the experiences of individuals who do not identify as straight. CIRCLES® addresses gay sexuality but only in relation to HIV, thus perpetuating a harmful stereotype about gay sexuality as promoting HIV transmission. With a specific focus on HIV/AIDS education, CIRCLES® capitalizes on more mainstream sex education approaches that

focus on disease prevention at the expense of discussing pleasure and diversity in sexuality.

As a whole, I do not seek to determine the educational effectiveness
of the various sex educational materials; instead, I consider the meanings and messages that are reinforced in these materials.[12] Since professionals in educational and residential settings frequently use these
curricula, an analysis provides an understanding of how sex is managed and taught in group homes and classrooms across the United
States.[13] I suggest that, historically, sex education for individuals with
intellectual disabilities has failed to address the multiple and varied
ways in which people express their sexuality both in and out of all
kinds of relationships. Rather, sex education is used to instruct people
with intellectual disabilities that sexual expression is best done by either self-pleasuring through masturbation or with heterosexual partners without the possibility of reproduction. Nondisabled students are
taught in sex education that sexual activity and reproduction ought to
occur within the bounds of traditional family, an option not widely
envisioned as viable for intellectually disabled individuals by professionals and sex educators. This way of conducting sex education shows
the struggles of liberal ideology versus religious conservatism, while
the pleasures of sex for individuals are lost in a discourse of abuse and
disease prevention. The collective weight of these two competing ideological camps serves as a normalizing discourse that obscures the desires and rights of individuals that do not fit within this dichotomous
framing. Discussing the fear of sexual pleasure Abby Wilkerson remarks, "Cultural erotophobia is not merely a general taboo against
open discussions of sexuality, and displays of sexual behavior, but a
very effective means of creating and maintaining social hierarchies,
not only those of sexuality, but those of gender, race, class, age, and
physical and mental ability."[14] In this chapter, utilizing Wilkerson's
theorization, I trace how sex education unqualifies certain bodies for
sex and marks practices as deviant and abnormal, constituting a mechanism of sexual ableism.

This discussion of sexuality (and which sex acts are "appropriate") is tied to notions of risk. Even if we don't acknowledge it, we all
negotiate levels of risk daily. Certainly, individuals choose to engage
in activities that are potentially risky, or at the very least could affect

their future. Having sex without a condom or dental dam is the clearest example of this when pregnancy, HIV, or another sexually transmitted infection is a risk. Passion, spontaneity, inebriation, or apathy might motivate actions. Desire to engage in "risky" sex might also motivate certain choices constructed as "unsafe." Tim Dean's work on barebacking, which in its most broad interpretation is sexual activity without protection, helps to illuminate choices that some gay men make in relationship to discourses of risk and intimacy. Of the universality of barebacking, Dean writes, "Let's face it: at some level we all enjoy barebacking, even if we consistently use prophylactics. I think that most heterosexuals would find it hard to commit themselves to a life in which sex *always* involved condoms."[15] Dean continues, "These days virtually everyone imagines that the safe-sex maxim 'Use a condom every time' does not apply to him or her but to those whose pleasure seems less significant or legitimate than his or her own. Fucking without a condom is often regarded as a privilege of the normatively coupled in the age of AIDS."[16] The poles of risk, desire, and pleasure intersect to motivate action. Sexual ableism functions to label certain sexual activities (e.g., gay barebacking sex) as risky, while not necessarily others (e.g., heterosexual hooking up). Dean complicates the assumption that risky sex doesn't add to a sense of well-being or a satisfying life: "Barebackers' abandonment of condoms is motivated not only by a lust for enhanced physical sensation but also by a desire for certain emotional sensations, particularly the symbolic significance attached to experiences of vulnerability or risk. Rather than mindless fucking, bareback sex is an activity deeply invested with meaning."[17] Feelings of kinship, desire, and negotiations of culture and identity motivate action.[18] To deny individuals with intellectual disabilities the opportunity to engage in risky sex, even if they know the activity is coded as such, further reinforces sexually ableist notions of harm reduction that can perpetuate assumptions that intellectual disability warrants protectionism.

Education that centers on individuals with intellectual disabilities as passive receptors, as opposed to active agents in their own sexual development, helps to disguise how individuals make operative choices as sexual beings. Individuals, including those with intellectual disabilities, are "agentic sexual subjects," who are able to contribute to the development of sex education materials that reflect their experiences and desires.[19] Sex education for people with intellectual disabilities can equip individuals with self-respect, respect for other people, sexual knowledge that facilitates their sexual expression, as well as a comfort in expressing nondominant ways of sexuality.

Professional Literature on Sex Education

In the 1960s, two events led to a greater focus on sexuality for individuals with intellectual disabilities. The first involved the growing influence of the philosophy of normalization, which advocates for an increased level of control by people with intellectual disabilities over their daily life choices, and of the notion of "dignity of risk," which recognizes the rights of all people as self-determining individuals to take risks and make mistakes.[20] Constant protection, regardless of impairment or disability, limits individual potential to make decisions that can result in failure. Normalization and dignity of risk appreciate that equipping individuals with knowledge of sexuality still affords the responsibility to determine individual sexual decisions. Alongside these philosophical developments within the profession and society, deinstitutionalization resulted in larger numbers of individuals with intellectual disabilities living in the community. Professionals and families were, however, concerned that those outside the institution would experience sexual abuse and manipulation.[21]

The promotion of sex education offered one way to equip individuals with the tools needed to recognize sexual abuse. Since its inception, a primary function of sex education in the United States has been preventing sex abuse and exploitation. The dominant discourse of sex education delineates sexuality as a non-pleasurable, potentially dangerous public health activity. In the exploration of sex education for people with intellectual disabilities, the rhetoric of harm reduction is significant throughout. Reducing the potential for sexual abuse and, to a lesser extent, sexually transmitted disease is the primary goal in sex education for people with intellectual disabilities. Patrick White's assertion about the homogeneity of sex education materials for blind individuals is comparable to the relative similarity among sex education materials for individuals with intellectual disabilities.[22] White writes that sex education "is characterized by a relentless focus on the problem of whether (and how) to educate the blind about sex. It eschews the task of giving a broader account of blindness and sexuality, as might be gained from ethnographic or autobiographical accounts."[23] The questions about how to educate are central to the development of sex education materials for individuals with intellectual disabilities.

Since the 1970s, many prominent professionals and educators have upheld the belief that individuals with intellectual disabilities have the right to sex education. This abiding belief motivates their work to create sex education curricula.[24] However, it is questionable whether the education materials, their delivery, and the educational outcome of learning can ensure the right-to-have-sex of people with intellectual disabilities, partly due to constraints of the broader social and institutional settings where they are situated. A close examination of sex education materials and their changes not only provides a gauge to ascertain what professionals and educators think about sexuality in relation to the norms of their times, but also illustrates what types of sexuality and expressions of sex are seen as appropriate, or normal, for this population. By extension, we can infer the ways that these professionals define the rights and freedoms of sexuality for people with intellectual disabilities and what these estimations tell us about the sexual status of people with intellectual disabilities.

In 1971, researchers and educators convened at Hot Springs, Arkansas, to discuss the sexuality of individuals with intellectual disabilities. This was one of the first comprehensive conferences discussing the sexuality of individuals with intellectual disabilities in the United States. Prior to this conference, multiple discussions were held, communicating that people with intellectual disabilities ought to be given the opportunity to create meaningful human relationships, including those of a sexual nature.[25] The Mental Retardation Program of the National Institute of Child Health and Human Development funded the 1971 conference. Individuals from the fields of biology, medicine, psychology, anthropology, sociology, genetics, education, theology, social work, and the law all attended and participated. The various papers and discussion from the conference were collected and published and a report was created for the President's Committee on Mental Retardation.

In her welcoming remarks at the 1971 conference, Jeannette Rockefeller of the President's Committee on Mental Retardation said the following:

How, in the special circumstance of the mentally retarded, do we separate fact from myth? . . . Our struggle now is toward a confluence of these characteristics, compassion and change, relative to the mentally retarded. What are the rights of the mentally retarded? How much freedom are they entitled to as private individuals? At what point and to what extent does the so-called normal element of society impose its judgment in such questions and then pursue what have been and what will be the consequences of wrong judgments both in the lives of the retarded and in society itself? You, as professionals, know best of all there will be no final, perfect answers. But, also as professionals, you find nowhere an option to discontinue this search.[26]

The questions posed by Rockefeller have remained central to discussions that determine what to teach in sex education for people with intellectual disabilities. The decision about what to teach and how to teach about sex often falls between moral suppression and a promotion of sexual rights. In other words, the answers to the questions about what rights and freedoms individuals possess often influenced efforts to create and disseminate sex education materials. In addition, the individuals whose sexuality is being discussed (and debated) are not present, highlighting how others make sexual ableist determinations through a denial of disabled perspectives.

At the same conference, Warren Johnson, one of the earliest advocates for comprehensive sex education for people with intellectual disabilities, delivered a treatise on the characteristics and subject matter of successful sex education programs. Johnson aimed to dispel myths about the sexuality of people with intellectual disabilities and stressed the importance of educators putting aside their moral beliefs about sex in general and people with intellectual disabilities in particular.[27] Historically, individuals with intellectual disabilities were seen as "sexually promiscuous," especially fecund, and in addition their offspring would also be intellectually disabled and potential criminals.[28] Sex education, Johnson argues, is "tangled up with moral theology parading as virtue, and with misconceptions parading as matters of health or decorum."[29] Traditionally, however, the Christian Right has endlessly tried to connect a sense of conservative morality with any public discussions and education about sexuality.[30] Alternate moralities are ignored, marginalized, and disrespected in this discourse. In contrast, Johnson argues that sex education can equip individuals with intellectual disabilities with the tools necessary for "their guilt-free enjoyment of life, their personal and social awareness, their ability to contribute to a world that 'cares' for them—cares not in the custodial sense of the word, but in the rationally loving sense of concern."[31] It is worth noting that Johnson contrasts sexual freedom against feelings of guilt and moral beliefs as well as discourses of health and decorum. The desire to distance sex education from morality and public health concerns highlights the complicated relationship that exists between health, morals, and sexuality.

The themes of morality, health, and autonomy are not easily delineated in discussions of sexuality and sex education. Certainly, champions of sex education as empowerment of individual autonomy gladly link being sexual as a sign of good health and morality, while the argument that sexual relations outside of heterosexual marriage is an assault on Judeo–Christian morality still has traction in U.S. society. Sexuality itself is often coded as immoral or moral, healthy or unhealthy, celebrated or repressed. The rights of people with disabilities to express their sexuality can also clash with the discourse of protectionism that constructs disabled people as vulnerable to exploitation and abuse. Normalization theory and social role valorization pose long-standing critiques of this type of conservatism, and I argue that an individual's view of sexuality influences the delivery of education about sex.[32]

There is a paradox in that sex educators provide sanctioned knowledge of sex to individuals with intellectual disabilities through recognition that the personal moralities of the educators can influence the educational content and delivery. Much in the same way that morality influences debates around sex education for those outside special education classrooms, Johnson foresees this same dynamic occurring in discussion, promotion, and delivery of sex education for people with intellectual disabilities. Sex education is as much about teaching sex as it is about educators and parents negotiating their moral beliefs and influences. Connecting discussions of morality and pleasure, Wilkerson develops her concept of "normate sex" utilizing the works of Rosemarie Garland-Thomson, Judith Butler, and Gayle Rubin.[33] According to Wilkerson, normate sex is "location specific," "not merely draw[ing] boundaries between appropriate and inappropriate desires, behaviors, identities, and spaces," but also "effect[ing] a privatization of sex, regulating nonnormative sex or keeping it taboo and under wraps, through a vast array of state and cultural supports for normate sex."[34] The sexuality of individuals labeled with intellectual disabilities is often considered nonnormative; thus the delivery of sex education materials attempts to restrict sexual expression, which illustrates how sexual ableism operates.

Another outcome of sexual ableism is the effort to limit sexual knowledge and erase firsthand experiences of sexuality. Knowledge of sexuality allows for meaningful participation in society as adults and a sense of personal worth. Johnson argues that knowledge of sexuality and the ability to be sexual is fundamental to a more holistic sense of self. Behind the advocacy for sexual rights for people with intellectual disabilities is a belief that all human beings are sexual and need to express their sexuality. Myths of intellectually disabled sexuality and reproduction also function as historical context in which the development of sex education occurs and which it seeks to address.

The basis of the claim for comprehensive sex education made by Johnson and others is that individuals with intellectual disabilities are not given or allowed access to knowledge about reproduction, sexual gratification, and other aspects of sexuality. However, when it comes to sexuality and sexual expression for people with intellectual disabilities, it is generally agreed that one of three approaches can be taken: (1) eliminate sexual expression; (2) tolerate and accept sexual expression; or (3) cultivate sexual expression.[35] When we turn our attention to more recent research around sexuality and sex education for people with intellectual disabilities, these approaches to sex are seen as influences on the day-to-day programming that occurs in educational and residential facilities. Johnson contends that members of "special groups" are treated somewhat like children and "have tended to occupy a somewhat less than adult status even though chronologically adult."[36] People in these special groups are often on the receiving end of charity, assistance, and/or pathologization by medical and related fields. The position of receiving assistance or being diagnosed with impairment can help to contribute to a childlike dependency or treatment. Within the philosophy of eliminating sexual expression, addressing or promoting sexual education and expression for "special groups" often entails a belief that sexual expression is best suppressed by any possible means, including, if necessary, segregation or punitive measures. Individuals with intellectual disabilities who lived in institutions were often sterilized "in a futile effort to eliminate the evil of masturbation, that dire source of further mental, physical and moral deterioration."[37] The discriminatory concept of mental age also helps to create this dependency.

The second philosophical approach to sexuality, to tolerate and accept sexual expression, begins with the premise that sexual expression is something natural but that social circumstances might limit the opportunities for and appropriate settings of sexual expression. Individuals subscribing to this philosophy of sexuality believe that comprehensive sex education can bring about greater societal adjustment for people in "special groups."[38] Developing and promoting sex education is one of the primary ways of tolerating and even equipping individuals with knowledge for sexual expression and not violating public sentiment about sexuality. The problem arises when the promotion of sex education mimics harm reduction, essentially preparing individuals with intellectual disabilities to protect themselves from being manipulated or abused without addressing any other aspect of sexuality. My point is not to criticize education that helps prevent abuse and manipulation. Rather, individuals can be equipped to lead diverse sexually fulfilling lives while negotiating discourses of abuse and risk.

The third philosophical approach to sexuality and people with intellectual disabilities entails cultivating sexuality. This view contends that sexuality and sexual expression is central to a fulfilling and meaningful life. By association, people who are asexual, choose to be celibate, or have no opportunity for sexual release are unable to lead a meaningful life; a key component is missing. Not only is this approach problematic because of the belief that all individuals ought to be (or are) sexual, but also because the notion that without sexual expression individuals are somehow deficient in maintaining a meaningful life devalues individuals who for whatever reason choose not to engage in sexual expression. Notwithstanding those who abstain from sex for religious and cultural reasons, the emerging asexuality identity movement illustrates that an asexual lifestyle is a valid and meaningful way to live one's life.[39] Johnson, however, advocates that this type of approach or philosophy would not only try to educate individuals with intellectual disabilities about sexuality but also be "concerned with cultivating sexual potential so that it might play the fullest possible part in the life of an individual."[40] Approaching sex education as a tool to help facilitate sexual expression is beneficial, but also potentially normalizing to a population of individuals that have already been subject to assessments of abnormality.

These three philosophical approaches to sexuality illustrate varying degrees of regulation and repression of the sexuality of certain groups of individuals. Punitive approaches to sexuality, including sterilization and segregation, highlight a type of sexual paranoia that is attached to certain groups of people including those with intellectual disabilities. Promotion of sexuality for groups of individuals who are deemed "special" becomes a political endeavor in which the answer to repression becomes facilitation of sexuality through comprehensive sex education and other measures. Sex education becomes a tool that can be either withheld or promoted, depending on negative or positive assessments of sexuality. Educators' unease about sex can determine what is contained in sex education materials. Ideologies of sex education reveal more about the teachers than about the learners.

The body of literature on the sexuality of people with intellectual disabilities is substantial, and these materials reveal how cautiously sexuality is viewed and how it is believed to require structure and professional surveillance.[41] The major finding is that the population does not have an adequate knowledge about sex and sexual practices.[42] There appears to be a need for comprehensive sex education that addresses not only the mechanics of sex but the public health aspects as well. Outside the field of intellectual disability, similar conclusions have been reached about the lack of knowledge of sex for adolescents.[43] For example, in a study comparing sex education in the United States, the Netherlands, France, and Australia, researchers found that young people in the United States report higher levels of personal shame around sex and have higher numbers of sexually transmitted infections and terminated pregnancies than their peers in the other countries.[44] Arguably, abstinence-only sex education limits sexual knowledge, promoting incorrect peer-to-peer knowledge, which contributes to negative attitudes toward sex and unhealthy outcomes. Abstinence-only sex education is "successful" insomuch as students refrain from sexual activity prior to marriage, which largely does not happen. The problem arises when sexually active individuals are not exposed to a more comprehensive understanding of sexuality. Additionally, abstinence-only education often capitalizes on the assumption that individuals need to possess sexual knowledge that facilitates harm reduction (e.g., consistent use of condoms) without acknowledging the sexual lives of students.

There is also a belief that "appropriate sex education should assist to protect those with an intellectual disability from exploitation and lack of choice."[45] Some researchers point to an increasing risk of manipulation for this population, especially at the hands of nondisabled peers, often in the context of pornography, prostitution, and stylized sex (e.g., sadomasochism).[46] As Ann Craft and Michael Craft point out, educating individuals about sex can provide knowledge about what constitutes sexual abuse, the goal being that individuals are able to comprehend when they are in abusive situations.[47] With knowledge comes an understanding of how to avoid abuse if possible and to report it to staff members and other professionals that can assist in obtaining the appropriate remedy. The lack of education and access to education is a major theme in the research on sexuality and intellectual disability. Access and exposure becomes the "solution." However, access and exposure should not mimic abstinence-based approaches, but rather should include sex education that incorporates multiple forms of pleasure, same-sex practices as well as a discussion of safer sexual habits. Focusing solely on harm reduction or disease prevention enables discourses of sexual ableism to be prioritized, while agency and discourses of pleasure are hidden.

As a whole, the majority of the literature in this area reports perceptions that this population needs unrestrained access to sex education in order to learn general anatomical features, reproductive control, and practices of safer sexuality. For example, LeeAnn Christian and her colleagues' examination of staff attitudes regarding sexual expression of women with developmental disabilities finds that "particularly in the area of sexuality, which is already an uncomfortable area for many, the lack of a comprehensive policy, the lack of staff training, or a lack of knowledge about staffs' values and beliefs can lead to potential inconsistencies in how support is provided."[48] Christian recognizes that personal views of staff members can create inconsistent responses to sexual expression, especially if there is a lack of both training and comprehensive policies. Lacking implementation of these policies creates additional inconsistencies. The variables of policies and implementation illustrate that a negative philosophical view of sex for individuals with intellectual disabilities can have a detrimental correlation with the level of sexual freedom and advocacy that occurs in specific locations. Christian concludes her analysis with recognition that staff members should be willing to advocate for increased sexual freedom for individuals with intellectual disabilities, including "advocating for a double bed" or "fund raising for the counsel of a mother with a developmental disability who is at risk of having her parental rights terminated."[49] Those working in the field of intellectual disabilities can advocate for individuals' rights, but a repression of those rights can also easily occur. While access to sex education can potentially solve knowledge and comprehension issues, on a daily basis support staff can exert control to limit the sexuality, even in seemingly benign ways such as organizing a group outing instead of allowing for personal choice in how to spend an evening.

In sum, the research advocates for consistent approaches to sex education for individuals that teach people not only about basic anatomy but also about how to recognize and avoid potential sexual abuse and manipulation. However, I believe that this approach misses the idea of sexuality altogether. Focusing on abuse primarily results in a crisis response approach to sexuality. For example, when a person with an intellectual disability becomes pregnant or is diagnosed with a sexually transmitted infection, support staff might try to control the sexual activity of the individual instead of equipping him or her with knowledge that facilitates and informs his or her sexual choices. This approach fails to recognize an individual's right to sexual freedom. Instead of following a proscriptive mode of interaction when it comes to disease prevention, individuals with intellectual disabilities have the right to make choices in relation to disease, including choices that they know are risky. Additionally, the addition of reproduction and genital-to-genital intercourse is generally suggested for inclusion in sex education programs for adults. Proposals to include nonheterosexual and non-genital practices to sex education programs are not as forthcoming, despite the implication that individuals in gender-separate congregate living settings engage in same-sex sexual practices. Some researchers contend that when people with intellectual disabilities live in same-sex living situations, they become "gay by circumstances," often resorting to sexual relations with people of the same-sex because it is most convenient.[50] Not only does this hypothesis deny that some people with intellectual disabilities are gay, lesbian, or bisexual, using the "gay by circumstances" ideology can result in removing individuals from their same-sex partner because staff members think the relationship is merely one of convenience. White remarks how sex education for blind individuals reinforces practices of heterosexuality.[51] Sex education materials for individuals with a label of intellectual disability also mimic this heterosexualizing attempt, effectively flattening diverse expressions of sexuality. Despite heteronormative ideals in relation to sexuality, some individuals with intellectual disabilities identify as gay, lesbian, bisexual, asexual, and transgendered.[52] The Canadian film *Our Compass* shares the narratives of lesbian, gay, bisexual, transgender, and questioning youth with intellectual disabilities living in the Toronto area.[53] The film is an excellent resource to help challenge assumptions regarding sexuality, gender, and competence of individuals labeled with intellectual disabilities. The individuals in the film express their sexual and gendered lives informed by the intersection of ableism, classism, transphobia, racism, and homophobia. While comprehensive sex education may increase knowledge about sexuality, it rarely addresses issues related to nonreproductive sexual activities. In the next section, I examine sex education curricula that promote learning about anatomy and colloquial terms for sex as a way to facilitate increased sexual knowledge.

What's Dirty in a Word?

Sex educators discuss the importance of utilizing what is often called "street language" in their sex education sessions with adults with intellectual disabilities. Knowing a variety of names for sexual organs apparently not only offers a level of defense against ridicule from an individual's nondisabled peers, but also allows the educator, be it a parent, teacher, or staff member to utilize language or concepts that might be familiar to an individual when more clinical language might not be comprehended.[54] Using medical terminology and expressions to describe sexuality and anatomy can place the learner at a disadvantage when trying to understand the message.[55] Being open to the use of more colloquial terms can facilitate a level of comfort and desensi-tization, allowing for the opportunity to advance education beyond a simple anatomy lesson.[56] Using more complex terminology and ex-pressions to describe sexuality and anatomy also creates a barrier be-tween the educator and the individual with intellectual disabilities.[57] Warren Johnson and Winifred Kempton make the argument that being more comfortable using "street" or "vulgar" language allows for more effective communication between the learner and educator.[58] An assessment of vulgarity is entangled with notions about class, in which "gentility is positioned against its opposite, vulgarity, viewed in sexual and classed terms. It is precisely the distinction between vulgar and the genteel, and the performance or occupation of these behavior-ally located identities, that produces the causal narrative of boredom, desire, and stimulation."[59] Even the language of sex is programmed with class-based assessments of "respectability." The amount of edu-cational labor used to make sex education relevant to individuals with intellectual disabilities points to one way in which sex education is not only about delivering knowledge but also about educators confronting their own biases and preconceived notions and making professionals more comfortable by avoiding pretension around sex.[60]

Promoting "street language," however, is not a simple solution where a diversity of words equals successful outcomes. Individuals with intellectual disabilities also might find it incredibly condescend-ing that educators use language to position themselves as insiders in a community. I would argue that individuals hear and learn the mean-ing behind words such as "blow job" and "giving head" before they know the term "fellatio." However, I also recognize that many slang terms, often in relation to the female anatomy or sexual practices be-tween lesbian or gay individuals, include a complex and oppressive history. The use of these terms perpetuates that history of oppres-sion. Jessica Fields, in her observations of sex education classrooms in North Carolina, comments that "jokes about homosexuality and silence in the face of harassment contribute to sex education class-room curricula that are homophobic (encouraging a fear and loath-ing of one's own and others' same-sex desires, behaviors, or identities) and heteronormative (reasserting straight sexuality as normal, ex-pected, and dominant)."[61] Some consider insult and shame to be the key power dynamics within various expressions of sexuality.[62] Discussions of sexuality in the classroom often are accompanied by jokes between students and the exchange of derogatory language. Despite efforts to reclaim words like "queer," certain words continue to be associated with a lexicon of intolerance. It would benefit all students if educators were equipped to recognize situations in which these words come up in the sessions and address the discriminatory meaning behind such words with the students.

An example of what seem to be effective ways to utilize "street language" in sex education programs is illustrated in the film *What's Dirty in a Word?* (1980).[63] Created by the Institute for the Study of Mental Retardation and Related Disabilities at the University of Michigan, the film is part of the Human Fulfillment Series, an eleven-episode series that address the sexuality of individuals with intellectual disabilities. It uses a variety of techniques to make educators more comfortable with the use of more vulgar terminology and gives examples of activities that can be used, including something referred to as "Fuck You Bingo" (FYB). FYB is fashioned after traditional bingo with cards and a caller, but instead of numbers, slang terms are used. When a person has a bingo on their card they are supposed to yell, "Fuck you!" to indicate the end of the game.

Shot entirely in black and white, the film teaches professionals how to utilize sexual jargon, described as the "language of the people," and advocates that "dirty words are not dirty." The film opens with two people playing Scrabble, but instead of spelling more conventional words to score points, the board is filled with sexual words including "cock," "hump," and "jiz." This scene is illustrative of the film's tone; medical terminology has no place in *What's Dirty in a Word?* Rather, the film celebrates colloquial language in the hope of desensitizing teachers and students to the affect that the words hold as well as increasing sexual knowledge. Desensitizing sexual morals and taboos can reduce some sexual guilt that students might experience. Additionally, songs from the sexual musical *Let My People Come* are incorporated throughout.[64]

Besides FYB, the film also suggests an activity called "Language Bombardment" (LB), where a facilitator calls out a sexual term or body part and the pupils then shout out alternate words.[65] In the film, the facilitator lists "void in the jar" and some of the words suggested include "peeing," and "wet." Next, "anal sex" and "homosexuality" are suggested for LB. Some of the participant responses for these terms reinforce heterosexual privilege and homosexual oppression, thus highlighting the complex oppressive history that language can bring. Colloquial terms to describe nonnormative sexual practices are often deeply intertwined with histories of discrimination that in turn demonize these sexual practices and activities. Calling a practice "deviant" or "abnormal" potentially further isolates those individuals who seek to or already engage in those practices. In sex education efforts, individual experiences of oppression can be intertwined with the language that is expressed (or silenced).

As an example, John D'Emilio and Estelle Freedman discuss how, at the end of the 1970s, "conservative proponents of an older sexual order had appeared," which led to a great incorporation of sexuality into U.S. national politics with the emergence of HIV/AIDS and the sustained interests of feminism and gay liberation.[66] *What's Dirty in a Word?* is a reminder of historical times in which discussions about sexuality and sex education were largely dominated by the Reagan-influenced New Right and the Christian Right.[67] This historical context points to the need for facilitators to be especially adept at navigating the complicated phraseology that can be "street language"—what do various words mean and what are their relation to sexuality, anatomy, minority identities, hate crimes, and so forth? And how are certain words used to perpetuate discrimination and oppression? LB and FYB can be effective activities that release socially imposed tension and awkwardness around sexual language, but they also have the potential to reproduce hate speech.

Another approach to facilitating sexual knowledge is the use of explicit drawings and dolls to teach people about anatomy (abstraction or unrealistic drawings of male and female genitalia might be more difficult to comprehend for individuals with intellectual disabilities). Some researchers contend that the use of pictures and images, even explicit ones, is more effective than utilizing language alone.[68] Eliciting information, with the aid of images and pictures, can gauge the sexual knowledge of an individual and the kind of education that might be needed or beneficial to a particular group of learners. A distinction is made between eliciting information from individuals and giving it to them.[69] These images and pictures, however, are most likely "pink-skinned, slender, able-bodied, and conventionally modest female bodies" that affirm "normatively racialized and gendered ideas about a girl's and women's sexuality."[70] Clitorises are routinely absent on these representations of female bodies, while "discussions of erections and ejaculation support men's and boy's claims to pleasure."[71] Female sexuality is more closely associated with discussions of reproduction while male sexuality incorporates pleasure and reproduction. Women with intellectual disabilities have historically been constructed as especially fecund, thus supposedly warranting eugenic sterilization.[72] This attention to controlling women's reproductive abilities is reflected in sex education. While men with intellectual disabilities are also not encouraged to reproduce, contemporary efforts to sterilize or control their sexuality are not as evident. Women with intellectual disabilities, on the other hand, are placed on birth control, often without their knowledge, as a way to limit their reproduction.[73] While sex education materials are heavily dependent on visual representations of male and female bodies, there remains the potential of distancing discussions of pleasure, especially for female students, in favor of more focus on reproductive anatomy. The CIRCLES® curriculum, discussed below, is organized around photographs of situations, sexual and otherwise, that are shown to individuals along with a narrative to facilitate understanding. One of the most widely circulated sex education materials focuses on visual representations of sexuality.

Other materials suggest the use of anatomical dolls to illustrate male and female reproductive organs. At a rudimentary level, these dolls act as tactile tools that can be used to educate people about anatomy. However, the dolls require a certain amount of abstraction, since a plush doll, no matter how lifelike, is not sufficiently representative of a nude body without some sort of generalizability. White discusses how sex education for blind individuals also advocates the use of dolls and tactile models of genitalia.[74] White remarks, "Sex education does not teach the blind about sexuality per se. It teaches them only about the dominant model of sexuality, in which the binary categories of male/female are foundational. The foremost concern of sex education is thus to impart to the blind both the fact and the importance of biological difference between the sexes."[75] The same could be said of sex education for individuals labeled with intellectual disabilities. Sex education is about "assimilation" of those with intellectual disabilities "into the heterosexual matrix."[76] Individuals with the label of intellectual disability are configured outside this matrix when their sexuality is restrained or denied. Their queerness is illustrative of the instability of a system like heterosexuality, where the actualization of sexuality prompts family members, governments, and trained professionals to restrict and deny the very sexuality that sex education materials attempt to control.

Additionally, any choice of doll reinforces a type of anatomy that might not apply to all individuals, especially those with atypical sexual organs. Anne Fausto-Sterling comments that mixed-gender bodies challenge the constructed "normal" dichotomous gender system: "Bodies in the 'normal' range are culturally intelligible as males or females, but the rules for living as male or female are strict. No oversized clits or undersized penises allowed. No masculine women or effeminate men need apply . . . If we choose, over a period of time, to let mixed-gender bodies and altered patterns of gender-related behavior become visible, we will have, willy-nilly, chosen to change the rules of cultural intelligibility."[77] The seemingly benign use of dolls to teach anatomy reinforces the process of gender hegemony by illustrating the "ideal" (i.e., normal) body for students. Those without the ideal, normative body are made invisible in the representational silencing of the intelligible bodies. Finally, using a doll can mask other features of identity not tied to sex; for example, an agency serving a diverse clientele would require multiple dolls representing the palette of humanness.

Educational use of dolls to teach sex can facilitate creative understandings of sex and desire that foster imagination and playful ways to disrupt heteronormative regulation.[78] However, as with any sex education materials, there is also a strong chance that hegemonic understandings of sexuality can be reinforced. Nicholas Addison argues that the use of dolls can not only "reinforce stereotypical notions of heteronormative culture but also to invade and police the imaginative spaces that playing with dolls once afforded."[79] Additionally, there appears to be little flexibility for family structures not based on blood relations, thus limiting the strength of alternative kinship that queer life brings.[80] For instance, cross-dressing dolls are generally absent, as are the use of props with dolls that signal fetishes.

Outline drawings of male and female bodies are often used to assess the sexual knowledge of individuals with intellectual disabilities. While the methods discussed previously depend on a certain amount of generalizing based on assumptions of typical male and female bodies, these drawings allow for individuals to fill in a representation of their own bodies. Less prescriptive curricula where female genitalia are not represented as designed to receive male genitalia allow for a type of re-imagination and counter-narrative to more dominant understandings of the sex-gender system. Enabling students to draw images and likenesses of their bodies, which are not necessarily aligned with a two-sex model, enables an explicit recognition of wider diversity of sex and biology. There is a sense of creativity in allowing students the opportunities to personalize sexuality instead of subjecting them to educator-approved ways of expressing it.

Uses of "street language," so-called anatomically correct or explicit images, and more creative methods of instruction all seek to increase sexual knowledge. Regardless, if the methods are effective, they have the potential to reference a history of discrimination and oppression based on different anatomies, but also can reinforce a certain type of heterosexual-based sexuality. Queer sexuality, for example, might be pejoratively referenced, as it was is in the clip from *What's Dirty in a Word?* Balancing the utility of using and learning street language, for example, with educating individuals about the oppressive history that certain words have requires an adept facilitator; speaking to the oppressive history that certain words reference brings an added sense of justice to the already potentially political process of educating individuals about sex and sexuality. Maintaining a sense of creativity in the process of developing and delivering sex education helps avoid dichotomous ideologies, which regard alternative sexualities as deviant. A reluctance to embrace creativity and maintain openness can allow sexual ableism to continue its hegemony as a mode of regulation and a system of qualification, which then justifies exclusion.

In the last section of the chapter, I analyze the widely used CIRCLES® series to examine how sexuality is taught for people with intellectual disabilities, including aspects of sexually transmitted infections such as HIV/AIDS. The analysis below reveals how this widely used curriculum reinforces heterosexual privilege and sexual ableism at the expense of a more creative understanding of sexuality.

CIRCLES®

The CIRCLES® series is one of the most widely used curricula to teach health promotion, sexuality, and social relationships. An examination of the thirty-year-old series offers a narrative of historical progression tracing out the relatively static ways sexuality has been taught to individuals with intellectual disabilities. The CIRCLES® sex education materials were developed to teach individuals with intellectual disabilities about social norms, as they relate to sexual and nonsexual relationships. CIRCLES® "takes the abstraction of personal space and relationship boundaries and makes them concrete and specific,"[81] utilizing behavioral psychology to teach students responses to social situations.[82] In order to accomplish this educational goal, CIRCLES® employs six concentric circles to illustrate the concepts of relationship boundaries, personal space, and "appropriate" contact.[83] The circles are most often represented on a large poster or a mat, where pictures of various people can be attached to reinforce the meaning of the circles. The innermost circle is the "purple private circle," which has only room for one picture, the individual undergoing the education. The circle is supposed to "convey the specialness and autonomy" of the individual.[84] One of the creators of the program describes the inner purple circle as representing that the individual "deserves to be treated like a king or queen."[85] Individuality plays a major role in CIRCLES®, where, at the end of each vignette, a series of prompts ask individuals to reflect on how to personalize the education to their own situations. The "luxury of individuality" as a given norm in this education reveals class-based assumptions not necessarily afforded individuals with intellectual disabilities. Sometimes it is difficult to be the "queen" or "king" of your body when personal care is provided by other people, because many individuals with intellectual disabilities are not able to demand respect from their care providers. However, refocusing the education on individuals' decisions about their lives and allowing them to access their bodies is one of the primary goals of the education.[86] As part of teaching decision making, Story 10, "Talking It Over," from the video series CIRCLES®: *Safer Ways,* tells the story of two white adults, Lorraine and Steve. Lorraine and Steve decide to be sexually active while using condoms. After watching the brief story, students are asked if they know how to obtain and use condoms and if they would make a similar decision about using condoms, if they were sexually active.[87] One of the implications of teaching individuals about contraception is to recognize that they are sexual beings and can be trusted with determining their own reproductive and sexual health outcomes.

The second of the concentric circles is the "blue hug circle." This circle represents those individuals that are the closest to the student: mother, father, boyfriend, and girlfriend. The training manual for CIRCLES® dictates that there are very few people that an individual might hug.[88] A common perception of certain individuals with intellectual disabilities is that they are eternally happy and generous with hugs and affection, even with strangers. CIRCLES® addresses this by laying out which individuals from which it is appropriate to receive a hug. Kempton and Kahn discuss how one of the positive outcomes of sex education over the last few decades has been reducing the number of "inappropriate hug[s]" common prior to developed sex education efforts.[89] Nevertheless, dictating hugs and other expressions of affection has the potential to reinforce a certain type of monogamous relationship, intimacy, and sexuality wherein there is apparently no room between the circle of privacy and the circle of hugs for multiple partners.[90] This is but one of the ways in which assessments of normalcy and morality influence the delivery of sex education and help to enact sexual ableism. The focus on hugging also highlights a culturally specific approach that might not reflect standards of intimacy in other cultures.[91] Other countries might have different standards of acceptable physical contact, thus illustrating how content of sex education shifts based on factors such as geographic location or cultural mores.

The third circle is known as the "green far away hug circle." This circle is supposed to represent individuals that are supposedly less likely to receive any sort of physical contact like hugging. The example given of a person in this circle is a best friend that would receive a hug on his or her birthday.[92] This circle is supposed to be populated with extended family members and people who act like family.[93]

The fourth circle in the CIRCLES® curriculum is the "yellow handshake circle," which comprises people "whose name you know and who know your name."[94] This circle might include a larger number of acquaintances with whom a handshake level of intimacy is "appropriate." The handshake circle comes with a reduced level of trust in the safety of the relationship.[95] The goal of describing the reduced level of trust is to prevent individuals from abuse, sexual and otherwise, from strangers or those with limited levels of intimacy. Despite the goal of protection that runs through sex education, as I discuss in chapter 1, those that are more intimate with individuals with intellectual disabilities enact most sexual abuse. Protectionism is problematic to the extent that it denies agency and instead focuses on the perceived vulnerability of the subject. If the primary focus is on the protection of individuals, their ability to act intentionally in their sexual lives can be covered over in the discourse of protectionism. Comprehensive education would ensure that individuals with intellectual disabilities are equipped through education to recognize and report abuse as well as to live fulfilling sexual lives. And while it might be controversial, comprehensive sex education also equips learners to choose all types of sexual activities and behaviors, even kinds that are assumed to be (or actually are) risky.

Building on the theme of reduced potential for abuse is the fifth circle, known as the "orange wave circle." This circle includes individuals with "no physical or emotional closeness," translating to people that are only acquaintances by way of a wave.[96] While the previous circles can aid in identifying which individuals are appropriate to be intimate with and hug, for example, the orange circle dictates that all children should receive a wave and no physical contact.[97] When people with intellectual disabilities take an interest in children, known or otherwise, there is always the potential that what is innocent contact will be interpreted as sexual abuse. CIRCLES® not only hopes to protect individuals with intellectual disabilities from experiencing abuse, but also lays out concrete rules of social interaction that can facilitate individuals from being accused of abuse. The implication is that people with intellectual disabilities can be seen as potential predators as well as vulnerable to experiencing abuse and manipulation. This contradictory assessment of predatory and vulnerable reflects the limited ways in which individuals with intellectual disabilities are seen. One of the implications of this assessment is that outside the group home, individuals with intellectual disabilities are seen as predatory, especially in relation to children and others considered vulnerable. The uncertainty allows for increased professional attention to individuals' behaviors, since these behaviors supposedly put them at risk of experiencing or committing abuse.

The last circle is the "red stranger space." This space is unlike the previous circles, where there is a definite beginning and end to the boundaries of the circle, in that the red step is represented by a wave-shaped border. The waved border indicates that the number of individuals that populate this circle is limitless. Most of the people in this section are people that the individual does not speak to or touch, with the exception being what are called "community helpers." A community helper is someone who wears a badge, name tag, or uniform.[98] In this circle, individuals are supposed to adhere to this directive: "I do not touch strangers, strangers do not touch me. I decide who will be close to me."[99] This circle is reminiscent of the old adage, "Don't talk to strangers." The implication of this circle is that to remain safe, individuals should associate only with people they know. Understandably, individuals with intellectual disabilities can be seen as innocent and an "easy target" for sexual, physical, and emotional abuse. One way to counter this is to prescribe a rigid set of social interaction guidelines that individuals with intellectual disabilities should follow. The problem arises when these rigid guidelines for social interaction undermine an individual's self-determination. Placing a priority on protection contrasts with dignity of risk. Self-determination as a philosophy recognizes that individuals are capable of living purposeful lives while navigating and managing any risk or consequence of those actions. Sexual ableism attempts to limit action based on assumptions of competence or vulnerability.

As a whole, this rainbowlike progression of levels of intimacy from purple to red appears to reinforce a logical, easy to understand assessment of who is appropriate to touch, be intimate with, and who should be avoided. While I am not trying to dissuade efforts to increase protection and "appropriate" intimacy, the rigidity and prescription of social relations that the CIRCLES® materials promote are both patriarchal and heteronormative. At the same time, however, heterosexual parenthood in the nuclear family is discouraged. Besides the inner purple circle, in which there is room for one, the next circle lays out a prescribed sexuality and intimacy. Simplistically, intimacy is only allowed for parents, who are represented as a mother *and* father as well as a *singular* boyfriend or girlfriend. This approved family structure excludes queer and alternative lifestyles.[100] Those with multiple or frequent partners might be discouraged and judged as promiscuous by the facilitator. Additionally, there appears to be little flexibility for less-typical family structures not based on heterosexual family units. CIRCLES® dictates *the way* of approved social relations, masking a conservative political view of families with a discourse of protection against abuse and manipulation. This view of relationships and family makeup mirrors those views found with more liberal, homophobic constructs of sexuality. While debates around sexuality often pit conservative Christians against liberals, debates about sexuality do not always adhere to political or partisan traditions.

A tension in CIRCLES® exists between the content, which is largely focused on courting and heterosexual sexual activities between committed partners, and the assumption that individuals with labels of intellectual disability ought not be participants in sexual activities. Social acceptability for disabled subjects, as configured through CIRCLES®, is predicated on living nonreproductive, monogamous lives. While individuals with labels of intellectual disability can work against restrictive binaries of "good" and "bad" sexual activity, in a sense queering or cripping this dichotomy, their sexuality is assumed to be endlessly normative in CIRCLES® through prescribed social interactions.

How exactly does the prescription of social relations play out in discussions about HIV/AIDS? The *Safer Ways* curriculum is a multi-video instructional aid used to educate individuals on effective ways to avoid communicable disease and sexually transmitted infections including HIV/AIDS. Created originally in 1988, *Safer Ways* is the last program in the CIRCLES® series. As a whole there are thirteen stories, conceived of as vignettes where each story represents an effective way to maintain a "disease-free" life, as if one could perform a prescribed set of activities to be free of infection. Tim Dean remarks, "Although defined as the body's normal state, health also has been idealized as something for which one must strive; it is no longer something one possesses. When framed in terms of 'lifestyle,' everyday living is transformed into an interminable exercise in risk management."[101] In much the same way that the promotion of masturbation as approved sexuality limits the sexuality of certain populations of people while enforcing a conservative political agenda, *Safer Ways* also promotes this version of sexuality, health, and epidemiology. Even the title of the program reinforces this agenda, in not so subtle ways, where each letter of the title refers to "a major concept in limiting the spread of AIDS."[102] The acronym is as follows:

S for STAY HEALTHY: Eat right, get exercise and appropriate rest.

A for ABSTAIN: No sexual contact with others that involves shared body fluids.

F for FREE FROM ILLEGAL DRUGS: Avoid using IV drugs and shared needles.

E for EDUCATE YOURSELF AND OTHERS: Knowing how disease is spread gives power to make good choices.

R for RELY ON CONDOMS: If sexual activity is chosen, a condom is used.[103]

At the end of each story, this acronym is utilized to show the steps the characters use to remain "safe" from infection. The instruction booklet also prompts the teacher to reinforce the specific steps that were taken by the characters in the vignettes. For example, Story 12, "Safety Circle," shows Sam, a white male who is not currently sexually active, purchasing condoms at a drug store, in case he becomes sexually active at some point in the future. Sam is applauded because he buys the condoms and stores one in his wallet and the rest in a drawer in his room.[104] At the end of the story, we learn that Sam remains safe because he is abstaining and preparing to "rely" on condoms in case he chooses to have intercourse at some point, presumably when he is in a long-term relationship. Abstaining becomes a dominant mantra throughout the education; sexual and personal health incorporates exercise, eating well, and abstention. Many individuals, including seemingly committed couples, are commended for abstaining from sexual relations until marriage or some other point in the future because the risk of infection is apparently too great. Individuals with intellectual disabilities are encouraged, through a linking of abstinence with "good health," to refrain from sexual activity. Jan Zita Grover, in the foundation article "AIDS: Keywords," writes that notions of risk groups "roughly identified people whose membership in a group practicing certain risk behaviors was likely to bring them in contact with the virus."[105] Any uncertainties or reservations about sexual activity are momentarily appeased under the cover of abstention and self-denial, particularly through the construction of "high-risk groups."

The curriculum continues with discussions of drug use, sex work, and nonheterosexual sexual activities. Primarily, the subject content of *Safer Ways* discusses the importance of personal hygiene, diet, and exercise in maintaining a healthier and potentially disease-free life. When sexuality is discussed in the curriculum, it often involves a white heterosexual couple that appears to have been in a relationship for an extended period. While Story 8, "A Touch of Romance," praises Lynn and her boyfriend, John, for abstaining from sexual activity until they are married, Story 9, "His-Story, Her-Story" provides the narrative of Sarah and Robert beginning a sexual relationship only after they had STI tests and were married. Even though the narrative of "A Touch of Romance" clearly describes that Lynn and John have "strong sexual feelings for each other" before marriage, they ultimately deny the "tingley [*sic*] feelings they get when they are so close."[106] Positive sexuality, according to *Safer Ways*, is that which happens after marriage between heterosexual, "disease-free" couples. To be fair, Story 10, "Talking It Over," does present a couple that chooses to be sexually active outside of marriage; however, the curriculum recommends that the teacher assess whether this scenario is applicable to the students in the classroom and an "acceptable choice."[107] Students are not asked for their input regarding contraception. Rather, the instructor is encouraged to determine the appropriateness of this topic for their students, illustrating one way in which sexual agency is usurped by professionals.[108] When discussed, consistent use of condoms is seen as the next best defense against "the spread of AIDS" besides abstinence.[109]

What about those who are not in committed relationships or those who are not heterosexual? One of the thirteen stories in *Safer Ways*, "Fitness Fever," discusses a gay couple, Phil and Dan, who, according to the script, are "sexually faithful to each other."[110] While inclusion of nondominant sexualities might reach a wider audience, upon further investigation a certain view of gay sex is discussed in *Safer Ways*. The students learn that Phil and Dan have not known each other very long, but they are "very close" and have had sexual relationships with previous partners.[111] Although in a committed relationship, Phil and Dan are presented as having prior sexual experiences and, according to the curriculum instructional guide, teachers are supposed to use this story to differentiate "AIDS-safe activities from high-risk activities."[112] The educational goal of this story is to "disarm fears about casual contact with men who have chosen a gay lifestyle."[113] Not only is the language here homophobic, it also denies the reality that "chosen gay lifestyles" are pleasurable and central to an individual's sense of self. The diversity of experiences and practices are erased through the linking of identity (gay) to risk (AIDS).[114] As Jan Zita Grover remarks regarding risk groups, constructing a group of men as "risky" can further "isolate and condemn people rather than to contact or protect them."[115] In addition, individuals that identify as gay, or are questioning or curious of their sexuality, are further silenced in this type of phraseology.

The AIDS-safe activities discussed in "Fitness Fever" include swimming, lifting weights in a gym, and sharing a meal.[116] Perhaps the purpose of showing that Phil and Dan are "safe" doing these activities is to teach other students that they do not have to be afraid of participating in these activities with gay men.[117] Regardless of apparent levels of safety, the portrayal of gay sex as risky and potentially dangerous is reinforced in the curriculum, summarized in the admonishment to Phil and Dan: "When Dan and Phil are in private, they need to be AIDS-SAFER."[118] Even though the curriculum also instructs that "judgmental attitudes regarding either the nature of the relationship or the practice itself, are not appropriate here," there is a clear indication that the inclusion of Phil and Dan's story is not to provide a narrative about gay love and relationships, but to calm any nervousness related to casual contact with gay men.[119] Even after suggesting an activity in which students help to name "high-risk sexual activities," and we can assume that gay sex is at the top of that list, the curriculum prompts instructors to suggest masturbation as an appropriate method to minimize the risk of HIV/AIDS transmission in a gay relationship.[120] This suggestion of masturbation as a method of safe sexual activities for a couple relates to the discussion in the next chapter of masturbation training as one of the few sanctioned ways for people with intellectual disabilities to be sexual.

Constructions of activities and groups of individuals as risky links notions of disease to proscribed behaviors. Accordingly, as Jan Zita Grover remarks: "Diseases, we are taught, are often communicable, the general term applied to both infectious and contagious diseases. In discussions of AIDS, because of distinctions *not* made—between syndrome and disease, between infectious and contagious—there is often a casual slippage from *communicable* to *contagious*. From this semantic error flow many consequences, not the least of which is widespread public terror about 'catching' AIDS through casual contact."[121] In discussions of AIDS, CIRCLES® reinforces a linking of gay sex as risky, while trying to mitigate assumptions of risk for casual contact. Curricular confusion arises in constructing diverse populations as at risk or not because of sexual identity, assumptions of the meaning of disability, and sexual activity. While this particular curriculum is silent on issues related to mutual masturbation, the limited inclusion of gay male sex and obvious exclusion of lesbian sexuality, delineates the narrow pathway of appropriate sexuality discussed earlier—namely, between committed heterosexual partners utilizing a consistent practice of condom usage. Condoms and abstinence are presented as the universal panaceas for HIV transmission between heterosexual couples; queer individuals and those with high-risk sexual activities best masturbate or use condoms as a last resort.

One other issue ought to be discussed in relation to the neoconservative political view of sexuality that *Safer Ways* endorses. As part of the discussion on HIV transmission, intravenous drug use is represented twice in the curriculum. In Story 13, "Just Say No!!" Marguerita and Lynn refuse to inject drugs with an acquaintance. As a whole, this vignette is benign—not many would argue for frequent sharing of needles between injecting drug users. The other story, "The Wasteland," makes stereotypical connections between drug users, sex solicitation, and risk of transmission. "The Wasteland" tells a story of Zeke, a wheelchair user, who happens to be the only visibly disabled individual in the curriculum, despite being a sex education program targeted directly at individuals with intellectual disabilities. In the story, Zeke is on his way home from work when he comes across an old co-worker, Rose. Rose is injecting drugs in a vacant lot, and asks Zeke to join her. He says no, presumably due to a fear of contracting HIV. After Zeke refuses the drugs, Rose proposes sexual intercourse with Zeke—not only is she a drug user, she is shown willing to engage in casual sex. On Rose's body, two of the "high risk" categories of HIV transmission collide—sexual solicitation and intravenous drug use. Under highly dramatic music, Zeke refuses Rose's latest offer, "does a wheelee [*sic*] and leaves Rose in the background."[122] Zeke remains AIDS-SAFER by abstaining not only from drug use but also from sex with a drug user.

Safer Ways reinforces a type of morality that continues the metonymic stigma associated with HIV transmission: those who "spread" and "infect" others with HIV are drug users, sex workers, homosexuals, and those with multiple partners.[123] The way to remain safer is to keep these individuals in the outer levels of your personal circle: yellow handshake, orange wave, and red stranger. CIRCLES® encourages a cordoning off of those who can make you unsafe; the lines of the circles are solid and there appears to be very little movement allowed.[124] While in the most distant circle the red stranger space is represented by a wavelike border indicating that people can enter and exit into this stranger zone frequently, the ability to move from orange to blue, for example, is not discussed. *Safer Ways* utilizes spatial separation as a stopgap to failed prevention of HIV transmission—for example, one should only engage in sexual relations within a committed relationship (even while utilizing condoms), and one should not have any physical contact or connection with anyone in the outer levels of the circle. Ultimately, safety (and perhaps health) occurs via deliberate and purposeful separation.[125] Focusing on abstinence as a way to avoid sexually transmitted infections, however, does not result in decreased levels of these infections.[126] Traditional ways of promoting abstinence as effective public health policy, as seen in CIRCLES®, do not always afford the protection promised. Sex and sexual encounters are generally seen as dangerous in CIRCLES®, as a way of experiencing abuse, manipulation, and disease infection. Instead of educating individuals about the possibilities and pleasures of sex, CIRCLES® ultimately tries to limit the sexual expression of individuals with intellectual disabilities.

Moving toward Pleasure and Agency

This chapter traces the various ways in which sex education activities for individuals with intellectual disabilities prescribe what is seen as appropriate or *normal* expressions of sexuality. Some efforts, like *What's Dirty in a Word?* give individuals an increased lexicon to describe sexuality, reproduction, and anatomy. Knowing the multiple and varied names for "penis" might not provide increased opportunities for sexual interactions, but it might allow for comprehension of a joke of a sexual nature on a television sitcom. A knowledge of colloquial sexual terms helps to facilitate a discussion of sex and sexuality. Likewise, using graphic images or models can give tangible examples to individuals of a certain kind of anatomy—that which is photographed and reproduced in the materials. The problem is that this type of activity capitalizes on representing the "typical" vagina, albeit with a missing clitoris. What makes it possible to include diverse bodies in sex education, such as those without typical genitalia, including those undergoing gender transitions, intersex individuals, and persons with smaller or larger genitalia? By promoting "street language" and images of anatomy, sex education lays out a very particular view of sexuality for individuals with intellectual disabilities—one where that same knowledge can perpetuate discrimination of atypical bodies and queer individuals and allow dominant expectations of heterosexuality to prevail.

When sexuality is specifically addressed, as it is in *Safer Ways*, in terms of abstinence and heterosexuality, this narrow version is endorsed as an effective way to limit the transmission of HIV. Those who choose not to, or simply do not, practice heterosexuality are further ostracized in this neoconservative view of sexuality, which favors nonreproductive heterosexuality between committed partners. Within the reviewed educational materials, sexuality is calculated and deliberate. All spontaneity has been replaced with lengthy discussions of appropriateness and reduction of risk. The underlying message is that individuals with intellectual disabilities are not able or are unwilling to participate in spontaneous passionate sexual activity; it is best to leave that to their nondisabled peers. But spontaneity in sex is also absent in sex education curriculum in general education classes, despite research indicating that adolescents continue to have intercourse earlier and more frequently than their cohorts from earlier generations.[127] The inadequacies contained in sex education materials for disabled individuals mirror those found in sex education materials in general, including exclusive focus on the gendered "harms" of sexuality (e.g., "Don't get pregnant, contract HIV, or get raped").

Desire and pleasure are also missing in these sex education materials. As Michelle Fine discussed over two decades earlier, "A genuine discourse of desire would invite adolescents to explore what feels good and bad, desirable and undesirable, grounded in experience, needs and limits."[128] Allowing students to access their own experiences of what feels "good and bad" in discussions of sex mirrors research findings that students often supplement what they learned in sex education classrooms with their own experiences and discussions with peers.[129] Sexual pleasure can challenge gendered aspects of power "by introducing women's capacity for self-determination."[130] For example, feminist-based sex education that not only addresses gender inequality but also discusses desire and pleasure separate from male heterosexuality demonstrates the transformative potential of sex education.[131] Sex education can both empower individuals and provide them with the tools to avoid sexually transmitted infections. Traditionally, public health promotion in sex education has overshadowed discussions of pleasure in sexuality, as if these are incompatible.[132] Pleasure and desire often include alternatives to vaginal intercourse, including mutual masturbation.[133] Allowing a discussion of pleasure back into sex education classrooms "would release females from a position of receptivity, enable an analysis of the dialectics of victimization and pleasure, and would pose female adolescents as subjects of sexuality."[134] Sex education has the potential to reinforce gender inequality; a discourse of pleasure that allows for alternate sexualities to be discussed is one way to mitigate this inequality.[135] Unfortunately, even when specific sexual activities like masturbation are discussed for people with intellectual disabilities, discourses of pleasure get lost. Sex education can meaningfully incorporate discussions of pleasure and sexual agency alongside equally compelling discussions of remaining safe and healthy in sexuality while avoiding the promotion of sexual ableism. Changing the content and delivery of sex education materials for those with intellectual disabilities can provide the impetus to transition sex education as a whole into a more balanced conversation between pleasure and protection.

Instead of merely advocating for increased exposure and access to sex education, an examination of the content of sex education is needed in order to envision what can be taught. This chapter offers one attempt to historically examine the contents of sex education curricula. Additionally, protectionism as a goal denies the reality that individuals are already and always active sexual agents, in a sense already doing it and knowing it. Gender and heteronormative assumptions in sex education should be thoroughly reexamined and challenged. The notion of power that comes from age, ability, gender, class, and race differences should be named in order to facilitate negotiations among individuals. Integrating sexual pleasure into sex education is a worthwhile endeavor largely absent up to this point. An incorporation of pleasure has the potential to make unpleasant sexual experiences visible while respecting individuals with intellectual disabilities as sexual agents with diverse sexual needs and interests as well as a range of both strengths and vulnerabilities. Like Lena in *Yolk*, individuals labeled with intellectual disabilities are able to exercise agency to navigate restrictive environments to express their sexual selves. Comprehensive sex education that addresses sexual pleasure and intimacy as well as aspects of reproduction, safety, and disease prevention will benefit all, regardless of disability status. The problems identified with sex education materials for those with disabilities are also relevant to sex education in general. Sustained focus on reducing harms and enforcing heterosexuality does not adequately enable individuals to be informed agents of their sexual lives.

The next chapter continues the discussion about appropriate sexuality with an examination of masturbation training for individuals. I make connections between people with intellectual disabilities and prisoners. We will see how masturbation as a prescribed action is not only the answer to behavioral issues but also a potential solution to the "problem" of sexuality for individuals with intellectual disabilities.

3 Sex Can Wait, Masturbate

The Politics of Masturbation Training

The 2008 Australian film *The Black Balloon* narrates the story of teenager Thomas (Rhys Wakefield) and his older brother, Charlie (Luke Ford), as they adjust to life in a new town in New South Wales.[1] Charlie is autistic, and his autism is presented as causing obstacles to sexual self-fulfillment and brotherly unity. In particular, Charlie's masturbatory habits provide dramatic obstacles to Thomas and his budding relationship with classmate Jackie (Gemma Ward). Unlike the scene in *Yolk* discussed in the preceding chapter, wherein Lena uses a stolen copy of *The Joy of Sex* to explore her own body, Charlie's public masturbation at a dinner table birthday celebration falls back on the trope of inappropriate public masturbation perpetrated by individuals with the label of intellectual disability.

At the celebration for his sixteenth birthday, Thomas's parents, Maggie (Toni Collette) and Simon (Erik Thomson), present their son with L-plates, thus signifying their formal acknowledgment of Thomas's transition into adulthood, marking a time in the not-so-distant future when Thomas can drive without supervision, which he imagines as a time of freedom.[2] At this moment, the promise of freedom—from parents and disabled brothers—highlights the different life options for the brothers. After the presentation of gifts, Maggie and Simon proceed to cut the birthday cake and dish up ice cream, not noticing that Charlie has his hand down his pants masturbating. Jackie first notices Charlie masturbating, exclaiming, "Oh, my God!" Almost immediately, Charlie's parents spring into action, signing, and vocalizing that Charlie is supposed to masturbate in his bedroom. The viewer gets the idea that Charlie's public masturbation is a regular occurrence. In the process of restraining and redirecting Charlie, Thomas's birthday cake and celebration are ruined. Quite literally, Charlie's sexual behavior becomes an obstacle, foreshadowing a time when Thomas will have to watch over his disabled brother, which is imagined as infringing on his impending freedom and his own exploration of sexuality with Jackie. Charlie's public masturbation in *The Black Balloon* is not just an action of a disabled adolescent, but also is configured in the film as signifying a threat to Thomas and his future life. Charlie's sexual behavior, as we will see below, would seem to facilitate placement into a masturbation-training program.

Eve Sedgwick in "Jane Austen and the Masturbating Girl" writes:

> I want to argue here that the status of the masturbator among these many identities was uniquely formative. I would suggest that as one of the very earliest embodiments of "sexual identity" in the period of the progressive epistemological overloading of sexuality, the masturbator may have been the cynosural center of a remapping of individual identity, will, attention, and privacy along modern lines that the reign of "sexuality," and its generic concomitant in the novel and in novelistic point of view, now lead us to take for granted. It is of more than chronological import if the (lost) identity of the masturbator was the proto-form of modern sexual identity itself.[3]

Additionally, in *Abnormal,* Michel Foucault discusses the emergence of the "masturbator" as a universal subject in the eighteenth century, naming masturbation as "the universal secret shared by everyone but disclosed to no one."[4] Taken together, these arguments convey the notion that masturbation and the masturbator are foundational in the development of sexual identity, but beyond that, surveillance, study, and discourse surrounding masturbation illustrate the potential seismic force contained within the practice itself. Put simply, claiming masturbation as a sexual practice and identity challenges conventional understandings of sexuality and sexual identity as binary or categorical.

Given the productive materiality of masturbation, including mention in film and theories of sexuality, this chapter traces the ways in which it has been studied and subsequently regulated through sexology and sex education in Western contexts as a way to manage the sexuality of people with intellectual disabilities. Masturbation training in sexology and sex education represents one of the few sanctioned approaches for individuals with intellectual disabilities, and similar approaches to masturbation emerge in prisons, nursing homes, and residential institutions. The complicated relationship between HIV and masturbation also plays an important role in this discussion. The discourse around disease and infection prevention at times reinforces masturbation as a suitable sexual activity. In exploring how and why masturbation is either promoted as an appropriate sexual activity or as a sign of deviant sexuality for people with intellectual disabilities, a larger analysis is required in order to connect the organizational, political, and spatial contexts of masturbation training for individuals with intellectual disabilities. How is masturbation, as well as other forms of sexual activity, regulated, thus manifesting sexual ableism?

Sex education materials for individuals with intellectual disabilities generally promote appropriate sexuality as nonreproductive, solitary, yet oriented toward the opposite sex. Expectations of pleasure and desire are absent from sex education, perhaps because educators' discomfort with disabled sexuality results in limited promotion of sexual activity. Neoconservative ideologies of family, reproduction, and disease masquerade as discourses of prevention while dictating specific kinship structures for individuals with intellectual disabilities. Reflecting these educational ideologies and methods, masturbation training in the case of individuals with intellectual disabilities reveals similar assumptions about nonnormative sexuality, discipline, and surveillance. Masturbation training teaches individuals how to masturbate in safe, appropriate, and effective ways.

Using as a point of departure two scenes from a 1975 American film, *The ABC of Sex Education for Trainables,* in which two people are either praised or reprimanded for masturbating, I show how sexuality for individuals with intellectual disabilities is simultaneously programmed, restricted, and professionalized by different training methods for the purpose of curbing public masturbation.[5] The assumption that individuals with intellectual disabilities ought not to masturbate publicly or with multiple partners underscores most discussions. Generally, denying individuals the ability to consent to mutual or more public forms of masturbation results in the promotion of masturbation as a private, solitary act. Eugenic thinking—that the reproduction of generations of people with intellectual disabilities is against social evolution—also influences the discussion. Finally, expectations of appropriate sex/gender roles influence discourses about how to practice "appropriate" masturbation. The restrictive binaries of good and bad, appropriate and inappropriate, dominate discussions of sexuality for people with intellectual disabilities, and they demand explanation and critique. In the end, a paradoxical question arises: where can one masturbate in private when one is incarcerated in a facility that denies, disallows, and prohibits privacy? Obtaining privacy to express sexuality as an extension of personhood becomes a necessity for individuals with intellectual disabilities. Masturbation and the promotion of the training for individuals with intellectual disabilities provide, I argue, a unique vantage point to discuss how the sexuality of institutionalized groups such as prisoners, people in group homes, and other types of residential institutions falls under regulation and restriction in everyday life, and reveals underlying assumptions of sexuality as grounds for institutionalization.

The ABCs of Sex Education: Masturbation as Sex

Events in the 1970s changed public perceptions of sexuality and reproduction in the United States. These events are commonly called the sexual revolution. Sandra Leiblum and Raymond Rosen describe the 1970s as displaying a "burgeoning of enthusiasm for all things sexual—from 'masturbation training groups' to Sexual Attitude Reassessment seminars, from 'sex shoppes' and California hot tubs to 'swinging clubs,' from 'open marriage' to the flourishing of casual and anonymous sex."[6] *Roe v. Wade* legislated a woman's right to choose an abortion to end a pregnancy in the first trimester while the Hyde Amendment restricts federal funding for these abortions, the result being that even with legal abortion, poor women and women of color still are subjected to reproductive control and sterilization abuses in the United States.[7] Half of U.S. states removed sodomy statutes from their laws, and the American Psychiatric Association in 1974 removed homosexuality as a diagnosable mental disorder.[8] Pornography was also highly visible, with "thousands of movie houses featuring triple-'X'-rated films" and adult bookstores selling "hard-core sex magazines and paperbacks" throughout the United States.[9]

This redefinition of sexual practices and norms was made possible partly through the development of a market for sex, pornography, sex therapy, and other things related to sexuality. With this new market came consumers with their purchasing power. Simultaneously, many in the United States also saw individuals with intellectual disabilities living in deplorable conditions, particularly because of Geraldo Rivera's investigative reporting about Willowbrook State School. Allison Carey describes how during the 1970s additional focus was given to the sexual needs of individuals with intellectual disabilities.[10] Accordingly, attitudes toward masturbation and individuals with intellectual disabilities softened in the 1970s. For example, professionals advocated the use of lemon juice as opposed to electric shock therapy to "correct" masturbation behavioral issues.[11] In one such intervention, parents and teachers would carry portable containers of lemon juice that would be squirted into an individual's mouth when he masturbated in a public location.[12] Lemon juice was also used when an individual would masturbate "excessively." J. William Cook and colleagues conclude that lemon juice as a masturbatory deterrent is both effective and more humane that subjecting individuals to electric shock therapy. Abby Wilkerson quotes an example from 1993 that reports an instance where residential staff taped sandpaper inside a boy's thighs to prevent public masturbation.[13] This more contemporary example helps to complicate Sedgwick's claims that masturbation and "the history of masturbation phobia—the astonishing range of legitimate institutions that so recently surveilled, punished, jawboned, imprisoned, terrorized, shackled, diagnosed, purged, and physically mutilated so many people, to prevent a behavior that those same institutions consider innocuousness itself—has complex messages for sexual activism today."[14] Sedgwick, writing around the same time the sandpaper example is published, overlooks the continuous regulation of masturbatory practices of individuals with intellectual disabilities. The language of disability utilized in her prose—diagnosed, physically mutilated, purged, surveilled—underscores the ways in which management of disability facilitates prevention of masturbation. While the linkage between masturbation and genesis of disease has been discredited, the desire to prevent masturbation has not. The control and restriction of masturbation for some individuals but not others illustrates how sexual ableism depends on assessments of ability and competency interlaid with notions of appropriateness.

In 1975, Planned Parenthood of Southeastern Pennsylvania helped produce a film titled *The ABC of Sex Education for Trainables*. *ABC* acts as a training film—instructing staff members about sex education while also providing content to teach. An older white professional man,

Richard Dix, a television actor from the 1970s and 1980s, narrates the film. At the beginning the A, B, and C of sex education are explained as: (A) awareness of bodies and feelings, (B) the mechanics of reproduction, and (C) training in responsibilities and social behavior. The twenty-minute film is divided into three sections, often cutting back to the narrator in between reenactments of professionals teaching and individuals with intellectual disabilities learning about sex.

The film currently has a fairly significant cult following. For example, the movie can be viewed on websites such as YouTube. There are also groups dedicated to the film on Facebook that keep appearing and then being shut down, often because of mocking and ableist language that appears in these spaces. This international attention, fueled by the Internet, is not coming from individuals with intellectual disabilities, but rather from nondisabled individuals who are interested in the film for its content. Much in the same way that the movie *Reefer Madness* is viewed and openly mocked for its portrayal of the harmful effects of marijuana usage, *ABC* is likewise mocked for showing the sexuality of intellectually disabled individuals.[15]

The Internet response to the film displays how the sexuality of people with intellectual disabilities is received in this age of globalized sexual identities.[16] One of the better-known scenes in the film involves a female teacher asking a group of co-ed students with disabilities the various names for penis. The students shout out the following: prick, peter, cock, rod, dick, meat, ding-dong, wand, wiener, tool, and joint. The film recommends this naming activity as an appropriate and effective training technique to reduce apparent stigma around the male sex organ. However, many in the Internet communities referenced above find this scene pejoratively hilarious, thus pointing to one way in which the sexuality (or sexual knowledge) of intellectually disabled individuals is ridiculed by the larger public. These comments are often layered with discriminatory and hateful language based on ableism and male superiority that not only sees sexual knowledge as objectionable but also evokes historical sentiments about sterilization and elimination as effective ways to manage the sexuality of people with intellectual disabilities.

In one of the reenactments in the film, there is a younger-looking white man, perhaps in his middle to late teens, lying alone on his bed with a blanket covering all of his body except his face. The boy, identified as Ricky, is clearly masturbating, although the viewers only see the blanket rise and fall around his waist. As Ricky is masturbating, his mother suddenly appears from behind the closed door to his room. His mother tells Ricky that she saw what he was doing and that she knows it feels good. She then tells him that it is respectable that he is doing it in the privacy of his own room and that she will knock next time before she enters the room. As a whole, the scene is reminiscent of many younger males' experiences of being discovered masturbating; however, since Ricky's mother walked in on him masturbating, the mood is especially embarrassing. Of course she is not acting appropriately in this scene, as she enters his room without knocking, but she uses her violation of personal privacy as an opportunity to teach a lesson that is already known, as Ricky is not masturbating in public.

This scene contrasts with a later scene in which a group of individuals with intellectual disabilities are drawing. As the group members draw pictures of their choosing, one individual, Sandy, a white woman, is touching her genital area on top of her clothes while seated at the table with the others. Sandy is told by the professional overseeing the drawing activity that her behavior is not appropriate in this public setting. Sandy ignores the prompting of the professional and resumes touching her clothed genital area. At this moment, the narrator explains that sometimes individuals need to be removed from public settings for displaying sexual activities. The film *Dealing with Sexually Inappropriate Behavior: Masturbation and Sexually Provocative Behavior* promotes a similar type of management for public masturbation in nursing homes.[17] While the film explains that sexual activity is a need, it also encourages nursing home staff to send residents who masturbate publicly to their rooms. The film also discusses how residents have little to no privacy in the nursing home, thus effectively making private masturbation more difficult because nursing staff have unrestricted access to patient rooms. Moreover, one nursing supervisor in the film comments that nurses have observed male patients urinating and quickly assumed they were masturbating, suggesting that some staff members are always on the lookout for "inappropriate" sexual activity. Much like disabled people's sexuality, older people also face discriminatory views from various professionals as well as the general public about their sexuality.[18] Barriers to sexuality for elderly persons, especially in nursing homes and assisted living facilities, include privacy, lack of information, and staff oversight.[19]

In *ABC* Sandy is represented as inappropriately sexual, while Ricky is displaying his sexuality properly. The presence of other people and the spatial difference between Ricky's bedroom and Sandy's workshop are important factors in determining the appropriateness of masturbation highlighted in the film. In addition, the combination of female gender and intellectual disability frequently results in intellectually disabled women being seen as exceedingly sexual, thus recalling histories of eugenic regulation of sexuality for this population, whereas physically disabled women often report being seen as asexual.[20]

These two scenes highlight a binary between "tolerable" and "intolerable" sexual activities within a limited parameter of masturbation. While good sexuality happens in private, individuals are not always afforded privacy, even when they are in their own rooms. There is no guarantee that mothers, nurses, roommates, and staff will not enter one's room. A lack of privacy reflects an individual's status as disabled, where "professionalization hinges on being able to invade privacy while divorcing that invasion for its sexual associations."[21] In certain locations, including nursing and group homes, the relationship between sexuality and privacy is directly related to professional assessments about competence and assumed dangerousness. Benign activity has the potential to be considered sexual. Touching of the genitals is seen as sexual regardless of the intent. Even if the touching is sexual in nature, individuals are often moved to their rooms without an explanation of why the activity is inappropriate. The binaries of good and bad, appropriate and inappropriate, private and public, point to the contested terrains in which many individuals with intellectual disabilities negotiate their sexuality.

Frequency of Masturbation

Masturbation issues, including frequency and location, are often discussed in the professional literature. While *ABC* does not address how to teach individuals masturbation techniques, masturbation training has a long history in sexology in general and intellectual disabilities in particular.[22] Regulating masturbation becomes a tangible way to secure good health and prevent "degeneration." Foucault posits that three distinct figures emerge as abnormal at the end of the eighteenth and beginning of the nineteenth centuries: the "monster," the "individual who cannot be integrated within the normative system of education," and the "masturbator."[23] Paying attention to the masturbator is important because "masturbation becomes the cause, the universal causality of every illness."[24] In other words, because masturbation seemed to explain the somatization of illness, "sexuality enables everything that is otherwise inexplicable to be explained."[25] In an effort to diagnose and explain the biological, masturbating takes on mythical meaning.

Havelock Ellis, a sexologist in the early twentieth century, thought that when women masturbate they experience "marital aversion," and thus eventually upset gender roles for men and women by making women not dependent on men for marriage, support, and ultimately sexual gratification.[26] In contemporary sex therapy, it has been hypothesized that teaching women how to masturbate to orgasm could be an effective way to counter hypoactive sexual desire disorder, which indicates low desire for engaging in sexual activities.[27] Sexologists caution that masturbation training can "lead to consistent orgasms, which could increase sexual desire."[28] Consistent orgasms are believed to stimulate consistent sexual interest while mitigating low sexual desire. The underlying belief is that sexual desire is normal and that low desire is a condition that needs to be corrected with sex therapy. While historically masturbation was thought to cause degeneracy and mental illness, it "continued to be a morally fraught, much thought-about arena of human sexuality—indeed a critical component of what came to be understood as 'sexuality'—long after it stopped being regarded as a cause of real physical harm."[29] The meaning of masturbation fluctuates based on historical situations. The rhetoric of masturbation, as beneficial or harmful, works as covert and overt mechanisms for controlling sexuality in Western civilization throughout the twentieth century.[30] This historical context is important to underscore when thinking about how masturbation practices for certain populations, including those with intellectual disabilities, become monitored. Why are the masturbatory practices of certain groups of individuals consistently scrutinized?

When it comes to frequency of masturbation, Alfred Kinsey and his associates determined that 92 percent of males and 62 percent of females interviewed had masturbated at some point in their lives.[31] The *Hite Report* in 1976 found that 82 percent of females interviewed masturbated, while the *Janus Report* of 1993 found that 55 percent of males and 38 percent of females were regular masturbators, meaning daily to monthly masturbation.[32] Additional studies completed in the 1990s found that a significant percentage of men and women masturbated on a regular basis.[33] These studies confirm that masturbation has been a conventional practice for the U.S. public historically, and has also been a constantly monitored and recorded practice as a central part of sexuality. As Alan Soble notes, "We [the U.S. public] advertise our marriages and brag about our affairs, but keep our masturbatory fantasies to ourselves. The masturbatory closet remains shut."[34] Even if the majority of people masturbate, they rarely talk about it.

These studies seek to confirm that individuals masturbate with some frequency; however, regularity does not necessarily foster open communication. Rather, silence about sexuality operates to confirm a "psychic disavowal" where "power acts to cover over anomalous forms of sexuality, it serves to generate a resistance that transforms the discourse in general."[35] Margrit Shildrick argues that efforts to guarantee sexual citizenship, particularly citizenship for disabled people, in line with Foucault, "invites new forms of governmentality" where discourses of desire and pleasure are rarely addressed in discussions of disability and sexuality.[36] Discussions of disabled sexuality should take up "the emergence of new forms of embodied selfhood that takes account equally of the intersectionality of sociopolitical context, the meaning of intimacy and the erotic, and the psychic significance of the cultural imaginary."[37] Discussions of masturbation reveal that, even if a significant number of people masturbate with some frequency, there remains an implication that certain individuals' masturbation practices need to be regulated. This control and oversight narrows the scope of sexuality and by extension recreates the primacy of reproductive heterosexuality as the outcome of this regulation, thus effectively illustrating one of the ways sexual ableism operates.

The masturbation practices of prisoners have also been the subject of study. Prisoners live in congregate settings, much like individuals with intellectual disabilities. Comparing these groups is instructive when considering how masturbation becomes promoted or regulated as a type of sexual activity above other forms of activity. Prisons are one location in which masturbation is openly regulated and often completely forbidden. In 2007, an inmate in a Florida prison was convicted of indecent exposure for masturbating alone in his cell.[38] A female corrections officer observed the inmate masturbating from the video monitoring room in the jail. As a result of the conviction, the inmate received an additional sixty-day sentence. Similar bans against masturbating in prison have been upheld in other U.S. states despite court challenges. Christopher Hensley and his associates conducted a study exploring masturbation and consensual same-sex activity in a male maximum-security prison. Their study found that 99 percent of those interviewed had masturbated while in prison, with 78 percent masturbating more frequently (from two to three times a week up to more than once a day).[39] They also conclude that white prisoners are more likely to engage in same-sex sexual activity, and those who have a higher level of education masturbated less frequently.[40] The authors argue that condom distribution should be widely adopted in prisons to encourage safer sexual practices, and inmates should be allowed to masturbate without reprisal from authorities.[41] In another study, Hensley and colleagues researched female masturbation in prison. They conclude that the number of women who report having masturbated while in prison is twice the number reported in similar studies on masturbation frequency outside prison.[42] They report that women in prison turn to masturbation more frequently as a way to reduce sexual tension, and that those who participate in same-sex sexual activity in prison have higher rates of masturbation.[43] They recommend that masturbation should be permitted in prisons to reduce transmission of HIV and other sexually transmitted infections.[44] Prisoners remain sexual during incarceration, potentially even more so; however, sexual practices like masturbation are often treated as behavioral infractions and grounds for the charge of sexual offense.[45]

A significant amount of the sexual activities that occur in prison are masturbatory in nature, despite the prohibition against it. While prisoners "ought" not to masturbate, but do so to achieve sexual gratification, individuals with intellectual disabilities "ought" to masturbate to reduce behavioral issues, not for sexual gratification. While both prisoners and those with intellectual disabilities experience attention to their daily activities, the opposite commands reflect two different conceptualizations of sexuality for the two groups: for inmates masturbation is a kind of sexuality, and for people with intellectual disabilities masturbation is a tool for behavioral modification.[46] In prisons, individuals who masturbate are often punished; however, masturbation for those with intellectual disabilities is seen as a benefit allowing for an appropriate articulation of sexuality, while mitigating behavioral issues, such as aggressive actions toward others. What are the assumptions that make these opposite perceptions of masturbation possible? Why does the meaning behind masturbation change in these locations? And how does the attention toward masturbation reveal similarities, despite perhaps differing management of those who masturbate? Additionally, how does aversion factor into decisions to monitor masturbation of certain populations? The logic of sexual ableism creates situations where individuals are unable to express their sexuality, linked to attempts at restriction and oversight by others, here prison officials or staff members in locations with individuals with intellectual disabilities.

Yet masturbation for individuals with disabilities has been configured as one of the only ways to express sexuality, assuming that interpersonal sexual intimacy is not readily available. Anthony Walsh argues that teaching individuals to masturbate and providing them the space to do so empowers them to express their sexuality.[47] Paul Cambridge and colleagues explain five key issues regarding the masturbation of people with intellectual disabilities: (1) inability to masturbate properly and achieve orgasm; (2) improper masturbation that may pose dangers, including contact with clothes, people, or objects; (3) too much masturbation; (4) public masturbation and other inappropriate practices; and (5) the use of objects that harm the individuals in question.[48] If an individual is considered to display one of these behaviors, most likely they will be referred to some sort of masturbation behavior intervention and assessment. The goal for such an individual is to learn how to masturbate "appropriately." Of course, there is a certain level of subjectivity in these criteria: Is daily masturbation considered too frequent? Does the use of sex toys make the act appropriate or inappropriate? While it is generally considered that masturbating in a crowded café is inappropriate because of social mores, if an individual chooses to masturbate with other individuals watching or participating, would that action warrant masturbation training? Masturbation training generally does not recognize mutual or group masturbation as an achievable outcome. Participating in more public sexual activities, or even consenting to group sexual activities, could unnecessarily warrant masturbation training for the parties involved, to discourage such practices. The reasons for entry into training point to one way in which masturbation becomes more about behavior modification to replace sexual relations with others than a form of sexual experience. Public or group expressions of sexuality involve complex assessments of competency, social respect, and other legal considerations, but limiting masturbation as forbidden to be seen by anyone else clearly demonstrates the understanding of it as a substitute for sex, not as a less restrictive and more diverse sexual activity.

Masturbation training becomes a disciplinary tool that is utilized not to facilitate sexual pleasure, but rather to place parameters on the act of masturbation. These parameters include the primacy of privacy and reduction of harm to self and others. Orgasm attainment is also listed as a goal for training, pointing to one way in which training can act as a conduit toward one pleasurable ending. The meaning behind the goal of orgasm attainment might vary, however, since some consider the inability to orgasm as one of the reasons individuals might display aggressive or problematic behaviors.[49] Sexual pleasure can be one of the unintended outcomes of the training. The discourse of harm reduction and behavior modification usurps an assessment of masturbation as an act of sexuality for the means of pleasure. The primacy of sexual pleasure is largely absent for individuals with intellectual disabilities, while masturbation training provides a façade of an endorsement of sexuality for individuals. While a Facebook fan page for *ABC* declares, "Sex can wait, masturbate," the film encourages individuals to masturbate in locations approved by the staff for such an activity. This public and professional attention toward the masturbation techniques or the habits of individuals with intellectual disabilities highlights not only individuals' possible sexual activity but also the ways in which their sexuality is discussed and potentially regulated. Denna McGaughey and Richard Tewksbury caution, in relation to prison sexuality, that "sexual behavior, which is generally considered in mainstream society to be private, becomes a public/social issue within the context of institutionalization."[50]

Masturbation and HIV

While correlations between frequency of masturbation, sexual experiences, and the level of sexual desire are established for certain groups of individuals, including prisoners, the relationship between masturbation and HIV is still being explored. John D'Emilio and Estelle Freedman discuss how in the United States gay men adopted mutual masturbation practices in response to the AIDS crisis.[51] As a striking comparison, inmates in prisons are often forbidden to masturbate, and the act of masturbation (despite its usual solitary nature) is one of the classified sexual activities by state prison officials that can potentially spread disease.[52] In addition, masturbation is assumed to increase sexual desire, which in turn leads to greater frequency of sexual practices that are "unsafe" or "risky." As Jean Stengers and Anne van Neck argue, masturbation flourishes in locations of repression so that, despite regulations, it most likely continues in prisons.[53] The solitary nature of masturbation allows for some creativity as to where and how an individual masturbates. However, a lack of privacy in situations where activities are regulated can result in these activities being monitored as well. The relation between HIV and masturbation takes on different meanings when aligned with differing markers of identity, such as race and class. Therefore, the contradictory assertion that some individuals should masturbate to express sexuality safely (individuals with intellectual disabilities), while others (prisoners) assumed to be at "risk" of contracting HIV when masturbating, as all sexual practices become risky, highlights how the relationship between sex and infection is not equally applied to all populations. Assumptions that individuals with intellectual disabilities do not have sexual partners, let alone HIV, also influences the endorsement of masturbation as a safe alternative to vaginal, oral, and anal intercourse.[54] Masturbation training for individuals with intellectual disabilities through sex education and individual counseling not only addresses reduction of behavioral issues but also introduces a discussion of masturbation as a safer-sex practice. Encouraging individuals with intellectual disabilities to masturbate is widely accepted as a means to teach practices that can reduce HIV/AIDS transmission rates, especially among men who have sex with men.[55]

Interestingly, a pair of studies conducted on African American women and college-age students, respectively, concluded that those who masturbate regularly also had multiple sexual partners and by extension are at greater risk of being infected with HIV.[56] Beatrice Robinson and colleagues argue that women who masturbate frequently, especially early in life, have "some increased HIV risk, perhaps through the mechanism of increased interest and desire."[57] They also reference additional studies that show a "negative relationship between masturbation and sexual variables related to safer sex."[58] Thus, if one masturbates more, one is also more likely to practice unsafe sex. For example, Kenneth Davidson and Nelwyn Moore conclude that consistent and regular masturbation can make individuals less likely to use contraception and more likely to have a sexually transmitted infection.[59] Steven Pinkerton and colleagues assert that for the college-age women in their study, "masturbation is clearly *not* being used as a substitute for intercourse and, therefore, cannot be assumed to decrease HIV risk on that basis."[60] The contention again is that frequent masturbation results in increased sexual desire, where sexual desire is the apparent barometer to measure HIV risk. This correlation between sexual desire and risk of HIV does not take into account how racism, classism, and sexism work as combined systems of oppression in the lives of individuals in relation to risks. Asking a male partner to use a condom is not always an option when a person is in an unequal relationship. There might be a lack of comprehensive sex education and access to reproductive technologies in certain geographical areas heavily populated by racial minorities and those with low incomes. The causal linkage between masturbation frequency and HIV risk can cover other structural factors that make an individual more likely to contract HIV or another sexually transmitted infection. Finally, even the correlation between frequency and risk of infection is not unilateral, as seen in the hypothesis that frequent masturbation might have a negative relationship with HIV risk, meaning that individuals could possibly have higher risk if they did not masturbate.[61]

The correlation between masturbation frequency and the claim of health is somewhat of an enigma. There is a belief that masturbation can help individuals with low sexual desire to reach a "normal" and "healthy" amount of sexual desire.[62] In contrast, some researchers contend that frequent masturbation can place individuals at increased risk to contract HIV and other sexually transmitted infections. While masturbation has been credited as making individuals more comfortable with their bodies as well as having increased levels of self-esteem, it continues to be stigmatized, notwithstanding its casual linkage with sexually transmitted infections.[63] Neoconservative ideologies in the United States often influence discourses of morality in relation to sex education. Masturbation as a type of sexual activity is wrapped up in this discourse as well, where masturbating as an act of sexuality is coded as immoral and inappropriate.[64] The discussion and promotion of masturbation continue to be controversial in U.S. sex education policies, which mirrors the broader sociocultural and political context of sexuality. Generally in the United States, masturbation as a group practice is consistently not discussed.[65] Despite domestic uncertainties when it comes to the relationship between masturbation and human sexuality, there is still a movement to align abstinence and masturbation in global efforts to reduce HIV transmission. Thomas Laqueur notes, "To date no mainstream politician has been willing to publicly defend masturbation as a morally innocent and socially benign sexual practice."[66]

Masturbation remains a controversial practice for sexual promotion because of moral issues and social taboos. For example, sex education rarely discusses masturbation as a type of sexual activity. However, the link among abstinence, masturbation, and condom usage helps to cement a certain philosophy of sex that limits those individuals who can reproduce. The implication is that if people want to be sexual, masturbating allows for sexual activity without fear of reproducing. Jennifer Nelson traces how U.S. foreign population policies around sexuality are inconsistent, especially in relation to populations of color.[67] Coerced sterilization and testing of birth control on women of color are examples of these types of U.S.-driven global population policies.[68] Efforts to sterilize individuals are linked with promoting masturbation as various modes of restricting sexuality and denying reproduction. The multiplicity of meanings and policies surrounding masturbation reveals societal unease with the sexuality of certain marginalized groups.

How to Teach: Do You Know How to Masturbate?

If individuals are masturbating or attempting to masturbate unsuccessfully, how can they be taught suitable ways of practicing "solitary sex with release"? Professionals working in the field of intellectual disability contend that successful masturbation can eliminate an array of behavioral issues. Masturbation is seen as a benefit insomuch that it allows for a reduction in potential disruptions in the institution or group home, but is not seen as an asset for sexual experience. Whatever the ultimate goal of training, be it reduction in "problematic" behaviors or an altruistic desire to teach ways to orgasm, there are developed techniques employed to train individuals with intellectual disabilities "effective" and "appropriate" ways of stimulation.

Frederick Kaeser advocates a type of masturbation training in which professionals train adults with intellectual disabilities in a hand-over-hand approach on an individual's penis or clitoris.[69] Kaeser argues that this approach can raise ethical concerns involving a paid staff person masturbating a disabled individual in his or her room. The ethical issues arise from the assumption that individuals with intellectual disabilities are unable to consent to a type of sexuality in which a staff member might touch individuals' genitalia to facilitate orgasm in order for them to subsequently learn how to masturbate. In addition, there is an ethical consideration of whether government-funded staff can provide a type of facilitated sexual service through a hand-over-hand approach to masturbation training. Even though personal assistants bathe, toilet, and interact with individuals on a highly personal level involving physical contact, the incorporation of sexuality as part the job requirement can be an entirely different consideration. On some level, the ability of the government to fund sexual services or sexual surrogacy becomes a key ethical point in this discussion. Kaeser considers that the benefits of training individuals how to masturbate to orgasm in their rooms are more important than any ethical concerns. In his discussion of masturbation training and Kaeser's article in particular, Tobin Siebers makes the following observations about the benefits of masturbation training for institutional settings:

1. to help patients with mental disabilities understand that sexual acts should be private, allowing authorities to eliminate offensive behavior from public spaces;
2. to provide patients with a means of releasing tension and controlling frustration, creating a more passive and manageable population for caregivers;
3. to teach safer methods of masturbation to patients who are injuring themselves in the pursuit of sexual pleasure; and
4. to introduce the pleasures of sexuality as part of typical human existence to people for whom these pleasures are unknown.[70]

While some of the benefits assumed with masturbation training include the importance of sexual activity in private and prevention of self-injury, it is important to note that the benefits are available for both the individual and the institution. Furthermore, the assumptions regarding the benefits of masturbation training are not generated from the individual but rather used as rationale and justification for the training. Individuals are not asking for the training. In fact, as discussed earlier, masturbation training usually occurs when a staff member observes an individual masturbating in public or using devices or objects that the staff member considers inappropriate or harmful. Masturbation training can be restrictive (or normalizing) if individuals actively choose more public displays of masturbation, in a sex club for instance or in front of other people, when staff deem these public displays inappropriate.

A more docile (or passive) group of individuals with a reduction of behavioral issues makes the institution seem more "pleasant"—for staff at least. Siebers contends that masturbation training is "not a neutral activity" because it "provides instruction in political agency in addition to helping the patient achieve sexual agency, declaring victory when the patient manages to achieve orgasm unassisted on a regular basis."[71] Masturbation is coded with notions of sexual autonomy and manageable behaviors. Of course, this assumes that masturbation is a solitary act and not one between consenting parties, including couples with intellectual disabilities—a situation that is strongly discouraged in group homes. Individuals who masturbate become willing agents in their own sexuality. But if masturbation training becomes a stand-in for other types of sexual activity and is used solely as a tool of behavioral control, then victory cannot be claimed for the individual's side, only for the institution. An individual's right to express sexuality can be co-opted by a discourse of harm reduction that ultimately favors the cohesion of institutional living. A "problematic" masturbator challenges a group home or institution's culture of behavior modification.

Although Kaeser's concern with educating individuals to learn techniques for self-arousal and release is practical, this professional attention toward masturbation training and surveillance points to the potentially restrictive locations in which individuals with intellectual disabilities live and attempt to be sexual beings. Moreover, hand-over-hand masturbation training most likely is illegal in many locations and can be seen as a type of sexual abuse.[72] Facilitated sexuality remains a controversial topic because of the blurring of boundaries between personhood and governmental assistance for sexual release. Not all individuals with intellectual disabilities are assumed able to consent to sexual relations. The politics of facilitated sexuality and the issues of consent for individuals with intellectual disabilities deserve further exploration within disability studies.[73] Shildrick remarks that facilitated sex "draws attention to the difference of anomalous bodies" in part because "the very notion of such hands-on involvement is particularly disturbing for both the wider public and the participants."[74] There are of course individuals that prefer to participate in and receive facilitated sexual encounters.

As an alternative to hand-over-hand training, some researchers advocate the use of pictures, videos, anatomically correct dolls, condoms, vibrating pillows, and handheld vibrators as tools that can potentially help individuals masturbate.[75] Alternative methods to teach people how to masturbate include using a model penis or vagina to demonstrate the technique, while avoiding any physical contact between staff members and service users.[76] Others contend that individuals with intellectual disabilities need to be taught to masturbate to climax to avoid behavioral problems.[77] These behavioral problems are, of course, coded in medical and moral terminology. Problematic behaviors assume a standard set of social mores that should not deviate from Judeo–Christian morals of social interaction. For example, sexual activity becomes appropriate only in the confines of an individual's residence. Coding an activity or action as a "behavioral issue" gives support staff license to correct the aforementioned behavior into something more "appropriate." The binary of appropriate and inappropriate surrounds the discussion of masturbation training. Even so, the reduction of behavior problems is a widely circulated positive outcome of masturbation training without any evidence that a reduction occurs or if the training facilitates individuals' satisfaction. As Siebers notes, "To fail in masturbation training is to fail to become an autonomous agent, but this failure has everything to do with prejudices against disability because achieving both political and sexual agency relies on the presupposition that the body and mind are nondisabled and will function properly if trained."[78] Thus, the discourse of sexual autonomy largely requires an idea that successful sexuality can be formed and manipulated. Individuals with intellectual disabilities supposedly need assistance to become sexually autonomous; failure here not only means a loss of autonomy but also perhaps a return of behavior issues, as identified by staff members. The attention on behavior modification serves as an illustration of the professional oversight available in discussions of sexuality for people with intellectual disabilities. Sexual training is cloaked in the rhetoric of sexual fulfillment. The meaning-making of masturbation reveals a specific assessment of what is deemed an appropriate expression of sexuality, in a location marked by professional oversight and reduced freedom.

One inventive approach to masturbation training comes from Family Planning New South Wales. A pair of books, *About Masturbation: For People with an Intellectual Disability: For Males* and a similar version for females with intellectual disabilities, takes a more holistic approach to addressing masturbation for individuals with intellectual disabilities.[79] Each book contains not only specific recommendations, resources, and guidance for support people and staff, but also a story about masturbation that can be shared with the individuals with disabilities. The male story involves an unnamed man, who upon being aroused in public, or as the book refers to it, when "he feels sexy," returns to his room and masturbates to orgasm. The story then shows the man in his bathroom cleaning semen off his hands. The version for women with intellectual disabilities presents a similar story about a woman going to her private room to masturbate and then to the restroom to clean up afterward. Additionally, both books contain drawings of male and female sexual organs that can be used to teach individuals about anatomy and sexuality. What is unique about these books is that they present masturbation as part of everyday life and something natural for individuals to do. There is no talk of special approaches or potential behavioral issues; rather, the books offer a sex-positive approach of providing individuals with the space and resources needed to explore their own sexuality through masturbation. This type of approach recognizes that individuals with intellectual disabilities have the right to sexual expression. This recognition challenges the culture of protectionism and harm reduction, reflected through a discourse of sexual ableism entrenched in discussions of sexuality for people with intellectual disabilities. Masturbation training in this context facilitates an expression of rights, instead of attempting to mold an individual's behaviors to fit the culture of the group home or other institution. Masturbation training can allow for an increased array of sexual knowledge and experience. Masturbation and the meaning behind it reveal assumptions about disabled sexuality in general; disabled people are deemed appropriate to be trained for sexual activity rather than disallowed of sexuality in the name of failed autonomy and consent.

While the methods of how to train individuals to masturbate might vary from location to location, there is consensus that individuals ought to be given the space, privacy, and resources (e.g., lubrication, vibrator) to masturbate in their own rooms or bathrooms, in contrast to more public locations, such as living rooms and workplaces. Again, the assumption is that masturbation is a solo activity done in private. The two scenes discussed above from *ABC* reflect these general norms: masturbate in your locked room using any tools necessary to facilitate the activity. The problem with this line of thinking is that individuals in group homes often have roommates and doors that do not lock. Tools to facilitate masturbation might not be available either. So the question remains: when and where can you masturbate if you do not have your own room, any time to be alone, or a well-sealed bathroom compartment? Individuals with intellectual disabilities in congregate living are not automatically afforded privacy or the option to be sexual by themselves or with others.

While an individual's masturbation habits and frequency can remain unspoken, for some individuals there remains a tremendous amount of attention on their masturbatory behaviors. While prisoners masturbate with some frequency, the practice itself is coded as a behavioral infraction. Despite a perception that masturbating reduces an individual's risk for HIV, a growing body of research is making connections between frequent masturbation, increased sex drive, and risk of infection. At the same time, masturbation training is promoted tentatively, as a way to correct hypoactive sexual desire disorder. Nursing homes are also considering how to address public expressions of masturbation in ways similar to those advocated by *ABC,* including removal and redirection, without considering the spatial setup to limit privacy in most institutions. Finally, individuals with intellectual disabilities are often encouraged to masturbate not only to eliminate potential behavioral issues but also to quench their sexual drives. The result is that masturbation is strongly influenced by institutional discipline, while additionally inscribing the primacy of nonreproductive sexuality directives on individuals' sexual actions.

This chapter begins a discussion of the politics of masturbation, and more specifically the sexuality of people with intellectual disabilities in the context of other institutionalized lives. In doing so, I charted the connections between the regulation of sexuality for people with intellectual disabilities and other groups of individuals similarly regulated. A significant focus on appropriate methods of masturbation and lack of focus on other ways of expressing or practicing sexuality bring forth a very rigid view of sexuality that reinforces the necessity of masturbation as a substitute for sexual intimacy, supposedly to reduce behavioral issues and tension buildup, while simultaneously enforcing notions that certain groups of people should not engage in sexual intercourse. Perhaps this is because of the inability or unwillingness to consider that people with intellectual disabilities are able to consent to sexual activity or have reproductive rights. Or perhaps it is because of the view that some groups of people should not participate in forms of sexual activity other than autoeroticism.

While equipping individuals with the knowledge, supplies, and techniques to masturbate is potentially important in developing a more integrated sense of self, equal attention should be given to whether individuals are given the opportunity to be sexual and free from restrictions placed on their sexuality. Furthermore, what is not recognized or discussed in masturbation training materials for people with intellectual disabilities is that individuals might not want to be sexual, or that they may identify as asexual. Individuals who prefer to participate in mutual masturbation, either with a partner of the same or opposite sex or some other combination, are not addressed or discussed. Mutual and public masturbation challenge the entire rhetoric behind masturbation training and expose the spatial division between private and public. Masturbation is seen as a solitary act, best done in private, preferably when the staff members of the group home sanction it. Masturbation for people with intellectual disabilities is not seen as a spontaneous event, but rather as the way to satisfy biological sexual urges and mitigate behavioral issues that trouble the authority of those regulating such individuals.

4 Reproductive Intrusions

The Fight against Forced Sterilization

In a 2005 editorial in the *Chicago Sun Times,* bioethicist and lawyer Katie Watson questions, "To be blunt, families give up a lot to care for a cognitively impaired child. Is it so wrong to ask the disabled individual to give up the right [to] have children in return? Might this be a fair exchange?"[1] In answering her own questions, Watson refers to case law that has been clear about the inability of the state to interfere in the reproductive freedoms of another: "The law says no person's reproductive options are contingent on the needs, desires or judgment of another. Why should persons with disabilities be the exception?"[2] The distinction between state intervention and reproductive rights and freedoms proves central in determining whether the desires of individuals with intellectual disabilities are respected regardless of parental and guardian desires. Conflicting desires, entrenched in assumptions about intellect, ability, and appropriateness, can influence reproduction of women (and to a lesser degree men) with intellectual disabilities. In this chapter, I explore a court case in Illinois, the one Watson references, where a young adult woman with an intellectual disability petitioned the court to stop an involuntary sterilization procedure. The court ruled that permanent sterilization would cause psychological damage to the young woman, even though the court was convinced she did not have the capacity to parent. Activists emboldened by the court case petitioned the state legislature and governor to pass a law preventing involuntary sterilization. I consider the desire of disabled people to parent as a legitimate expression, outside of discriminatory assessments of parental appropriateness. In what follows, I offer observations about the reproductive rights for women with intellectual disabilities living in an ableist, racist, classist, sexist, and heteronormative society.

The State and Its Ability to Prevent Reproduction

One of my main efforts in this book has been to develop a theory of sexual ableism to highlight the ways in which notions of competence, appropriateness, and ultimately able-bodiedness surround discourses of sexuality and reproduction. Sexual ableism is the system of imbuing sexuality with determinations of qualification to be sexual based on criteria of ability, intellect, morality, physicality, appearance, age, race, social acceptability, and gender conformity. Both the court case Watson references and the example from the documentary *Unlikely Travellers,* discussed below, illustrate how sexual ableism operates in the lives of individuals labeled with intellectual disabilities.

On January 9, 2003, a guardian petitioned the Illinois court to authorize a tubal ligation procedure on her niece, a then twenty-four-year-old young woman with an intellectual disability. The young woman, referred to as K.E.J., was sexually active and her aunt was concerned that less permanent birth control methods would not effectively prevent a pregnancy. According to court documents, the guardian acknowledged that her niece was "unable to comprehend the possibility of pregnancy or handle the responsibility that it would bring."[3] K.E.J. was receiving regular Depo-Provera injections to prevent conception, but as a result of these injections she had gained fifty pounds, had elevated blood pressure, and experienced a loss of hair.[4] As a result of this initial petition by the young woman's guardian, a five-year protracted court case ensued, resulting in a judge upholding a previous court's ruling that a tubal ligation was not in the best interests of K.E.J. Because of this court case, the Illinois legislature passed a law outlawing sterilization of individuals with intellectual disabilities without court proceedings. Activist efforts in Illinois, including those by the organizations Equip for Equality, a protection and advocacy organization, and FRIDA, which stands for Feminist Response in Disability Activism, a Chicagoland-based feminist disability activist organization formed in the wake of this case as well as other more public issues, including the controversy surrounding Terri Schiavo in Florida, directly influenced the court case and legislation.

Regarding the court case, I am interested how K.E.J.'s desire to reproduce and parent were discounted but also simultaneously used as evidence testifying to the apparent cruelty of the tubal ligation procedure because of its apparent permanence. In his final appellate ruling,

Judge Joseph Gordon remarks that part of his reasoning for upholding the lower court's denial of the guardian's petition is that there are "less intrusive and less psychologically harmful alternatives to a tubal ligation."[5] As part of the court proceedings, K.E.J.'s father remarked that his daughter's wish to be a parent, combined with her understanding of the inability to do so with a tubal ligation, could bring about severe depression and crush her "hope" to have a child.[6] Her father testified that the procedure would "take [her desire to raise a child] and crush it and take her whole wish and fantasy totally away."[7] This crushed "wish" and "fantasy" were used as rationale against tubal ligation; the father's choice of words illustrates the potentially restrictive environment in which K.E.J. remained a sexual being. Her desire and fantasy of family successfully gender her. It is crucial to consider why K.E.J.'s "wish" or "fantasy" warrants state intervention and surveillance. How is her wish read through the system of sexual ableism? How can we imagine a future where her wish and desire need not be regulated or restricted, or seen as disqualifying due to her disability? Can her disability ever be seen as compatible with a desire (and ability) to parent?

In the discourse presented in the court case, K.E.J.'s impairment supposedly meant she was unable to take care of a child. In the courtroom her intellectual disability was equated with justification for active measures to prevent pregnancy. Although tubal ligation procedures are potentially reversible, K.E.J. understood the procedure as foreclosure of her future ability to reproduce and become a parent. At a 2005 bench trial, K.E.J. testified about her desire to parent, "I will love taking care of them. I will love, you know, to see how they grow."[8] K.E.J.'s articulation illustrates the extent to which reproductive desires are constructed in society. In fact, K.E.J. is articulating a desire that many young women her age have regarding their imagined, current, or future families. Her disability does not negate that desire. All too often, desire to parent is seen as natural but tangential to identities and other issues presented as "pressing" and "real," which are seen as compromising the capability to parent.

Judge Joseph Gordon, writing the decision for the appellate court, remarks:

> We find the testimony of K.E.J.'s father regarding the likely effect of a tubal ligation to be persuasive: because K.E.J. dreams of having children someday, he stated that a tubal ligation would be

likely to induce severe depression in her, as she understands the permanence of the procedure. While other methods of contraception also have the effect of preventing pregnancy, they are much less intrusive in that she does not object to their use, as they allow her to maintain her hope for the future. However, this must be weighed against the testimony that if she were to have a child and it were taken away, it would be a highly traumatic event for her.[9]

Despite her desire to reproduce and parent, the court ruling did not advocate for her right to parent, or even determine how to manage her reproductive ability. Rather, the court ruling merely limited potential birth control options to seemingly less invasive ones, such as birth control pills or patches. The judge takes for granted that any future children could be taken away as well. It is striking that the judge here doesn't imagine a situation in which K.E.J. might retain custody of her child, regardless of whether he disagrees with this assessment of terminated parental rights. As we are not able to explicitly determine his view on the situation, the fact that he remarks that K.E.J.'s parental rights most likely would be terminated reflects the reproductively ableist environment in which many individuals labeled as intellectually disabled are framed by the discourses of appropriateness, fitness, and competency.

The judge's ruling and assessment of K.E.J.'s future reproductive abilities raise important questions at the intersections of intellectual disability, sexuality, reproduction, and competence. What justifies the assumption that the young woman's desire to reproduce seems inappropriate and potentially harmful? Why is her desire to mother seen as a threat to herself and her yet-to-be conceived and born child to the degree that the child would automatically be removed from the mother? When it comes to intellectual disability and motherhood, it would seem that mothering is only qualified by assessments of supposedly measurable intellect and assumed ability to take care of offspring. This illustrates links between sexual ableism and the ability to reproduce. In a twist of judicial irony, the court sees that her desire to reproduce and parent was unrealistic, but ending that desire was deemed harsh; her desire (although not recognized as valid in the courtroom) and the potentiality to realize that desire are still intact. Her desire to parent is only seen as valid provided it remains constructed as a "wish" and not "reality." In essence, having these desires properly genders and "ages" her, where intellectual disability assumes childlike rationality.[10] Why is it fantasy that the young woman would want to have a child? Does she have any reproductive rights? If she didn't assume that the tubal ligation was permanent, the court presumably could have ruled in favor of the guardian. Expressing her desire to parent secured her future potential to reproduce, but the possibility that her child could be taken away also remains a possible future outcome.

In an amicus curiae brief authored by Katie Watson and other bioethicists in support of K.E.J., the issue of reproductive rights is central to the argumentation in asking the appellate court judge to uphold the lower court's ruling to not allow sterilization. As part of their brief, the amici begin with two assertions to help illustrate the gravity of this particular case on the reproductive rights of individuals with intellectual disabilities. First, they remark that guardians "request to sterilize their wards with some regularity" and that "it is estimated that guardians ask physicians to sterilize their wards approximately 1–3 times per month throughout the Northwestern medical system" (a Chicagoland university connected multi-hospital system).[11] Next the amici remark how Illinois is one of seventeen states that do not have "a specific legal standard for when a guardian may decide to permanently deprive a ward of the possibility of becoming a parent, even over the ward's explicit objection."[12] And because of this, the amici "are concerned that Illinois law currently leaves its cognitively impaired citizens vulnerable to sterilization for the benefit of others, a practice from a dark historical era to which we should never return."[13] Calling on the eugenic history of forced sterilization and usurping of reproductive potentiality, the amici urge the court to adopt a best interests standard in determining the outcome of the case.[14] In his appellate court ruling, Judge Joseph Gordon cites the following from the 1942 Supreme Court case *Skinner v. Oklahoma*:[15] "Marriage and procreation are fundamental to the very existence and survival of the race. The power to sterilize, if exercised, may have subtle, far-reaching and devastating effects. In evil or reckless hands it can cause races or types which are inimical to the dominant groups to wither or disappear. There is no redemption for the individual whom the law touches. Any experiment which the State conducts is to his irreparable injury. He is forever deprived of a basic liberty."[16] Judge Gordon explains that in citing *Skinner v. Oklahoma*, he is remarking how these words serve as a "warning for us to proceed with caution" not only because of the impact of the procedure in question but also because of the eugenic history of involuntary sterilization, although the judge remarks the K.E.J. case "does not technically" raise eugenic concerns because K.E.J.'s impairment was acquired as a result of trauma opposed to being congenitally obtained.[17] The judge is making a technical distinction, stating that eugenics only applies to preventing reproduction of those with hereditary disabilities. However, eugenic efforts to restrict reproduction have never just been directed at those with congenital impairments. Disability studies activists and scholars would easily contend the judge's assertion, because limiting the reproductive potential and ability of disabled people or those assumed to have disabilities, especially along a discourse of competence and "fitness" to parent, is seen by many as a continuing reminder of the legacy of eugenics. Naming what classifies as eugenics helps to trace linkages between "past" and "present," which continues to have drastic effects on the reproductive potentiality of individuals including disabled women. Watson remarks that "allowing guardians to permanently block their ward's reproductive desires with the muscle of the courts and the knife of medicine is a discriminatory step back toward a shameful era to which we should never return."[18]

FRIDA in a blog post from January 3, 2006, comments that "the controversy" as it pertains to the K.E.J. case "is not over birth control or sterilization per se. Millions of people with and without disabilities have made the decision either to use birth control or get sterilized, as a matter of personal choice. Instead, the issue is whether the court will respect [K.E.J.'s] basic human right to make her own reproductive choices, or give that right to her guardian."[19] Throughout the entire proceedings, K.E.J. was quite clear about her desire to parent. A lawyer for Equip for Equality, Byron Mason, in a *Chicago Tribune* article specifically addresses self-determination and rights discourse: "Regardless of whether a person has a disability, a person has a right to make certain fundamental decisions about their own body."[20] Disability activists and K.E.J.'s legal team tried to change the discussion from her supposed unfitness or inability to parent to a broader discussion of rights of bodily autonomy.

In an interesting choice of words, the attorney for K.E.J.'s guardian, Lester Barclay, remarks in the same *Chicago Tribune* article, "This lawsuit was not about placing any restrictions on [K.E.J.]. It was only about looking at her desire to be free and recognize her desire to engage in sexual conduct . . . This is why we appoint guardians."[21] It would appear, at least according to this lawyer, that desire to engage in sexual conduct and desire to parent in the future are mutually exclusive. Freedom to engage in sexual relations, according to the lawyer, ought to be maintained, even if this means that the ability to reproduce is restricted. In fact, many of the journalistic accounts of the case report how K.E.J. was sexually active at the time of the initial request for sterilization by the guardian, offering at least some rhetorical weight to understanding the motives of the guardian, as if her sexual activity, with its attendant risk of pregnancy, warrants drastic measures to prevent reproduction. K.E.J.'s guardian was not denying that K.E.J. could participate in sexual activity. Rather, parental fitness proved central in the legal and journalistic accounts. Much of the recent research into reproduction, intellectual disability, and supposed parental fitness addresses how parents with intellectual disabilities often have to navigate government and social service agencies that question, if not openly challenge, their abilities to parent.[22] Despite the very public nature of this case, it would appear that the parental and sexual rights of individuals with intellectual disabilities are largely subject to personal assessments of competence and appropriateness. The sustained focus on managing and controlling the reproductive potential of women (and to some extent men) with intellectual disabilities illustrates the restrictive environments in which they raise children, while constantly trying to prove parental abilities. Margrit Shildrick remarks that the focus on controlling the reproduction of individuals with intellectual disabilities points to mainstream "ambivalence, or more clearly a disinclination, towards recognizing and giving value to difference at the margins," which could be seen as a "psychic disavowal that in turn partially drives governmentality."[23] This increased governmentality in the arena of intellectual disability and reproduction makes it difficult for individuals to retain their rights—sexual, reproductive, parental, and otherwise—thus highlighting one way that discourses of sexual ableism are reinforced.

Necessary to Restrict Rights?

In December 1971, the United Nations General Assembly adopted a declaration on "The Rights of Mentally Retarded Persons."[24] The declaration is one of the first to explicitly address individuals with intellectual disabilities on an international level. It acknowledges the language of rights put forth under the Universal Declaration of Human Rights (1948), the two International Covenants on Human Rights (1966), and the Declarations of the Right of the Child (1959) to assist individuals with intellectual disabilities "develop their abilities in various fields of activities and of promoting their integration as far as possible in normal life."[25] The summary of rights includes seven explicit statements of rights, beginning with the assertion that individuals with intellectual disabilities have "to the maximum degree of feasibility, the same rights as other human beings."[26] The short declaration includes an understanding that individuals have the right to health care, rehabilitation, education, and economic security, including a decent standard of living, the ability to live with family and participate in community, as well as be free from abuse and exploitation.

However, the statement ends with the guidance that because of "severity" of disability, individual rights can be restricted or denied based on an "evaluation of the social capability" of the individual by "qualified experts."[27] The declaration clearly lays out the apparent need to restrict or deny individual rights because of disability. Rhetorically, rights become conditional—there is a condition or diagnosis that can limit the actualization of human rights. Thus, the individual with an intellectual disability has to demonstrate an ability—or social capacity—to exercise rights that can be read by a qualified expert to demonstrate competence. Tellingly, the declaration does not explicitly address issues related to reproduction or sexuality, although the right to medical care could reasonably be extended to a right for reproductive care including obstetrics and gynecological treatment. The declaration has been criticized for explicit mention of the need to limit the rights of individuals because of apparent severity of disability.[28]

The 1975 United Nations Declaration on the Rights of Disabled Persons also does not mention issues related to sexuality or reproduction except for similar language around the right to medical treatment. The 1975 declaration mentions that disabled people have "the same civil and political rights" as other human beings, although it carries forth the language from the 1971 declaration that the rights of some individuals with intellectual disabilities might be suppressed or limited because of assumed severity of impairment.[29] Again, the rights mechanism from the UN sets out conditions for the actualization of rights based on disability status. While the 1970s marked a transition internationally from the custodial impulse to house individuals in large institutions, the language of protection still held tremendous authority, particularly around fears of abuse or manipulation.[30] The professional consensus held that individuals might need to have their rights constrained or withheld in order to protect those same individuals from supposed harm or abuse. Janet Lord discusses how both the 1971 and 1975 declarations were seen by disabled communities as "reflecting medical and charity models" instead of advocating for equality.[31]

George Lee, the first general secretary of the National Society for Handicapped Children, now known as MENCAP, addressed the apparent need to regulate the sexual rights of individuals with intellectual disabilities—particularly around issues of reproduction—in a 1974 treatise on the subject.[32] In his brief essay, based off a lecture given at a 1972 University of Delaware conference on the "Rights of the Retarded," Lee addresses the issue of limiting rights:

> With the international growth in awareness of the ethical, as well as the arithmetical, considerations leading to population control, we surely have a duty to avoid if possible a collision between "new" basic rights and the long-standing rights of others. In this case, such conflicting rights might be regarded as: (a) the right of society at large to resist the unnecessary growth of the social, educational and welfare burdens arising from the birth adversely affected by environmental factors and, more importantly, (b) the unassailable right of the unborn child itself to receive an initial fair chance in life; to develop in a stimulating environment his innate potential to the full; and to be free of the emotional problems which almost certainly will later arise should it be his misfortune to be born to retarded parents.[33]

Lee tries to reconcile what he considers "new" rights, of which he would include sexual and reproductive rights, with the long-standing rights of others. He articulates a position that restricts abortion access and ties ableist projections to disabled individuals and their offspring. His particular brand of utilitarian determination of rights severely limits the right of reproduction for individuals with intellectual disabilities. Of note is how he structures the potential rights of children and unborn fetuses as more pressing than those of individuals with intellectual disabilities. The rhetoric of rights for children has long attempted to demonize those constructed as unfit to parent. Individuals with intellectual disabilities share this demonized status with sex workers, women of color, gays and lesbians, prisoners, and immigrants, thus illustrating how the rhetoric of parental fitness and sexual ableism expands outside the absence or presence of impairment. Lee's prioritizing of the rights of children of individuals with intellectual disabilities centers on his belief that the child will be raised in an environment that will curtail potentiality and not offer a "fair chance in life."[34] This concern for the well-being of children is frequently used as justification for the removal of children from parents with intellectual disabilities. Recent research in the social sciences has demonstrated that individuals with intellectual disabilities are capable of successful parenting.[35] In the case discussed above, K.E.J. was deemed unfit to parent, as the judge ruled that any children would be taken from her, resulting in her trauma. Despite the knowledge that Lee's remarks reflect a certain historical moment prior to the onset of self-advocates expressing their self-determination around a variety of issues including reproduction and parenting, the judge in the K.E.J. ruling is aligned with the language of Lee in making his judgment. It is important to note, however, that the judge's paternalistic, protective stance regarding K.E.J., while troubling, is done to prevent K.E.J. any future projected harm or suffering, while Lee does not focus on the interests of those with intellectual disabilities at all. All too often, the unfortunate weighing of rights fails to recognize the rights of individuals with intellectual disabilities to determine their reproductive futurity.

More recently, disability rights has "gate crashed" the international human rights stage with the United Nations Convention on the Rights of Persons with Disabilities (CRPD)—a convention that "embraces a social model of disability and articulates the full range of civil, political, economic, social, and cultural rights with specific application to disability."[36] The CRPD has one explicit mention of sexuality and reproduction, under Article 25, on health, stating that state parties shall "provide persons with disabilities with the same range, quality and standard of free or affordable health care and programmes as provided to other persons, including in the area of sexual and reproductive health and population-based public health programmes."[37] There are three additional sections mentioning parenting, under Article 23, concerning respect for home and the family:

1. States Parties shall take effective and appropriate measures to eliminate discrimination against persons with disabilities in all matters relating to marriage, family, parenthood and relationships, on an equal basis with others, so as to ensure that: . . . (b) The rights of persons with disabilities to decide freely and responsibly on the number and spacing of their children and to have access to age-appropriate information, reproductive and family planning education are recognized, and the means necessary to enable them to exercise these rights are provided; (c) Persons with disabilities, including children, retain their fertility on an equal basis with others

2. States Parties shall ensure the rights and responsibilities of persons with disabilities, with regard to guardianship, wardship, trusteeship, adoption of children or similar institutions, where these concepts exist in national legislation; in all cases the best interests of the child shall be paramount. States Parties shall render appropriate assistance to persons with disabilities in the performance of their child-rearing responsibilities . . .

4. States Parties shall ensure that a child shall not be separated from his or her parents against their will, except when competent authorities subject to judicial review determine, in accordance with applicable law and procedures, that such separation is necessary for the best interests of the child. In no case shall a child be separated from parents on the basis of a disability of either the child or one or both of the parents.[38]

The explicit mention of sexuality, reproduction, parenting, and custody in the CRPD seems to illustrate a new understanding of the rights of disabled people. Certainly, the CRPD is much more expansive than previous UN human rights documents and declarations, thus mention of aspects surrounding sexual and reproductive rights would seem to reflect the work of disabled activists in countries throughout the globe. During the past twenty years the reproductive rights for disabled individuals, particularly disabled women, have been more widely discussed. Additionally, the emergence of critical disability studies has taken up reproductive rights and engaged with other fields, including feminism, sociology, philosophy, and psychology. While there is significant research on reproductive rights as they relate to selective abortion and parenting, there still remains a need to theorize the reproductive experiences of women and men with intellectual disabilities.[39]

Allison Carey frames the ambiguity of rights for people with intellectual disabilities as an issue where various constituents "have different visions of what rights people should hold," including "whether they should have the right to the full range of reproductive choices, including sterilization, or the right to bodily integrity, which may preclude sterilization."[40] Carey continues that often the rights of individuals depend on what she calls "controlled integration"—"rights granted to them often situate them within environments that impose supervision and demand conformity."[41] The apparent need to control the integration of individuals with intellectual disabilities through conditional rights is certainly clear in the earlier UN Declarations. Additionally, the more recent CRPD still maintains the best interests standard as justification for removal of children from their disabled parent(s). The best interests standard also remains under the purview of experts. It would appear that international consensus regarding the rights of parents has remained consistent, in that disability status can potentially negate custody. The language of conditionality in rights maintains the mentality that individual rights can be usurped at any time by an entity, including governmental action or judicial ruling, in effect upholding the primacy of sexual ableism: "Procreation by people with intellectual disabilities often is perceived as creating an additional burden on family and society with children who cannot be supported socially or economically by their already dependent parents."[42]

Carey remarks that often rights for people with intellectual disabilities encourage placement in "structured and supervised environments that encourage conformity to the rules and expectations of society."[43] She continues that "the line between rights and restrictions becomes precariously thin," especially the right "to privacy in reproductive decision making," because there is "no back door through which the control of people with intellectual disabilities may be ensured."[44] Admittedly, there remains a significant amount of bias—or to borrow Licia Carlson's term, "cognitive ableism"—around intellectual disability.[45]

Intellectual disability itself seems to warrant state intervention regardless of the presence of abuse or neglect. Unfortunately, a diagnosis of intellectual disability seems to signal a deficit in intellectual capacity, thus seeming to indicate that individuals should not have unrestricted rights to sexuality, reproduction, and parenting. The meaning-making of intellectual disability as an impairment category sets up the apparent need to restrict rights. Susan Parish discusses how in several states, "the existence of mental disability in a parent is sufficient to terminate his or her custody, regardless of the care provided to the child."[46] States often use "standards that are significantly more strict" for parents with intellectual disabilities while not also considering other circumstances, including "domestic abuse, poverty, inadequate social supports, and successful completion of rehabilitation or training programs."[47] The National Council on Disability's report "Rocking the Cradle" documents how, in the United States, removal rates of children from their parents with intellectual disabilities is as high as 80 percent.[48] The National Council on Disability argues that removal of children from parents based solely on the disability status of the parent is a violation of the Americans with Disabilities Act. The organization Through the Looking Glass works with parents with disabilities to retain custody.[49]

The burden of proof rests with the disabled parent. Quoting Robert Hayman, Parish discusses how courts in determining parental fitness defer to experts in determining the "nature and impacts of the alleged disability," which shifts the focus, requiring the disabled individual to prove their fitness, rather than having the state prove inability to parent.[50] Assumptions about competence, self-determination, and adaptability, as they relate to intellectual disability, become central in judicial decisions. All too often, parents with intellectual disabilities are assumed unable to take adequate care of their children based on a diagnosis of intellectual disability. Certainly the case involving K.E.J. was informed by the assumption that her disability status limited (or more accurately restricted) her ability to parent. The lack of imagination that her disability could be compatible to and even enhance—not spoil—her ability to parent reflected ableist tendencies in assessments of reproductive futurity. Disability configured only as limitation denies the epistemological insights generated from an experience of living with impairment. To categorically deny ability to parent based solely on disability denies the adaptive and creative ways that disabled individuals parent and provide support to their children. The rights of a yet-to-be conceived embryo were weighed against K.E.J.'s expressed parental desires. The notion set forth in UN conventions, that the rights of children might take precedence over the rights of disabled parents, acts as a specter over K.E.J.'s reproductive outlook. The gendered limiting of reproduction illustrates how disability status cannot be understood without attention to other identity categories. Disability status and gendered existence constrain K.E.J.'s reproductive rights, thus connecting her to a long string of disabled women whose reproduction has been controlled by husbands, partners, guardians, institutional staff, and state legislators. In the next section, I examine a documentary film representation of a father with intellectual disabilities whose parental rights were terminated, connecting the language of rights restriction with the ableist interpretation of intellectual disability equating inability and incompetence, while teasing out the differing gendered experiences.

Stanley and the *Unlikely Travellers*

The 2007 Australian documentary *Unlikely Travellers,* by the controversial director Michael Noonan, better known for his PhD project, "Laughing at the Disabled," documents a two-week vacation to Egypt taken by six adults with intellectual disabilities and their support staff.[51] Described as "a no-holds barred insight into the lives of intellectually disabled people, *Unlikely Travellers* helps to allay our preconceived perceptions about people with disabilities whilst taking these 'unlikely travellers' on a deeply moving, hilarious and insightful journey of self-discovery in a strange land away from the comforts of their normal protected environment and family support."[52] While the entire documentary is fascinating for its portrayal of Western-centric perceptions about Egyptian culture as well as romance, sexuality, and intellectual disability, I want to limit my exploration to one of the travelers, Stanley King.

As part of the documentary, Noonan offers brief vignettes that help the viewer become better acquainted with the six travelers. Stanley is a white man with an intellectual disability, perhaps in his middle-to-late thirties, who lives alone in his own apartment. Stanley used to be an animal trainer in the circus, and his experience and knowledge of camels are advantageous to the group. Stanley tells how he met his ex-wife, Michelle, at the cinema in 1995. While the details of their courting are vague, we learn that Stanley and Michelle got married and shortly thereafter Michelle gave birth to a premature son, Andy, the first of three children. Stanley and Michelle stayed in the hospital for forty-one days after Andy was born to take care of him; the allusion is that there must have been some underlying health issue with Andy's premature birth. Samantha and Joseph, their other children, were also born premature. We learn from Stanley's narrative that the Department of Family Services took all three of Stanley and Michelle's children. Michelle left Stanley in 2000 because, according to Stanley, "she got sick of the department taking our children and stressing her out so much." Stanley then shares that "the Department of Family Services broken our marriage. And I did not like that. I went downhill, really down."[53] Since the breakup of his marriage, Stanley started a window-washing company that he says provides him joy. He also states for the camera that he has not had a girlfriend since the dissolution of his marriage. The absence of a girlfriend changes momentarily in the film, as Stanley and another traveler, Natasha Dengate, have a brief relationship, confined to the duration of the Egyptian trip. As indicated by Stanley's desire to enter into a relationship with the potential for marriage, the union with Natasha quickly develops into expressions of love and commitment.[54]

Despite Stanley's overwhelming desire to spend time with his children, he remains unable to do so. One of the most poignant moments of the film occurs when the travelers return to Australia after their vacation. At the airport, the various family members are present to welcome their loved ones home. Stanley has no family or friends there to greet him; the lack of visible connection to others stands in stark contrast to the other travelers, who have extended networks of support.[55] In the largely hetero–patriarchal space where the travelers are defined as children by their relationship to their parents, Stanley's estrangement is magnified; he remarks of the experience that "when everybody else's family was there and my children were not there, I think it was unfair and I felt lonely."

Three months after the end of the trip, the director provides an update on the travelers. Stanley and Natasha's relationship has ended and, while Natasha's parents indicate it was Natasha's choice to end it, Natasha in a separate interview indicates that she wishes her parents would let her make her own choices. There remains some uncertainty as to whether the dissolution of Stanley and Natasha's relationship resulted from their own wishes or if it was due to external pressures. One of the final shots of the film shows Stanley alone, leaving his apartment to go fishing. The solitary nature of fishing highlights his enforced isolation from his children. His desire to parent his children is hindered by support services and government bureaucracy with notions of appropriate parenting. Similar to the forward-thinking assessment that K.E.J. would be unable to parent and that having her child taken from her would be traumatic, Stanley is also faced with forced isolation from his children and potential sexual partners. Stanley's experiences here illustrate how traumatic K.E.J.'s imagined loss of children would be. His estranged children and K.E.J.'s loss of future children connect the two where state intervention and sexual ableist assumptions limit their abilities to reproduce and parent. Additionally, both individuals desire to parent, while this desire is actively stifled by others. The film doesn't offer any explanation as to why Stanley's parental rights are terminated. The absence of an explanation might be based on the "apparent" reason of his disability. Part of my effort in this chapter is to name this desire to parent as legitimate. I am also seeking to respect an individual's grief when they are disallowed to parent.

In their article "Men in the Lives of Mothers with Intellectual Disabilities," Tim Booth and Wendy Booth revisit three research projects they completed in the preceding ten years to examine the roles men with intellectual disabilities perform in parenting. Their goal in reexamining their research is to "critically examine the view that mothers with intellectual disabilities are generally used, abused, and abandoned by the men in their lives."[56] In their examination of the research into parenting and intellectual disability, the authors conclude, "Men—as husbands, partners, boyfriends, lovers, or fathers—play little more than a walk-on part."[57] Others have remarked how fathers are neglected in the research.[58] Booth and Booth report that the men in their study largely were supportive of their families and aided in providing increased human capital, including personal skills and accomplishments.[59] The authors recommend that service agencies which offer support to parents (primarily women) with intellectual disabilities also engage men, both with and without intellectual disabilities, in order to support the family structure.

The examples of K.E.J. and Stanley encourage us to wonder what an ethics of reproductive rights look like for men and women with intellectual disabilities. Is U.S. society ready to meaningfully recognize the desires to parent and consider the right to parent for individuals with intellectual disabilities? In the last section, I engage with Tanya Titchkosky's "politics of wonder" to consider why the precedent in legal cases and international human rights documents places the rights of parents with intellectual disabilities in direct conflict with the rights of children.

Wondering Why the "Need" to Limit

If the international consensus is that individuals with intellectual disabilities are more likely to be unable to effectively parent, the question becomes, To what extent have assumptions of unsuccessful parenting been the product of ableist constructions of intellectual disability, which are themselves grounded in questionable assessments of competence, self-determination, and intellect? Or to be more explicit, are widely held beliefs of intellectual disability the result of falsehoods and unfair generalizations? How have "we" come to understand intellectual disability? And how has that understanding led "us" to consider individuals with intellectual disabilities as potentially ineffectual parents?

Tanya Titchkosky describes the politics of wonder as "a wondering about that which organizes bodies and social spaces and their worlds of meaning" by being "restless with the concept of certainty by returning to its production and not permitting it to remain unquestionably certain."[60] For Titchkosky, the politics of wonder "leads us to ask if we might come to know disability differently by wondering how people have already come to know disability with certainty."[61] Rethinking the who, what, where, when, and why of disability, according to Titchkosky:

> makes possible something other than the repetition of more of the same. A restless return permits us to wonder about what is already said and done—and it is political to the extent that it can forge new imaginative relations to what is already well-established, powerful, and serving as the taken-for-granted constitutive grounds of future action, thought, movement, and feeling. A politics of wonder allows us to remake our lives together by wondering about the shape they hold and the meaning already ascribed to them. A more traditional social science procedure would require the identification

of problems, the development of an explanation theory as to the problems' causes, and the development of solutions. In contrast, the approach here puts the identification of problems, the explanation of said problems, and the development of solutions all on the same level. All these activities are the stuff of social life in regard to which the theoretical imagination needs to return and to wonder, "How *is* 'what is' accomplished and what does it mean?"[62]

Historical and traditional understandings of disability are examined to determine how individuals think they know what they know—and in turn, how assumptions of knowledge bound to assessments of disability limit the imagination to see disability in new and dynamic ways. The assumed certainty of knowledge around intellectual disability gets illuminated in the politics of wonder.

Intellectual disability seems to warrant "unlimited permission to deal with disability" in programmatic and legal endeavors that restrict autonomy in the name of paternalism.[63] The meaning-making of the impairment diagnosis, for some, warrants an intrusion into private decision making, thus rendering these decisions worthy of public scrutiny, if not regulation. For example, Bryan Turner discusses how individuals with intellectual disabilities might need others to act as their protectors or guardians because of disability status.[64] Tobin Siebers points out that privacy is not always afforded to disabled individuals because of their living arrangements, assistance from others, or other remnants of disability bureaucracy.[65] A diagnosis of intellectual disability, because of the way services are often rendered, too often means that individuals are in residential locations where privacy is not expected. Further, reproductive decisions are made without an expectation of privacy, where guardians or professionals consult physicians to manage reproductive health, including prescriptions of birth control or sterilization procedures. K.E.J.'s experience illustrates the tenuous relationship between individuals and those effectively charged with protection or support. Additionally, Stanley's incident of losing custody points to the larger experience of individuals with intellectual disabilities having their children taken away from them. It becomes imperative to articulate how often parental and reproductive rights are terminated because of already constituted understandings of intellectual disability.

David Eng highlights that constructs like privacy and intimacy are tied to white racialized standards that invite certain expressions of "queer liberalism" where "intimacy as a racialized property right—one predicated on a long U.S. history of racial subordination and the legal protection of white privilege—now serves to constitute normative gay and lesbian U.S. citizen–subjects as possessive individuals."[66] These expressions of privacy and intimacy help enforce normalcy insomuch as "whiteness as property has now evolved to create new queer subjects for representation, demanding a more thorough investigation of the degree to which (homo)sexuality and race constitute and consolidate conventional distinctions between the time and space of civilization and barbarism."[67] I would add to Eng's statement that an investigation should also consider how able-bodiedness is tied to conditions of respectability and normativity, particularly around judgments of which bodies are endowed with citizenship claims and rights to privacy, intimacy, and reproduction. A politics of wonder around intellectual disability, reproduction, and parenting invites a critique of the intersectional (and interlocking) ways in which race, class, gender, and able-bodiedness construct the ideal being, who can lay claim to rights, often at the expense of other subjects. A politics of wonder demands that K.E.J.'s "wish" of children be respected and not used a sign of inappropriateness warranting state intervention. In discussing transnational adoption, Eng remarks that there is "an unexamined belief in the traditional ideals of the nuclear family as the primary contemporary measure of social respectability and value," which means that the "enjoyment of rights is, of course, ghosted by those queer and diasporic subjects—unacknowledged lovers, illegal immigrants, indentured laborers, infants left behind—consigned to outcast status and confined to the margins of globalization."[68] I am struck with the notion of ghosting of subjects as I remember the scene of Stanley fishing alone or K.E.J.'s experiences, mitigated through trial transcripts. A model of parenting—embedded in a nuclear family—fails to reflect the reality of a diversity of individuals. Using standards that exclude queer and diasporic subjects, including K.E.J. and Stanley, only further highlights the ways in which an expansion of rights, without attention to the intersectional ramifications embedded in the attainment and construction of these rights, can render some subjects as never being able to meet the criteria or standards for the attainment of the afore-mentioned rights. The communality of disability gets foreclosed in a dyad model of parenting that endorses a set of behaviors and practices that ensure the attainment of rights.

In thinking about intellectual disability and reproduction, we can wonder why the rights of individuals have traditionally been seen as incompatible and why an attainment of rights is conditional. A politics of wonder demands a rethinking of the traditional ways of programming, managing, and funding disability while also imagining a future that transforms this history into a more equitable arrangement. Connected to the wonder, we can forget normative notions of family; according to Judith Halberstam "we must *forget* family in our theorizations of gender, sexuality, community, and politics and adopt forgetting as a strategy for the disruption of the regularity of the Oedipal transmission."[69] K.E.J's case and Stanley's narrative raise important questions regarding parental ability and governmental responsibility to protect and perhaps facilitate rights. Katie Watson connects parental support to physical access for those with mobility impairments: "Parenting support for the cognitively impaired is like ramps for those in wheelchairs—small modifications that ensure the only limitations are those caused by disability itself, not our society's response to it."[70] The move to place parental support on the same level as physical access seems to me like a fruitful vantage point from which to explore the construct of reproductive rights and what is needed to ensure the ability of individuals to access parenthood. What would it mean if societies and communities affirm the reproductive and parental rights of individuals from all types of identity categories?

Reproductive rights as a construct seek to ensure the potential for people to exercise their desire to reproduce or not, outside of coercive and restrictive environments. Many women with intellectual disabilities, as well as women of color, prisoners, poor women, and those at the intersections of these categories, are not always able to exercise their reproductive rights. In the next chapter, I seek out conversations about what reproductive rights, outside a discourse of "pronatalism," would look like if all women, including those with intellectual disabilities, were not just allowed to reproduce of their own volition but also supported and respected about their reproductive life and potentiality.

5 Not Just an Able-Bodied Privilege

Toward an Ethics of Parenting

In an interview with the Mother's Movement Online, feminist historian Rickie Solinger discusses her photography exhibit "Beggars and Choosers: Motherhood Is Not a Class Privilege in America," co-curated with artist Kay Obering. Solinger comments that the exhibit "interrupts the curriculum" by asking viewers (especially on college campuses) to "rethink what they 'know' about who makes a legitimate mother—and who decides. The exhibition becomes an occasion for offering social justice perspectives and good information about the experience of mothering in the United States in the early twenty-first century."[1] Accordingly, the exhibit offers images of women "clearly engaged in being loving, attentive mothers—with strength, dignity, and determination."[2] One of the images in the exhibit includes a photograph from Nancy Pastor's collection "Jasmine's World." Jasmine is a young girl being raised by two parents with intellectual disabilities. In this chapter, I am tracing out the meanings of including a representation of intellectually disabled parents within an exhibit that specifically addresses the lack of diversity in representations of motherhood.[3] Specifically, I am arguing that by including an image of disabled parenting in the exhibit, the coalitional potential between disability studies and reproductive justice is actualized. While expanding a conversation of sexual pleasure for individuals with intellectual disabilities (as I have done in earlier chapters) challenges the rhetoric concerning sexuality, to limit the focus on sexual pleasure does not necessarily challenge broader questions of reproductive control. In this chapter, I explore the implications of advocating for a theory of pleasure through reproduction and offer observations about the reproductive rights for women with intellectual disabilities. Additionally, I argue that subjugated knowledge of persons with a label of intellectual disability and their experience of "misfitting" challenge frameworks of competence and fitness, especially as they relate to parenting.[4]

The website for the social justice organization Generations Ahead published an open letter titled "Robert Edwards, Virginia Ironside, and the Unnecessary Opposition of Rights."[5] The letter illustrates the interconnectedness between disability rights and reproductive rights and justice. A portion of the statement reads, "As people committed to both disability rights and reproductive rights, we believe that respecting women and families in their reproductive decisions requires simultaneously challenging discriminatory attitudes toward people with disabilities. We refuse to accept the bifurcation of women's rights from disability rights, or the belief that protecting reproductive rights requires accepting ableist assumptions about the supposed tragedy of disability. On the contrary, we assert that reproductive rights include attention to disability rights, and that disability rights require attention to human rights, including reproductive rights."[6] In discussing this statement and the potential for coalitional politics, Alison Kafer remarks that often the justification to end pregnancy on the basis or assumption of disability is realized through "trafficking in discriminatory stereotypes about disability."[7] These stereotypes of disability include the notion that raising a child with a disability is always emotionally and financially difficult. Other stereotypes specifically make suppositions about the overall quality of life of the disabled individual. These assessments often make the mathematical claim that disability negates a sense of purpose or overall well-being. The statement above advances the important reproductive justice coalitional work between disability rights and women's rights under the umbrella of reproductive rights. Kafer continues:

> We need to expand the terrain of dialogue, moving away from such a limited focus on suffering, quality of life, and unlivable disabilities—notions that often perpetuate ableist assumptions—and toward creating opportunities to support reproductive justice for all, including for and by disabled people. Continuing to accept disability as the reason to keep abortion legal, and casting abortion as the only reasonable choice when dealing with disability, is a narrowing of both abortion rights and the terms of debate. So, too, is the assumption that the meaning of "suffering" or "quality

of life" is self-evident and monolithic; rather than using these concepts as if they "obviously" led us to only one conclusion, we could attend instead to their shifts in meanings across different registers, contexts, or bodies/minds.[8]

I take Kafer's insistence to move beyond the dialogue of suffering and ableist trends as my starting point in this chapter. Here, I am interested in the further coalitional work between activists in the reproductive justice arena, those who fight against reproductive violations of individuals with disabilities, and the reproductive potential of individuals with intellectual disabilities. In the previous chapter, reproduction of women with intellectual disabilities was framed largely as a negatively formulated rights issue that focuses on instances of violation. Often the claiming of rights (to marry, have sex, die, give birth), however, is performed at the expense of other groups. For example, in claiming the right to die, some advocates construct disability or illness as a condition warranting physician-assisted suicide, thus rhetorically constructing the lives of those inhabiting these categories as less livable or already mostly dead. Despite the potential limitations of a rights-based approach, various advocates find that legal and legislative venues are more apt to ensure limited intrusions into the reproductive lives of individuals if the language of rights and violation are strategically used to generate action.

I am advocating that the reproductive wishes of individuals with intellectual disabilities be respected and legally, culturally, and socially supported. While I risk further separating constituents, including those in queer theory, reproductive justice, and disability studies, for potentially upholding reproductive norms, this claim is an effort on my part to interject the conversation of qualifications for parenting, which makes imaging parents with intellectual disabilities almost impossible, with an explicit intellectual disability analysis. Individuals with intellectual disabilities ought not be excluded from the ability to reproduce and raise children based solely on their disability status.[9] My intent in this chapter is not to further isolate those for whom reproduction is not desired or to portray these individuals as deviant or exceptional. Queer theorists such as Lee Edelman are quite persuasive in advocating for antifuturity by rejecting the "child" (and reproduction and normativity).[10] Edelman in particular is critical of attempts to secure rights, in marriage and reproduction, as too normative—and distancing from queer radical potential. Others in queer theory, including José Muñoz, have criticized antifuturity that "moves to imagine an escape or denouncement of relationality as first and foremost a distancing of queerness from what some theorists seem to think of as the contamination of race, gender, or other particularities that taint the purity of sexuality as a singular trope of difference. In other words, antirelational approaches to queer theory are romances of the negative, wishful thinking, and investments in deferring various dreams of difference."[11] Muñoz's comment regarding distancing from "particularities that taint the purity of sexuality" as "wishful thinking, and investments" in "various dreams of difference" helps to articulate my position in this chapter that the dream of family or wish of children does not necessarily have to be made at the exclusion of the desire to not parent or to have childless futurity.

While it might seem that I am "fighting for the children" in this chapter, I would claim that in advocating that individuals with intellectual disabilities can parent, I am queering the very notion of family and parenting to a relational model outside normative constructions of futurity, which paradoxically depends on the very liberal constructions of rights that Edelman critiques. I am disrupting the narrative that children of disabled parents need to be protected because of the "selfish" reproductive desires of their parents (and supposed parental unfitness).[12] Additionally, I am highlighting the need for reproductive justice movements and organizations to include disabled women as subjects and partners in their analysis and social justice efforts. In mapping out the queer terrain of reproduction and parenting for individuals with intellectual disabilities, I am compelled to disidentify with both camps (rights-based liberal theory and anti-futurity queer theory) in order to articulate a perspective that expands current conceptions of reproduction and livability. In this chapter, I take up an expansive reproductive justice framework to explore the reproductive lives of individuals with intellectual disabilities. This analysis is informed by critical disability studies and queer theory approaches that force an uneasy coalition between these fields, which are typically constructed as tangentially related or perhaps theoretically oppositional.[13] My goal in advocating for the parental and reproductive rights of individuals with intellectual disabilities is not to replace one mode of normativity with another but rather to smash open or *crip* the boundaries of family to create space for intellectual disability. I meditate on the potential connections, conversations, and issues of contention to consider the reproductive and parental possibilities of individuals with intellectual disabilities.

Images of Motherhood and Misfitting

In the United States, individuals with intellectual disabilities were subjected to eugenic control of their reproduction through the use of coerced sterilization, institutionalization, and invasive birth control methods similar to the kind of reproductive control experienced by people of color, immigrants, and the poor, many of whom were labeled as having intellectual disabilities. Dorothy Roberts documents how, after the 1927 *Buck v. Bell* decision, eugenic fervor to control the reproductive potential of those deemed feebleminded shifted to the sterilization of women.[14] "Feebleminded" was the all-encompassing word used by eugenicists to classify racial, ethnic, disabled, and sexual others.[15] Prior to the *Buck v. Bell* court decision, much more attention was given to policing men's ability to father children, yet after Carrie Buck was deemed unfit to mother, "sterilization was viewed as a way of allowing mentally deficient women to be released safely from institutions in society, eliminating the chance that they would bear children who were expected to be wards of the state."[16] Women of color, poor women, disabled women, non-Western women, and those at the intersections of these categories, have experienced various means of reproductive control, including forced sterilization, equating welfare eligibility with a required prescription of Norplant, and delivery of other forms of birth control without their consent or knowledge.[17]

There are gendered and sexual myths of intellectual disability, including the beliefs that women with intellectual disabilities are extremely fecund, or particularly vulnerable to experience sexual abuse. Men labeled with intellectual disabilities are supposedly prone to sexually abusing women with intellectual disabilities, as well as children. These myths continue to influence the delivery of sex education in special education classrooms and group homes. For example, as seen in chapter 2, sex education materials specifically instruct men with intellectual disabilities to only interact with children by waving or using some other socially distant method of interaction, to ensure that they would not be accused of sexual abuse. While there are fairly extensive examinations of how the reproductive rights of women with intellectual disabilities are violated by forcible application of birth control pills, IUDs, and involuntary sterilization, as well as the legal and cultural ramifications of reproduction, there is limited focus on men and women with intellectual disabilities as agents of reproduction.[18] Disabled people, as parents and reproductive beings, warrant deeper analysis in reproductive justice and critical disabilities studies.

At various times since the 1960s, the U.S. government, state legislatures, and to some extent the general public have debated the qualifications of motherhood. What makes a good mother? Can a mother be poor, disabled, an immigrant, of color, lesbian, a prisoner, or more than one of the above? What is the government's responsibility (if any) in providing financial assistance and other kinds of aid for poor and disenfranchised mothers? Ability to provide these essential resources, including access to abortion, birth control, and reproductive technologies, day care, health care, shelter, clean water, and nutritious food, have been central to these conversations. From the Hyde Amendment to welfare reform of the 1990s, from the lesbian baby boom to the global gag rule and discussion of women's rights, notions of appropriate motherhood have shifted. With access to reproductive technology and surrogates, especially from developing nations, more middle- and upper-middle class Americans, who are often white, heterosexual, and able-bodied, are able to have offspring. Charis Thompson, in her exploration of assistive reproductive technologies and how they are used to "make parents," remarks that these technologies continue to reinforce economic-based distinctions, while at the same time they can be used to help redefine family and kinship outside of a heteronormative model.[19] Additionally, as evidenced by U.S. white celebrity fascination with adopting children of color, the presence of (certain) white American families with children of color is becoming more common.[20] It would appear that the boundaries of mothering (and parenthood in general) are flexible. Yet as Solinger questions, "Why is it still necessary—or necessary again—to justify the motherhood of poor and other resourceless women, many of whom raise children alone under extremely difficult circumstances?"[21] Discourse of dependency on state support renders some mothers as potentially deviant. Membership in a socially disenfranchised group has the potential to warrant intrusion and oversight, in addition to assessments of parental fitness.

Illustrating the linkage between materialist concerns and assumptions of parental appropriateness, Dorothy Roberts discusses how "stratified reproduction"[22] and a neoliberal emphasis on privatization places responsibility on pregnant women to ensure the health and welfare of their children as opposed to the state.[23] Roberts connects this focus on privatization as a key element of the medical model of disability "embedded in a neoliberal health policy that relies on widespread use of genetic technologies to disqualify citizens from claiming public support and to avoid the need for social change."[24]

The women in Solinger's exhibit should be included in any discussion of neoliberal health care trends that emphasize privatization. As Ruby Tapia writes of the exhibit, "The truly re-visionary push of 'Beggars and Choosers' is toward an examination of the colliding and colluding politics that fix maternal images in the first place along a spectrum that ranges from the reviled to the revered."[25] The exhibit space asks participants to contemplate the long history of linking women and their value as mothers to their children in photographs, while also grappling with dominant discourses of parental fitness tied to classist, ableist, racist, and gendered assumptions.

One of Nancy Pastor's images from her collection "Jasmine's World" is included in the "Beggars and Choosers" photography exhibit. Pastor, an award-winning former photojournalist for the *Washington Times,* also photographed another controversial mother, Nadya Suleman.[26] Pastor describes "Jasmine's World" as "a collection about a developmentally normal child being raised by her mentally challenged parents. It is an ongoing story of a little girl's relationship with her parents and her struggle for normalcy in this extraordinary environment."[27] "Jasmine's World" is a collection of twenty black-and-white photographs documenting moments in the lives of Jasmine and her parents, Brenda and James.[28]

The image included in "Beggars and Choosers" from "Jasmine's World" is the first of the series. In the black-and-white photograph, four-year-old Jasmine is seated between her parents, her left arm in a fabric sling.[29] Jasmine is the only one who is directly gazing into the camera; her eyes are seemingly full of emotion. Jasmine appears content to be laying her body on her mother. Their physical closeness is

In the backseat of a car, Jasmine sits between her parents, Brenda and James. She is leaning on her mother. Jasmine's left arm is in a cloth sling. Jasmine is looking at the camera, while Brenda is looking at James. Photograph by Nancy Pastor.

highlighted here and in other images in the series. Her father, James, is looking at something in his hands, outside the focus of the camera. Brenda, Jasmine's mother, is looking at James. The exhibit contains the following caption with the photograph: "Four-year-old Jasmine sits between her parents, Brenda and James, who are developmentally disabled, in the back seat of their social worker's car. They are given a weekly allowance and Pat, their social worker, is driving them to do grocery shopping." While the caption does not comment on the sling or provide much more than the basic details of the captured moment, a quote from the social worker, Pat Hanson, displayed alongside the caption, opines as to why the parental rights of Brenda are controversial. The quote reads, "I know more about the situation than anyone around. A child has needs. And Brenda has needs. And Brenda was once a child who was thrown away. Brenda got her tubes tied when Jasmine was born. She knew her own limitations. But that desire to reproduce was strong. That desire to nurture was strong. On the one hand, they shouldn't have had children, but on the other hand, Jasmine is here. And Jasmine, Jasmine is a jewel."

Like many women with intellectual disabilities, Brenda was encouraged not to reproduce because of her "limitations." The social worker, however, remarks that Brenda's desire to parent was strong and natural. Hanson's words reinforce a linking of biology with gendered parenting expectations. Desire to nurture and reproduce are linked to Brenda's gender, while her motherhood is also exceptional in the sense that it is supposedly accepted that Brenda and James should not have had children. The competing discourses of gendered parenting expectations tied to biology and ableist prohibitions of parenting fixed to disability frame Brenda's reproduction and parenting. Notice, too, how we learn Brenda was "thrown away" as a child. This language of throwing away invokes trash. Brenda's experience of growing up after being thrown away mirrors the lives of many disabled children growing up in foster homes or state-run institutions and group homes. The social worker claims expertise and knowledge, stating, "I know more about the situation than anyone around," and acting as the voice of authority to frame the reproduction and parenting of Brenda and James through the figure of their daughter, Jasmine. While the social worker is not visually represented in the photograph, as she and Pastor are outside the frame, her voice intertwines her experiences with that of Brenda, James, and Jasmine.

The multiple frames—or framing—occurring in the photograph and accompanying text are illuminating when considering intellectual disability, parenthood, and reproduction. The framing of the photographer constructs Brenda and James as passive recipients of social supports. Additionally, the image of Brenda with Jasmine calls on a long history of women with their children, the most relevant being Dorothea Lange's 1936 photograph "Migrant Mother." In Pastor's photograph, the family is situated in the backseat of their social worker's car. Pastor is most likely sitting in the front passenger seat as she takes the photograph. The curator's caption also frames Brenda, James, and Jasmine as recipients of social services: "They are given a weekly allowance and Pat, their social worker, is driving them to do grocery shopping." Figuratively the backseat is a location of passivity, a place where individuals sit to be driven. Even if CEOs, celebrities, or others sit in the backseat to be chauffeured around, they are unable to directly affect the direction the car travels. Under the guise of safety, children, up to a certain age, are expected to sit in the backseat of the car, even if the front passenger seat remains open. The image and text accurately document the social service management of disability. The three individuals are seemingly passive recipients of state support; their agency is disguised. The only mention of agency is Brenda's desire to parent and her decision to tie her tubes after giving birth to Jasmine. James's experiences are not remarked on in the caption, other than through the statement "On the one hand, they shouldn't have had children, but on the other hand, Jasmine is here." The photograph, however, visually documents his presence. His fatherhood is not remarked on as exceptional as Brenda's motherhood is by the social worker.[30] James is present in the lives of Brenda and Jasmine, four years into the formation of this unit of intimacy.

The visual representation of the triad is based on their relationship to disability management, embodied for the viewer through the social worker. Her words are presented as authoritative because her image is rendered invisible. Materialist relationships, including lack of resources and reliance on state support, seem to create dependency. Brenda and James are connected to the social worker, Pat Hanson, through a disability bureaucracy that dissolves assumptions of privacy, agency, and self-determination, even if Hanson positively supports their parenting. They are assigned a social worker, presumably, because of their class and disability status. Rosemarie Garland-Thomson forwards a materialist feminist disability analysis of "misfit" and "misfitting." Garland-Thomson tries to track "how the particularities of embodiment interact with their environment in its broadest sense, to include both its spatial and temporal aspects."[31] I find this concept helpful in thinking about how Brenda, James, and Jasmine seem to misfit and are conceptualized as misfits by Pastor, Solinger and Obering, and the social worker. Misfitting is a central experience for disabled individuals, as "law or custom can and has produced segregation of certain groups; misfitting demonstrates how encounters between bodies and unsustaining environments also have produced segregation."[32] She connects the experience of misfitting to that of being denied citizenship and rights.[33] Garland-Thomson continues, "Misfit emphasizes context over essence, relation over isolation, mediation over origination. Misfits are inherently unstable rather than fixed, yet they are very real because they are material rather than linguistic constructions."[34]

Intellectual disability as a condition and diagnosis is often imagined as a stable and exact category, the assumption being that those labeled as having an intellectual disability are unable to do, comprehend, and manage certain concepts and tasks. What seems to partially misfit Brenda and James is the assumption that they are unfit or unable to parent their daughter, Jasmine, most likely due to assumed intelligence levels as well as material and support needs. Additionally, the materialist condition of poverty further illuminates how the family is utterly dependent on social supports and state oversight. The perspectives of Brenda and James are not shared in the captions and they are not reframed as powerful parents, like others are in the exhibit space. Accordingly, "the utility of the concept of misfit is that it definitively lodges injustice and discrimination in the materiality of the world more than in social attitudes or representational practice, even while it recognizes their mutually constituting entanglement."[35] While it appears that Garland-Thomson makes physical realities (and impairments) the main thrust of her embodied analysis, I want to further her claims onto individuals with intellectual disabilities.[36] Garland-Thomson writes that the experience of misfitting fosters subjugated knowledge "from which an oppositional consciousness and politicized identity might arise," helping to "foster intense awareness of social injustice and the formation of a community of misfits that can collaborate to achieve a more liberatory politics and practice."[37]

In a lecture at the Collège de France, Michel Foucault considers subjugated knowledges as a "whole series of knowledges that have been disqualified as nonconceptual knowledges, as insufficiently elaborated knowledges: naïve knowledges, hierarchically inferior knowledges, knowledges that are below the required level of erudition or scientificity."[38] Individuals labeled intellectually disabled are seen to not possess sufficiently elaborated knowledge; rather, their disability label is predicated on an assumption of naïveté.[39] Their impairment diagnoses construct Brenda and James as possessing insufficient knowledge to raise Jasmine, despite the insistence that she is wanted, needed, and desired. This assumed insufficient knowledge, however, is formed in relation to the experience of intellectual disability management and ableism. When a diagnosis of intellectual disability is predicated on assumptions of incompetence, the meaning-making of the diagnosis seems to warrant professional management and oversight. As such, the subjugated knowledge of Brenda and James is intimately tied to the knowledge of the oppressor. Foucault writes that a genealogy and uncovering of subjugated knowledge is "a sort of attempt to de-subjugate historical knowledges, to set them free, or in other words to enable them to oppose and struggle against the coercion of a unitary, formal, and scientific theoretical discourse."[40]

I am particularly interested in tracing out the possibilities of sub-jugated knowledge collected by a community of misfits. Misfits are assumed to not be productive and resourceful. Misfits have either lost their sense of purpose, or never have had their purpose recog-nized. While the concept of misfit seems to argue for an either/or formulation—you either fit or misfit—I am trying to expand the con-cept beyond the binary to further elaborate on the possibilities and potentialities of misfitting. What are the crip/queer possibilities of being a misfit parent?[41]

The crip/queer possibilities can be found in the subjects of "Jasmine's World," a collectivity of misfits in its own right. These misfits do not seem to enable liberatory politics or practice, but in this space of mis-fitting, the assemblage of diverse parts renders the whole possible. Brenda and James, through their experience of disability, informed by poverty, have become misfits. Scanning the rest of Pastor's series illustrates how Brenda, James, and Jasmine have become misfits; they seem to not quite fit their environments, but this lack of fitting can be rendered as a sense of power and resiliency. Visually their inter-connectedness is highlighted, illustrating their fit both within the space and with one another.[42]

For example, the third photograph in the series shows Brenda and Jasmine asleep on a couch. Shot from above, Pastor is artfully docu-menting a tender moment between mother and child. While the overhead angle makes the subjects appear vulnerable and small, the intercorporeal connection is nevertheless highlighted. Their legs are intertwined as they have adapted their bodies and physicality onto the couch. In particular, this image is inverted from a standard scene of mother and child at rest. Here, Jasmine and Brenda appear feet to feet,

Shot from above, the photograph shows Jasmine and Brenda asleep on a couch. Their legs are intertwined, as both are able to fit their bodies on the couch. Photograph by Nancy Pastor.

their legs helping to form a cohesive unit.[43] It appears that both mother and child are able to use the space populated with a drink cup, magazine, plush toy, phone, and television to catch a nap. Some commentators might pay close attention to the environment as opposed to the subjects, choosing to focus on the condition of the furniture or carpet as illustrating a space of poverty. I want to resist this reading for the moment to dwell on the potentiality of the pairing on the couch. This pairing becomes an interdependent unit, allowing a shared sense of purpose and mutuality. Their corporealities support each other, meeting the bodily need of rest. Mother and child, regardless of labels of disability or assumptions of intelligence, have emerged to form a unit of mutuality and sustainability.

One of the most common arguments for terminating the parental rights of individuals with intellectual disabilities is a concern that the child's intellect will surpass that of the parents. Pastor's description of Jasmine's developmental normalcy includes this concern as a specter. Here I find the concept of subjugated knowledge a powerful tool to help crip/queer this parental relationship configured as potentially limiting for Jasmine. In both images analyzed above, as well as others in the series, Jasmine and Brenda support each other through physical closeness and mutual expressions of care labor. The images themselves, without captions or accompanying text, do not disclose the presence or absence of disability. Rather, the images highlight the family resting, playing, cleaning, and doing other quotidian activities. Brenda's care and support of Jasmine, James's assistance and presence, as well as Jasmine's connection to her parents illustrates the crip/queer potential of these figures in unison, while external materialist forces and disability management attempt to render the unit broken. These three smash open the conception of family as a reproductive capitalistic unit; their documented dependence on state intervention and financial assistance reframes notions of family, care, and support away from a mode focusing on accumulation of wealth and a self-sufficient nuclear family.

Despite the potential for Brenda, James, and Jasmine to smash open conceptions of family, like other parents with intellectual disabilities Brenda and James lost custody of Jasmine, when she was around the age of six. In an e-mail correspondence with Pastor, she told me that Pat Hanson retained custody of Jasmine since birth but wanted Brenda and James to parent the girl. As such, Brenda, James, and Pat (and her husband) shared parenting duties based on both formal designations and informal arrangements. According to Pastor, when Jasmine grew older, the parenting duties proved too challenging for Brenda and James. Jasmine moved in with Pat and her husband, where she lived until Pat passed away. If Pat was not willing to allow Jasmine to live with Brenda and James, it is reasonably likely that Jasmine might not have had much experience interacting with her birth parents. This update, after the photographs discussed above were taken, demonstrates how the parental rights of individuals with intellectual disabilities can be tenuously and temporarily held together. The forces working against the crip/queer potential can significantly restrain alternative conceptions of family, especially when those models are predicated on able-bodiedness and capitalist productivity.

I will return to the possibility of subjugated knowledge emanating from misfits at the end of this chapter. Before continuing, however, I want to suture the various threads of this chapter together to connect the photographic representation of intellectual disability with Kafer's call for coalition and Muñoz's longing for various dreams of difference. The inclusion of Brenda and James in Solinger and Obering's exhibit fosters these coalitions between diverse subjects on the margins of reproductive potentiality. McRuer writes that a crip/queer perspective can "direct our attention back to those productively unruly bodies" by demanding "access to public spaces and conversations currently configured to reproduce only the limited perspective of the able body."[44] Disabled parents can challenge assumptions of parenting that perpetuate able-bodied norms. As Carrie Sandahl remarks, "As outsiders, queers and crips refuse to minimize their differences by passing as either straight or able-bodied. Instead, they appropriate and rearticulate labels that the mainstream once used to silence or humiliate them and that the liberal factions of their subcultures would like to suppress."[45] Considering disability as an experience that can enhance parenting (and childhood) drastically challenges ableist assumptions.

Coalitional Potential and Intellectually Disabled Parenting

I take seriously the need to facilitate cross-group conversations to reconsider the positionality of parents with intellectual disabilities as subjects of the reproductive justice movement. Reproductive justice acknowledges that restriction and oppression of reproduction are created by systems of domination that include power differentials based on race, class, ability status, sexuality, age, and immigration/citizenship status.[46] Reproductive justice organizations like Forward Together and SisterSong acknowledge that ableism is a key component in limiting the reproduction of individuals.[47] More coalitional work between reproductive justice organizations and disability rights organizations can be done, but dialogue between organizations and communities is happening. While the social worker's quote highlights Brenda's "choice" of getting her tubes tied after Jasmine's birth, I cannot help but wonder what goes unspoken in this declaration. It is as if Brenda's decision to end her reproductive potential renders her past discretion less objectionable. In the introduction to this chapter, I remarked that disability and quality of life are often configured as oppositional in theoretical calculations. The same assumptions about disability are invoked in the social worker's claim of Jasmine's jewel status. Jasmine's jewelness is positioned against the assumption of her parent's disability status as limiting. Quality of life and suffering are not monolithic concepts, and the social worker's claim can be resisted and *cripped* to illustrate the exclusionary ableist assumptions embedded in having disabled parents. It is also interesting to consider the social worker as a type of "mother" (or guardian)—she is the driver and provider, the authoritative voice on the experiences while begrudging the choices of Brenda, especially given the parenting arrangement discussed above. These power differentials help illustrate how disability management and service delivery can reinforce sexually ableist understandings of fitness for reproduction and parenting.

A significant portion of the research into the lives of parents with intellectual disabilities documents how their reproductive choices are met with disapproval from social service workers and agencies.[48] As part of an effort to address the overall disapproval, in the last two-plus decades a sizeable amount of research has been conducted on parents with intellectual disabilities in the United States, Canada, England, Australia, and New Zealand. In a comprehensive review of research into intellectual disability and parenting since the 1950s, Gwynnyth Llewellyn makes the incisive observation that "a clear relationship between parent intelligence and the child's educational achievement has not been established for any specified parent group."[49] Despite discriminatory assumptions that parents with intellectual disabilities are unable to successfully parent because of their supposed diminished intellect, more recent studies have determined that intellectual ability has very little to do with parental capacity.[50] Parenting is a "socially determined process" where a multiplicity of factors including upbringing, socioeconomic status, and discriminatory views influence parenting styles and content.[51] As Llewellyn observes, "The literature on parents with intellectual disability is founded on two interlinked assumptions. These are firstly, that parents are primarily responsible for child outcomes, and that, therefore, child outcomes are indicative of parenting adequacy; and secondly, that intellectual disability is in some way inextricably linked with the absence of parenting capability."[52] Additionally, a majority of the research was conducted on parents with intellectual disabilities who have been referred to a variety of social service organizations because of perceived deficiencies in their parental duties, including child neglect and abuse and unsafe living conditions, meaning that "the majority of findings come from studies in which the parents were already identified as needing assistance. Presumably, other intellectually disabled parents live in the community unknown to health, welfare, or protective authorities."[53] This oversampling bias of parents who have been determined as needing assistance has the potential to skew our knowledge base with an undue focus on parents in trouble. This brief review of the professional literature is important in order to contextualize some of the reasons for the inclusion of Pastor's photograph in the "Beggars and Choosers" exhibit, because disabled women reproduce and parent in restrictive and ableist spaces.

Solinger comments that "'Beggars and Choosers: Motherhood Is Not a Class Privilege in America' offers a vision of what *reproductive rights* could look like in the U.S. if having a baby were recognized as a *right*; if public policies and community attitudes did not aim to restrict legitimate motherhood to 'qualified' women."[54] The exhibit is very much about showing the struggles that these disenfranchised women face in obtaining some recognition as mothers while dealing with various bureaucracies; these struggles include widows living on government assistance, single mothers fighting with insurance companies, immigrant mothers filing immunization paperwork in English to secure access to schooling, and women in prison giving birth in shackles and handcuffs. Many of these images affirm the reproductive and mothering rights of these women by highlighting the difficult circumstances they face with limited resources. Pastor's photograph of Jasmine and her parents might be the exception in that it (and the series in general) concerns Jasmine's perspective of living with two parents with intellectual disabilities. Pastor is not as concerned with affirming the reproductive rights of Brenda and James as she is with representing Jasmine's world and the impact of having disabled parents. Jasmine's apparent nondisability might offer viewers some semblance of hope that she can emerge out of poverty, despite her upbringing.

The social worker remarks that Brenda "knew her own limitations" despite wanting to reproduce. Brenda's desire to give birth is seen as natural, albeit exceptional because of her disability status. Her decision to tie her tubes afterward, however, is seen as responsible. What would it mean if as a society the parenting and reproductive wishes of all women were celebrated, regardless of measures taken to provide adequate child care or prevent future pregnancy? Or as Solinger provocatively asks, what would reproductive rights mean if giving birth were seen as a right, regardless of membership within a socially devalued group? On the section of her website introducing "Jasmine's World," Pastor adds that "disability, poverty, and single parent limitations all affect the way families are perceived by the courts. However, the essential issues remain: who can judge the source and sufficiency of love? Which women have the right to mother their children?"[55]

As explored in the previous chapter, the judge in the Illinois case unjustly decided that if the young woman with an intellectual disability were to give birth, her child would surely be taken away. Unfortunately, this is still true for many parents with intellectual disabilities. Supposed parental unfitness or neglect, as well as discriminatory attitudes regarding intelligence, dominate these court proceedings. In many of these parental custody cases there remains a preoccupation with the ensuing moment when their children will advance past the parent's supposed intellectual age.[56] Margrit Shildrick discusses how sexuality and pleasure are largely ignored in legal and policy considerations except for the "major, but limited, concern in the area of sexuality and sexual relations [that] appears to focus primarily on regulating and monitoring the reproductive capabilities of men and women with developmental disabilities."[57] Shildrick continues, "Where that monitoring results in potentially severe restrictions that may deeply undermine the enshrinement of reproduction as a fundamental right of humanity, it demonstrates state power in a more classically repressive form that is at least open to challenge. In contrast, an insidious management by silence is extremely hard to contest."[58] The sustained focus on managing and controlling the reproductive potentiality of women (and to some extent men) with intellectual disabilities illustrates the restraining environment that many raise children in while constantly trying to prove parental abilities. Solinger's exhibit attempts to bring together in one location the various women whose difference at the margins is not recognized, or more explicitly, whose mothering is vilified. These women are represented as capable mothers despite encountering systematic opposition and barriers to their reproductive choices. Solinger remarks that "the subjects of 'Beggars and Choosers' express their motherhood in ways that show the viewer the connection between reproductive rights—the right to be a mother—and an essential claim of humanity. These photographs clarify the full meaning of reproductive rights: the right to decide when not to become pregnant or to have a baby *as well as* the right to decide for oneself to become a mother."[59] For the reproductive rights Solinger discusses to be fully actualized, a drastic reimagining of mothering would have to occur, including the recognition that parents with intellectual disabilities can be successful parents in ways that make sense to them. I hesitate to offer success as a criterion for evaluating parenting because I do not want to replace one system of evaluation with another; my point is that despite the disavowal that occurs, people with intellectual disabilities ought to be given the space, resources, and legitimacy in their desires to reproduce and parent. Though Jasmine is a "jewel" according to the social worker, what if she were not? Would it still be acceptable for Brenda and James to be parents if their child were not treasured? Does the lack of visible disability status for Jasmine (despite her sling) negate the supposed inappropriate reproduction and parenting? While Jasmine certainly can be a jewel, her parents' desire to create a child can be the criteria for celebration and pleasure as opposed to the outcome of their union.

To conclude this chapter, I want to revisit the notion of subjugated knowledge and place it in conversation with María Lugones's notion of playfulness to theorize the transformative pleasurable potential of intellectual disabled parenting and the need for coalitional work as evidenced in the "Beggars and Choosers" exhibit. Lugones writes, "to the extent that we learn to perceive others arrogantly or come to see them only as products of arrogant perception and continue to perceive them that way, we fail to identify with them—fail to love them—in this particularly deep way."[60] This failure to identify further divides marginalized individuals from one another while reconstructing dominant understandings of subordinate populations.[61]

The potential for acceptance, mutuality, and an agenda for change is reflected in the exhibition space of "Beggars and Choosers." Playfulness and pleasure emerge between subjects previously considered to be misfitting, deficient, and lacking in their ability to parent.[62] Playfulness emerges on the couch between Brenda and Jasmine in the photograph discussed above. Cross-agenda coalition facilitates a new imagining of connections that need not be contained within a heteronormative nuclear family unit. Rather, these coalitions of individuals retrace boundaries of community. Playfulness, pleasure, and "world"-traveling through the experience of misfitting actualize the coalitional potential. As Lugones remarks, "Through traveling to other people's 'worlds' we discover that there are 'worlds' in which those who are the victim of arrogant perception are really subjects, lively beings, resistors, constructors of visions even though in the mainstream construction they are animated only by the arrogant perceiver and are pliable, foldable, file-awayable, classifiable."[63] Brenda and James, like other parents with intellectual disabilities, are assumed deficient in their parenting by the arrogant perceivers as a result of ableism. Their experience illustrates the need for continual challenges to the able-bodied heteronormative family as the basis for rights entitlement. Individuals with intellectual disabilities are able to be meaningful collaborators in coalition with other individuals working on reproductive justice. Their unruly potentiality facilitates disidentification with entrenched assumptions of normalcy or productivity, misfitting their future with others toward new, pleasurable, and creative formulations of community.

6 Screening Sexuality

Media Representations of Intellectual Disability

In the previous chapters, I explored the sexuality of individuals with intellectual disabilities in relation to issues of sexual abuse, competency and agency, sex education, and sanctioned approaches to sexuality, namely, masturbation training and nonreproductive heterosexuality. In this chapter, I attend to the ways in which the sexuality of individuals with intellectual disabilities is represented in more popular forms of media. Specifically, I examine television movies, talk radio, and film from 1980 to the present to historically trace out the ways in which characters with intellectual disabilities are represented in relation to issues of sexuality and reproduction. I attempt to find representations of the themes discussed in previous chapters, thus locating these same themes in popular discourse. I have been operating on the supposition that cultural representations of intellectual disability present an opportunity to understand how the sexuality of this population is constructed. Additionally, there have been few comprehensive analyses of representations of intellectual disability undertaken in disability studies. I have explored in the previous chapters how the sexuality of people with intellectual disabilities is programmed and regulated by special educators, guardians, and parents, as well as residential staff in group homes and institutions. Complicated and potentially controversial constructs of competency, agency, and pleasure guided my inquiry. These same constructs once again serve as theoretical guideposts in this chapter's exploration of sex and intellectual disability through popular media.

I examine *I Am Sam* (2001) and *The Other Sister* (1999) as two mainstream Hollywood films wherein the sexuality of intellectually disabled characters is central to the plot. While there are many films that incorporate characters with intellectual disabilities, including the made for television films *Bill* (1981) and the sequel, *Bill: On His Own* (1983), both starring Mickey Rooney as an adult man who is learning to be independent outside an institution, *I Am Sam* and *The Other Sister* are unique in that they take up sexuality as integral to the characters' lives. Here I examine these films to explore how the sexuality of individuals is imagined, while maintaining critical attention to the professionalization of sexuality. Representations of male and female sexuality provide differing gendered expectations of sexuality and pleasure.

In the last section of the chapter, a somewhat unlikely source is examined. *The Howard Stern Show* is a satellite radio program heard on Sirius XM Radio by over a million listeners a week. Stern is also a best-selling author with his autobiography, *Private Parts*, which later became a feature film of the same title. He is known as a shock jock; he regularly participates in and promotes sexist conversations on his program, often using derogatory terminology such as "whore" and "slut" to refer to women who appear on the show. Stern has a regular group of guests, including two individuals with intellectual disabilities, "Gary the Retard" and "Wendy the Retard." On the program, Gary and Wendy are often subjected to ridicule that can only be described as ableism in its most oppressive forms. As part of the "humor" on the show, Gary and Wendy are mocked for their sexual knowledge and sexuality. This section examines Gary and Wendy and the messages of their sexuality that are reinforced on *The Howard Stern Show*.

Efforts to Study Representations of Cognitive/Developmental Disability

In his book *Inventing the Feeble Mind,* James Trent explores how mental retardation becomes understood based on developments in treatment, management, and social views:

> From the time people with the "thing," mental retardation, became social problems requiring help and treatment, the contours of this requirement have changed, sometimes dramatically, but the contours of our regard for people with mental retardation has not. This and that must be done to and for them; this and that must be learned about them and said about them to ensure progress in treatment techniques, professional influence, institutional funding, or social control. It is important to understand that this image of mental retardation as a "thing," the object of scientific under-

standing and intervention, conceals a history shaped by the implicit political choices of the mentally accelerated. In making care more scientific and professional, these political implications have been hidden, but they, more than our explicit "knowledge," have determined our fabrications of mental retardation and the gaze with which we regard and control mentally retarded persons.[1]

Trent sees intellectual disability as a "thing" that influences not only how individuals are managed (e.g., in institutions, sheltered workshops, special education) but also how professional knowledge has determined the treatment and social outlook of people with intellectual disabilities. This is an important place to start when thinking about representational theories of intellectual disability because the professionalization of the impairment that affects cultural understandings can help to explain the static representations of intellectual disability. Throughout the exploration thus far, I have highlighted how the sexuality of individuals with intellectual disabilities remains a "thing" requiring professional redirection (through masturbation training and prescriptive sex education). In fact, sexual ableism operates by constructing individuals with the label of intellectual disability as being unable to live and act in sexually deliberate ways. The subsequent construction that flattens and obfuscates diverse realities of individual lives seems to warrant professional intrusion and oversight. My argument is that professional interventions, education materials, and oversight of sexuality inform cultural representations and understandings of sexuality and vice versa. Often the very kinds of representations of intellectual disability are coded in professionalized assessments; characters are living in group homes or institutions, and physicians remind us of the "intellectual age" of the character throughout. Changes in professionally run living arrangements are often central to the plots of the films discussed below. A change in living situations offers conflict that is resolved in the film. The result is that the character with an intellectual disability can be interpreted as the "problem" that professionalization can "solve."

In *Images of Idiocy*, Martin Halliwell examines idiocy in modern fiction and film.[2] While idiocy does not fully translate to my efforts in this chapter, some of the analyses below will be informed by Halliwell's observations. He posits that the 1990s increase in representations of characters with idiocy (including some with intellectual disability) is a result of increased public awareness of disability, because of disability rights efforts and "millennial preoccupations with seismic change, with the idiot figure often representing a throwback to a previous era or a simpler way of life."[3] At the same time, Halliwell continues, with the impact of disability activism, these representations become "more accurate" even though it is difficult to "strike the right balance between accuracy and idiosyncrasy."[4]

More recently, there has been an increase in cultural studies of disability with a representational focus that engage with nonphysical or intellectual disabilities, configured more broadly. In his text *Representing Autism: Culture, Narrative, Fascination,* Stuart Murray remarks that the most cited scholars in disability studies, "who have produced excellent influential studies that have shaped the emerging forms of current critical disability scholarship, often make the linguistic slip whereby 'disability' in their writing comes to mean physical impairment."[5] Murray's work is foundational in carving out a space where "nonphysical" disabilities, especially autism, are seen worthwhile subjects of critical inquiry. My work is beholden to the efforts of scholars like Murray, which give critical attention to complex notions of intelligence, competence, and agency. Murray comments that "the attempt to understand autism through looking at it is central to many of the most contemporary narratives that deal with the condition. Especially in film and television, narratives are wrapped around this fundamental invitation to look at the individual with autism, and to try to see how the condition manifests itself."[6] Margaret Price's study *Mad at School: Rhetorics of Mental Disability and Academic Life* continues the important work of further advancing a critical exploration of intellectual/cognitive aspects of disability.[7] Like Murray, Price comments on how representations and deployment of mental disability take advantage of stereotypes to perpetuate false assumptions that try to traffic in reality.[8] Both authors' contentions about the representational (and discursive rhetorical) quality of disability help to contextualize the films analyzed below to consider how these representations of intellectual disability circulate assumptions of sexuality. Sharon Snyder and David Mitchell theorize that "we primarily come to know disabled people, both historically and in our own moment, through representations of their lives, experiences, and bodies that have been manufactured by those outside of the immediate disability experience. Unless one seeks out specific gatherings of people with disabilities, operates in allegiance with an independent living center, or is incarcerated along with dozens of one's fellow disabled citizens, one receives cultural perspectives on disability filtered through documents and images at best secondhand to these experiences."[9] I tend to agree with this claim, especially when it comes to representations of intellectual disability. Characters such as Corky Thatcher (Chris Burke) in the television series *Life Goes On* are the exception; when intellectual disability is represented, it is often with an individual without a cognitive impairment.[10] Rather, intellectual disability is presented by actors like Sean Penn *(I Am Sam)* or Dustin Hoffman *(Rain Man)* in which a nondisabled actor participates in what Tobin Siebers calls "disability drag," by mimicking clichéd behavioral traits of individuals with intellectual disabilities. Unlike queer drag, the subversive potential of disability drag is lost because it often capitalizes on stereotypes of behaviors that highlight the cognitive difference of the characters (such as Raymond's obsession with K-Mart in *Rain Man*). Siebers theorizes that "the modern cinema often puts the stigma of disability on display, except that films exhibit the stigma not to insiders by insiders, as is the usual case with drag, but to a general public that does not realize it is attending a drag performance."[11] The performances by these actors are not seen primarily as practices in performing disability, even if there is a tendency to award Oscars and Emmys to these same actors (e.g., Mickey Rooney for his portrayal of Bill Sackter, or Dustin Hoffman for his performance in *Rain Man*). These behaviors mimic stereotypes of intellectual impairment while distancing the reality of intellectual disability from the audience. Since a majority of representations in popular media are able-bodied actors portraying intellectual and developmental disability, and the remaining representations are caught in the trap of the "special"—education and Olympics—any theory of representation should focus on not only to what extent these representations reinforce oppressive ideas of disability, but also on how the lived reality of countless individuals trapped in congregate living and working situations is not (or is) adequately reflected in the representations currently available.

The Male Buddy Film: "Be a Regular Good Man"

The buddy film is a genre where the central plot involves two adult men engaging in an exploration of friendship, where their relationship becomes central to the plot. The result is that female/male relationships are pushed to the side. It has been argued that the emergence of the buddy film is a response to 1970s feminist activism.[12] However, the buddy film often reinforces hegemonic masculinity by collapsing "intermasculine differences by effecting an uncomfortable sameness, a transgression of boundaries between the self and other, inside and outside, legitimate and illicit."[13] Racial or ethnic differences are smoothed over by rearticulating masculine bonding. Also, there is often no room for both a buddy and a romantic relationship; even if one of the characters is married, his partner becomes an accessory to put on and take off.

Hollywood films involving men with intellectual disabilities since the 1980s have utilized the buddy film formula. While these intellectual disability buddy films speak about sexuality within the limited frame of threat, I argue that the apparent omission of sexuality in these films is a direct response to the perceived threat of male sexuality. This threat is manifested through a fear of men sexually abusing children. Purchasing sex becomes the approved way to express sexuality while perhaps also mitigating the threat of sexual abuse. As historical texts, these films also reflect U.S. society's management of intellectual disability, where the characters with intellectual disabilities are living in community settings while previously having resided in state-run institutions. This management of intellectual disability as a "thing" requiring professionalization is incorporated in many of the films analyzed in this chapter.[14] This professionalization helps to create an artificial separation between the characters and the viewer.

Bill (1981), a biographical made for TV film about Bill Sackter, a disability rights activist from Iowa City, tells the story of Bill (Mickey Rooney) moving out of an institution and into the larger community.[15] The film chronicles Bill's struggle to find employment as well as his friendship with a documentary filmmaker, Barry Morrow.[16] The subtitle of this section, "Be a Regular Good Man," comes from the film *Bill* and the sequel, *Bill: On His Own* (1983).[17] Bill frequently remarks that he wants to be a regular good man as opposed to a "crack-minded" or "low-grade" man. The repetition of "regular good man" illustrates to the extent in which Bill was told to act a certain way in the institution. His desire to be a "good man" has the potential to discourage alternate expressions of masculinity at the expense of a reinforced notion of "good manhood." The lack of explanation of what a "good man" might be in the film further creates confusion. This problematic notion of a "regular good man" might reinforce a certain type of male heterosexuality where women are seen as either sexual objects or maternal caregivers, if not both. Additionally, the struggle to not be crack-minded or low-grade invokes eugenic diagnostic practices where intelligence becomes a marker of moral aptitude.[18] The characters in these buddy films express a certain type of masculinity that strives for independence—an independence that is achieved through the establishment of support systems that highlight the instability of that same independence. As I explore these films, sexuality, independence, and masculinity will combine to create complicated views of these very concepts.

In the film, Barry Morrow (Dennis Quaid) is a documentary filmmaker who takes an interest in telling Bill's story. As Bill and Barry's friendship develops, largely through the telling of Bill's story via a documentary within the film, Barry helps to get Bill a job at the School of Social Work at the University of Iowa. Initially, Bill does a variety of menial tasks around the school, including scraping paint off rain gutters and raking leaves. While the administration, including Dr. Tom Walz, a forward-thinking department head, is supportive of hiring Bill, one of the preschool teachers at the school's day care, Florence Archer, is suspicious of Bill's motives. Florence is uneasy with the attention that one child, Amy Hill, gives to Bill as he cleans up, rakes leaves, and does other work outside during the preschool playground time. Florence confronts Tom, saying that his "programs to reform society," including employing Bill, put the safety of children at risk because no one can predict Bill's behavior. The apparent threat of sexual and physical violence against the children of the preschool is manifested as Florence's perception of intellectual disability. The perceived threat of individuals with intellectual disabilities sexually assaulting young children helps to shape not only sex education materials but also restrictive views on sexuality, a manifestation of sexual ableism.[19] The plot of *Bill* presents this threat of sexual abuse, even if Bill himself does not fit the stereotypical image of a sexual predator. Mickey

Rooney's intellectual disability drag is childlike, endlessly loving, and naïve. Although Bill has remained friendly with Amy, there is no indication that he is predatory toward her. Rather, Florence reads his impairment as a signifier of the threat of abuse. In the film, a meeting of the school's administration is called and a compromise is reached, with the aid of Barry's advocacy. Barry asks, "What is normal and abnormal?" While Barry's questioning of normalcy does not meaningfully challenge the construct of disability, the "threat" of child abuse is resolved. The solution, Wild Bill's Coffee Shop, is a canteen-type outfit where Bill serves coffee to the college students while they study.[20] Bill's new position, the one that effectively makes him a well-known figure, is created because of the threat of sexual and physical violence. Perceptions of violence shape Bill's future.

The threat of sexual and physical violence enacted by and toward a character with an intellectual disability is also central to another buddy film, *Dominick and Eugene* (1988).[21] Dominick (Tom Hulce) and Eugene (Ray Liotta) are twin brothers who live in Pittsburgh. Dominick has an intellectual disability and works as a garbage collector, while Eugene is a resident at a local hospital. Although the details are unclear—"Why am I like this?" Dominick asks Eugene—it appears that the brothers' father hit Dominick when he was a child, thus causing his intellectual disability through brain injury. Central to the plot of the film is Eugene's concern that when he leaves to complete his residency at Stanford University, Dominick will be unable to take care of himself: "But you're still able to think, and see, and hear, and keep yourself strong. You have to believe in your strength, Nicky." The theme of independence is principal in these buddy films of intellectual disability; in fact, the plot of *Bill: On His Own* is about Bill Sackter living independently after Barry moves with his family to California.

I Am Sam (2001) also capitalizes on notions of independence.[22] On the surface, *I Am Sam* is one of the few exemplary narratives of an individual with an intellectual disability living a relatively independent life outside of congregate living spaces. Halliwell considers this film to be "the clearest contemporary example of mainstream Hollywood trying to tackle the difficult issues surrounding representations of idiocy and its place within a more or less realistic social structure."[23] Sam Dawson (Sean Penn) works at Starbucks, where he regularly refills the condiment bar and knows the customers and their drinks: "That's a wonderful choice, Bruce." Outside the coffee shop, Sam and his daughter, Lucy Diamond Dawson (Dakota Fanning), live in an apartment heavily decorated with Beatles memorabilia. Their neighbor Annie Cassell (Dianne Wiest) provides child care and support to Sam and Lucy, while they provide Annie a sense of family and community. Right after Lucy was born, Annie taught Sam how to take care of her, including advising Sam to feed Lucy when the following shows were televised on Nickelodeon: *Hogan's Heroes, I Love Lucy,* and *I Dream of Jeannie.* In the rapid succession that the film narrative takes from Lucy's birth to right before her seventh birthday, Annie offers creative parenting advice and support to Sam. Rounding out the community of support around Sam and Lucy are Sam's friends, all with intellectual disabilities themselves: Joe (Joseph Rosenberg), Brad (Brad Silverman), Robert (Stanley DeSantis), and Ifty (Doug Hutchison).[24] Sam and his friends, who act as extended family to Lucy, regularly have outings at IHOP, sing karaoke, and watch movies at one another's houses.

The Bollywood film *Main Aisa Hi Hoon* (2005) is an almost exact replica of *I Am Sam.* Both leading characters work at a coffee shop, have unrelated adult women providing care labor for their daughters, and have a group of other men with intellectual disabilities as friends. Additionally, the custody rights of both Sam and Indraneel "Neel" Thakur (Ajay Devgan) are challenged—in *I Am Sam* by a social worker and in *Main Aisa Hi Hoon* by the grandfather (Rucha Vaidya) of Neel's daughter, Gungun. The similarities between the films are striking, but so are the differences. In *I Am Sam,* Lucy's biological mother is not central to the plot, while the first third of *Main Aisa Hi Hoon* tells the story of Neel and Maya Trivedi's relationship, including their sexual romance. Additionally, the end of *I Am Sam* finds Sam sharing parental rights with an adoptive family. In the Bollywood version, Neel and his lawyer, Niti Sinha (Sushmita Sen), marry in order to secure guardianship rights for Gungun. In one version the man with an intellectual disability is not seen as a worthy partner and sexual mate, while in the other, Neel and Maya's romance is not only central to the plot, but Neel's capability as a sexual mate also requires viewers to see Neel and Niti's marriage as both a way to secure guardianship for Gungun and a potential path to sexual fulfillment for both individuals. Sam does develop a fair amount of mutual sexual tension with his lawyer, Rita Harrison Williams (Michelle Pfeiffer), although the film endorses Sam as a friend of Rita's, not a lover.

Even though *I Am Sam* is at its core about the ways in which Sam tries to maintain custody of Lucy, his parenting skills are very much the result of the support and training he receives from those around him, none of whom are biologically related. Sam is very much part of a queer family network, where individuals not related by blood or marriage provide care labor and emotional support.[25] Martha Fineman argues that the labor of caretakers should be "treated as equally productive even if unwaged, and should be measured by its societal value, not by economic or market indicators."[26] The creative care giving that Sam gives to Lucy undermines "the autonomy myth" of families as self-sufficient units that do not rely on the assistance of others.[27] Effectively, the court ruling that temporarily removes Sam as Lucy's guardian reinforces the problematic notion of autonomy. Despite the queer potential in *I Am Sam* and *Main Aisa Hi Hoon,* both films ultimately reinforce a type of heterosexual masculinity and familial kinship that undoes the queer possibility that both films begin with, although *I Am Sam* does offer an extrajudicial arrangement where Sam and Randy Carpenter (Laura Dern), Lucy's potential adoptive mother, agree to share parenting duties regardless of the court ruling.[28] According to Robert McRuer, compulsory heterosexuality and able-bodiedness "depend on a queer/disabled existence that can never quite be contained, able-bodied heterosexuality's hegemony is always in danger of collapse."[29] Even though there is something queer about Sam remaining as a father figure to Lucy despite his marginalized social status, Sam's proclamation to Randy, "Because I always wanted Lucy to have a mother," acts as an endorsement of more traditional parenting and family structuring, thus potentially rendering a queer/crip existence dissolved. Sam's declaration effectively resolves the problem of disabled parenting in the film. I would argue that Sam's position as Lucy's father depends on his insight (and declaration) that Randy (and presumably her husband) can also act as parents to Lucy, regardless of what the judicial system might rule. This type of representation fails to challenge popular understandings of intellectual disability. Rather, the problem of disabled parenting is resolved by a white, middle-class, able-bodied, heterosexual unit that can provide Lucy the support she *supposedly* needs, as assessed by the justice system in the film. Sam as a character fails to act beyond a metaphor, a narrative prosthesis, where he brings love to those around him.[30] The audience can be content with the final parental arrangement because Randy's income and nondisability supplement Sam's love for Lucy.

Sam and Neel's intellectual ages are remarked as that of seven-year-olds, the same age of their daughters when the custody battles ensue. During the custody trial for Lucy, the prosecution questions, "How much insight or know-how will he bring to those sensitive subjects of a young girl's development?" The sensitive subjects that are referenced are menstruation and sexual maturity. While Annie retorts that any father would be lacking in sensitivity and insight when it comes to a girl's sexual development, the implication that Sam would be ill suited to aid Lucy is clear. While Sam and Neel are likeable characters, the representation of their intellectual capacity denies the possibility of parenting. However, prior to the legal challenges, both men utilize creative support networks to maintain nurturing kinship formulations. These films take advantage of stereotypical understandings of intellectual disability in order to reject the disabled, queer families. The filmic resolution to the problem of intellectual disability allows for a creation of family that utilizes heterosexual marriage to cover over any queer potentiality.

The last scene in the film shows Lucy playing a soccer match while Sam is the referee. Lucy scores a goal and Sam chases her around. The camera scans the crowd, showing Sam's friends, Rita and her son, as well as Randy and her husband. The traditional happy ending enables us to be relieved that Sam can remain connected with Lucy but that she will receive caregiving and constant support by Randy and her husband. It is only through the marriage of Neel and Niti that Neel is able to remain as Gungun's father; however, the court can only agree to the arrangement because of Niti's parenting (and nondisability). Despite evidence to the contrary, including the creative parenting and care labor arrangements in both movies, the judicial system effectively delegitimizes disabled parenting by restoring the primacy of heterosexuality, even as the characters try to create extrajudicial solutions.

Even though Sam is Lucy's biological father, his sexuality is not affirmed in the film. There is a connotation in the film that Lucy's biological mother might have tricked Sam into having intercourse in exchange for letting her stay at his apartment. Sam's apparent ignorance of sexuality is highlighted when he encounters a sex worker in a late-night diner. Sam is working on the International House of Pancakes word search puzzle, trying to find the word "carrot" to surprise Lucy. As he is studying the puzzle, a sex worker, Lily (Rosalind Chao), approaches Sam and helps him find "carrot" on the brainteaser. Sam, clearly impressed with Lily's skill, tells her that she is smart and "would be a good mother." Shortly thereafter a police officer confronts Lily and arrests Sam for solicitation. We later learn that the arresting officer thinks that Sam is the first person he has arrested that truly did not think that he was soliciting sex. Sam's lack of knowledge of sex work allows him to escape jail time and helps to illustrate his apparent childlike innocence and intellect. Sam is buying into the myth of a mother–father parenting approach. Lily can find a word on a word search puzzle, which Sam interprets as a sign of her intellect and thus her skill as a mother. These cinematic conventions to show Sam's childlike understanding of sexuality and parenting undermine the fairly sophisticated ways in which, up to that point, Sam negotiated child care and emotional support by utilizing his friends and Annie. As mentioned previously, the film hints at a growing romance between Sam and Rita but never allows this romance to develop, as Sam declares his role of friend to his lawyer.[31]

The predictable characterization of Sam as loving endlessly to the point of inspiration ("All you need is love") allows for others around him to be unified with their loved ones. While Sam is fighting for custody of Lucy, his lawyer, Rita, is examining her contentious marriage and estranged relationship with her son, Willy. Sam's love facilitates the reunion of Rita and Willy. Sam and other characters with intellectual disabilities help to unify families around them, often at the expense of their own personal desires. The unification of families points to the metaphoric potential that these characters contain in their representations. Intellectual disability acts as a plot device that unifies those characters without intellectual disabilities.

Before continuing to the next section, which addresses films that have female characters with intellectual disabilities, I briefly want to discuss another buddy film about intellectual disability. *Homer and Eddie* (1989) deploys some of the same cinematic devices of the previously discussed films, including the quest for independence and a reclaiming of masculinity.[32] Homer Lanza (James Belushi) is a young man with an intellectual disability, living in Arizona, who attempts to travel to Oregon to visit his dying father. We later learn that his father disowned him, most likely because of his intellectual disability.[33] Shortly after leaving Arizona, Homer is robbed and left penniless until Eddie Cervi (Whoopi Goldberg), a gender-queer hustler with a brain tumor, agrees to accompany Homer on the multistate journey on the promise of Homer's family fortune in Oregon. Eddie escaped from a psychiatric institution. Intellectual disability and mental disability are central to the stereotypical character development in this film to illustrate Homer's seemingly naïveté and Eddie's risk-taking behavior. Eddie resorts to using stolen credit cards or committing armed robbery to bankroll their travel. A few times in the film, Eddie tells Homer that in order to be a "man" he needs to do two things: obtain a credit card and have sex. Whereas getting a credit card legitimately while traveling is impossible, having sex, we learn, is not. Although Homer tells Eddie that he should be in the *Guinness Book of World Records* for the number of times he has been "laid," Homer's sexual naïveté confirms that he is in fact a virgin. Individuals with intellectual disabilities are continually represented as sexually ignorant. In order to "correct" Homer's virginity, Eddie takes him to a brothel in Nevada where her cousin works. This brothel is the exact opposite of the Bunny Ranch–type establishment with associated glamour and legitimacy. Rather, the brothel is a converted double-wide trailer. Eddie's cousin, Esther, agrees to have sex with Homer for thirty dollars. While Esther and Homer complete the sexual transaction, Eddie robs a gas station in order to pay for the intercourse. We do not see Esther and Homer have sex, but the film shows them afterward as Homer wonders if "he was good." Esther assures him that he was good if he enjoyed it, signifying that Homer's pleasure is of primary importance in this encounter. They then dance in their underwear together, embracing each other and talking about Eddie. Eddie facilitates Homer's sexual encounter as one tangible expression of friendship. At the end of the film, Eddie is shot to death while robbing a convenience store, complete with hallucinations of Jesus. The unlikely friendship between these two exploits melodramatic conventions (death, friendship, disability) to return

Homer to his biological family and community. Even though the film represents Homer as being sexually active, his innocence and lack of knowledge are reaffirmed through his sexuality.

Collectively these films navigate constructs of intellect and independence with notions of masculinity and what proper sexuality is or should be. When these male characters engage in sexual activities, their female partners are either purchased or not meaningfully incorporated into the plot. In the apparent struggle to affirm their practices of masculinity, female characters are seen as obstacles that these male characters need in order to find their path to independence. The characters' own agency is manipulated in the films not to bring about their own self-determination but to facilitate the unification of heterosexual family units.[34] Intellectual disability becomes a vehicle in these films, successful or otherwise, that allows others to learn about love and caregiving, often at the expense of the character with an intellectual disability. Sexuality is very much the catalyst for the change that occurs external to the male characters with intellectual disabilities.

In the next section, I look specifically at films with women with intellectual disabilities, primarily *The Other Sister* (1999) and *Molly* (1999).[35] These films were created almost a decade after *Dominick and Eugene, Homer and Eddie,* and the two *Bill* films. This historical difference allows for some comparison between the different time periods, but also makes a simplistic gender comparison more difficult. As an example, the struggle between community-based arrangements and more traditional state-run institutions continues throughout these films, often providing some conflict that requires resolution. In both films, sexuality is central to the plots but functions differently than in the buddy films. While family unification occurs alongside these female characters, the characters are also seen as sexually competent and even to some extent sexually desirable partners.

"Now You Can Do It": Female Sexuality and Intellectual Disability

The Other Sister is a Hollywood love story for a couple with intellectual disabilities. Carla Tate (Juliette Lewis) is a twenty-one-year-old woman with an intellectual disability living at Roselake, a residential school for children with intellectual and developmental disabilities. Carla's parents, Elizabeth Tate (Diane Keaton) and Radley Tate (Tom

Skerritt), placed Carla in Roselake when she was a young girl ("I don't want her to be retarded," Radley tells his wife. "Of course you don't," she replies.) The family's extreme wealth allows them to send their daughter to a private school instead of a state institution. The film begins with Radley coming to Santa Barbara to collect Carla and bring her back to San Francisco, where the family lives. Elizabeth is endlessly trying to maintain her family's social standing. She forces Carla to practice tennis daily because "well-bred" girls play tennis. The Tate family is not as "ideal" as they wish; one daughter has an intellectual disability and another daughter, Heather, is a lesbian. The last daughter, Caroline is engaged, and throughout the film her nuptials provide a comparison to the other daughters' lives. Heather and her partner, Michelle, are not accepted as a legitimate couple by the Tate parents. Carla and her boyfriend, Daniel (Giovanni Ribisi), are not accepted either. Parental recognition of lesbian and disabled love and sexuality drives the plot of *The Other Sister*.

Shortly after Carla returns to her parents' home, her self-determination conflicts with her parent's expectations of intellectual disability. Carla wants to go to college, become a veterinarian's assistant, and live independently. Elizabeth sees all these as dangerous and too risky: "She needed professional help. Now, it is Carla's turn and I am going to protect her. And nobody's going to tell me how to do it, not even you, Radley." Elizabeth's parental guilt over placing her daughter at the residential school makes her extra protective of Carla. Despite her parents' uncertainty, however, Carla moves into her own apartment and starts attending classes at a local polytechnic school. At school, Carla meets Daniel, a young man with an intellectual disability, who, like Carla, experiences ridicule from his peers and generally lacks family support for his life choices. Daniel does live alone, but we later learn that his divorced parents provide financial support in a piecemeal fashion. One of the mini-crises of the film happens when Daniel's father cuts off economic provisions when Daniel flunks a class. Daniel is forced to move to Florida, but halfway through the trip he returns to San Francisco and declares his love for Carla.

Early in the film, we learn that Carla has a curiosity and knowledge about sex. During the first family dinner after she comes back from the residential school, Carla asks Caroline and her fiancé, Jeff, if they "did it" yet. Carla then tells her family that a teacher at school told her that people who are in love "do it." Carla's mother replies that she is positive that the teacher said when people are *married* they have sex, effectively challenging Carla's knowledge of sexuality. For Carla, and presumably not her nondisabled sisters, marriage becomes a prerequisite for sexuality in the Tate family.[36] Before she moves into her apartment, Elizabeth attempts to have a discussion about sex with Carla. Carla asks her mother if this is "the sex talk" and then proceeds to share her largely anatomical knowledge of sex with her mother (e.g., the vulva, penis, semen). Carla also tells her mother that she learned about sexual abuse at school and was taught to say "no" if she finds herself being raped. Her knowledge of anatomy and abuse prevention mimics the content of the sex education materials examined in chapter 2; and it appears that her sexual knowledge is primarily for harm reduction—preventing sexual abuse—as opposed to facilitating sexual pleasure.

In the film, Daniel tells Carla that he is not a virgin and had a sexual encounter with a sex worker paid for by some "older guys." Since other, older men paid for the encounter, this could allude to public ridicule of Daniel's sexuality by nondisabled older peers or to a type of sexual charity, thinking that Daniel would not experience sexual intercourse that is not paid for. Either way, because Daniel is somewhat sexually experienced, the viewer's concern for Carla and Daniel's forthcoming sexual encounter is partially mitigated. Daniel tells Carla that he "finished" before he was supposed to during his rendezvous with the sex worker. Carla is at first upset by Daniel's revelation, but when Daniel confesses that he loves Carla, not the sex worker, she is put at ease and they embrace.

After they confess their love, Daniel and Carla focus their energy on entering into a sexual relationship. In a scene that highlights both naïveté and responsibility, Carla and Daniel discuss sexual positions by using a copy of *The New Joy of Sex* as an instructional aid.[37] They decide that certain positions look easier or more enjoyable than others. They are practically negotiating the limits of their first sexual encounter in a way that many couples in Hollywood films do not; the passionate spontaneity is absent. Daniel tells Carla that he brought condoms that he got at the free clinic, and that he practiced putting a condom on a banana. Daniel and Carla are well prepared for their sexual encounter, complete with adequate knowledge and contraceptives. The couple is utilizing their own sexual education and desire to plan their forthcoming intercourse. Individuals with intellectual disabilities are not often equipped with comprehensive enough sex education that prepares them to be active agents in their sexual lives. Individuals with intellectual disabilities are primarily taught harm-reduction approaches to sexuality that attempt to prevent sexual abuse and sexually transmitted infections but fail to prepare an individual to achieve pleasure in their sexuality. *The Other Sister* is exceptional in showing characters with intellectual disabilities actively seeking out a sexual relationship, on their own terms. After the correct position and protection are decided upon, Daniel wants to immediately have sex with Carla, but she decides she is not ready and would rather have sex on a holiday since it would be more "special" on Thanksgiving, which is the closest holiday. The careful planning highlights the couple's preparedness in this encounter. Even with the passion and spontaneity missing, it is remarkable that the film respects the sexual lives and choices of the characters.[38]

However, Pamela Block asserts that "through the lens of *The Other Sister,* the wrongs of the past and the barriers in the present are symbolically neutralized. In an illusory process of symbolic healing, the lived experiences of real women such as 'Deborah Kallikak,' Carrie Buck, Cindy Wasiek, and the young woman from Glen Ridge are justified, trivialized, and forgotten."[39] In other words, Hollywood's representational efforts, including *The Other Sister,* obscure eugenic and ableist influences that historically restricted the sexuality and reproduction of women with intellectual disabilities as well as more contemporary infringements of the rights women experience. Moreover, *The Other Sister* presents a narrative enabled by familial wealth and white racial privilege. This narrative obscures a whole segment of the population that is unable to live independently because of resources and class status.[40]

On Thanksgiving, Carla quickly eats dinner with her family and returns to her apartment so she can consummate her relationship with Daniel. After they have sex, Carla and Daniel see more of each other and Daniel gains some recognition from Carla's family. This recognition includes being invited to the annual Christmas family outing to the country club party. During the party, Daniel becomes drunk, hijacks the microphone, professes his love to Carla, and tells everyone that they "did it and it was so beautiful." In a dramatic moment, like the iconic wedding scene in *The Graduate,* Daniel proposes to Carla during her sister Caroline's wedding. Carla accepts, forgiving Daniel for disclosing the details of their intimate relationship to the entire country club. Despite Elizabeth's objections, Daniel and Carla marry; the minister exclaims, "Now you can do it," indicating that Carla and Daniel can kiss at the conclusion of the ceremony. They of course can also "do it," in the more colloquial sense, as their wedding sanctions their continued sexual relationship. The institution of marriage culturally, legally, and religiously sanctions the sexuality of all couples regardless of disability. The sexuality of individuals with intellectual disabilities is often sanctioned through committed heterosexual pairings. Carla and Daniel's nuptials illustrate the moralization of sexuality for individuals with intellectual disabilities through sex education materials and the discourse around masturbation training.[41] *The Other Sister* challenges stereotypes of sexuality insomuch as two individuals with intellectual disabilities are seen as capable of marrying; however, marriage as the end result has the potential to normalize sexual relations, while individuals and couples, including Heather and Michelle, who cannot or choose not to get married, are excluded from the "normalizing" authority marriage provides.

As the film concludes, Elizabeth shows up at the wedding and embraces Carla and Daniel, effectively welcoming them as legitimate members of the Tate family. As a way to resolve the previous intentional avoidance of Heather's partner, Elizabeth finally meets Michelle and welcomes her into the family as well. Both disabled and lesbian daughters are seemingly accepted into the family, enabled by Carla and Daniel's wedding. The most encouraging reading of this film finds the traditional parents, Elizabeth and Radley, as redefining family by including Daniel and Michelle into their household. As a text of social criticism, or liberal fantasy, *The Other Sister* weaves the narratives of Carla and Heather, disabled and gay, to highlight the ways in which white, conservative, upper-class families can incorporate their diverse children. Carla tells her mother at one point in the film, "You never look at me." The ending forces Elizabeth and Radley to look at Carla and by extension Heather, and recognize their choices. The conclusion, however, is anticipated throughout the film and the acceptance is tentative at best. Elizabeth and Radley *had to* accept their children's partners, if only to ensure the superficial diversity that disability and queerness can bring. Neither child's sexuality challenges the dominance of Radley and Elizabeth's social circle and its mores. Unlike Caroline's wedding in front of the entire country club, in a packed church, Carla's nuptials occur in an almost empty church. The contrast between the celebrations is stark. Even Michelle's introduction as Heather's partner is an isolated event, without larger family recognition.

Whereas *The Other Sister* is largely about parental recognition and family unification through an expression of love, *Molly* (1999) is about a brother and sister and their efforts to become better connected. Molly McKay (Elisabeth Shue) is a young adult woman with an intellectual disability who lives in an institution. In the film, doctors continually say that she has the mind of a child.[42] Her "childlike" mind is in conflict with her adult sexuality. Molly is sexually objectified as a woman while her disability disrupts her from achieving a sexually fulfilling life.

When the institution closes, Molly has to go live with her brother, Buck McKay (Aaron Eckhart). Even though they are related, the siblings have had limited contact and Buck is entirely unsure about how to integrate Molly into his lifestyle. Early on, Buck drops Molly off at the day care at his work, thinking that even though she is older, her "childlike" mind allows her to remain in the child-care facility. Scenes like this show the apparent incompatibility between Molly and Buck's lives. She likes to watch soap operas and movies; he likes to restore his boat and go to baseball games. Additionally, the apparent effects of Molly's intellectual disability are generally seen as incompatible with living an independent life.

Shortly after Molly and Buck start to live together, Buck takes Molly to another institution, where the doctors offer an experimental surgery to correct Molly's intellectual disability. This miraculous cure of intellectual disability is largely copied from the film *Charly* (1968), which is based on the novel *Flowers for Algernon*.[43] In all three versions, the character with an intellectual disability is offered a surgery to *cure* the intellectual impairment. The surgery works for a period of time, resulting in brilliance or savant-like behaviors, until the effects of the surgery fail and the character's prior intellectual capacity returns. The affect of this story is predictable, including amazement that the surgery works, hope and joy that the character is released from their intellectual impairment, and, finally, sadness at the prospect of the character becoming disabled once again. *Molly* follows this same story arc, and while Molly does become more knowledgeable about medical information, the primary benefit of the surgery is that the siblings become better acquainted with each other. Although not entirely related to sexuality, the fascination with curing intellectual disability is important to consider. A preoccupation with a scientific breakthrough that allows an individual to become nondisabled reveals a desire to cure disability through medical intervention. A cure becomes the solution. Here the cure is temporary; in the film, scientific advancements are not able to eliminate Molly's intellectual disability. The lack of a lasting medical intervention, however, does not jeopardize the sibling relationship between Molly and Buck.

Unlike other characters with intellectual disabilities, Molly is seen as sexually attractive despite (or because of) her intellectual disability. Either way, the film regrettably uses Molly's naïveté of sexuality to highlight how inappropriate her sexuality is, even though others in the film find her attractive. Allow me to illustrate this point with a few examples. Before the surgery, Molly is at Buck's place of employment. During a meeting with a group of Japanese businessmen, Molly enters the meeting room completely naked because she is warm. She had taken off her clothes prior to entering the boardroom. While Buck is embarrassed, the businessmen sexually objectify Molly and remark to one another, "Is this a great country or what?" Molly's public nudity highlights her impairment (for the viewer) and seeks to confirm her femaleness and sexuality (for the businessmen and the viewers). Additionally, racist Euro–American assumptions of Japanese businessmen as sexually depraved seemingly add to the construction of Molly's sexuality and attractiveness.

Another scene that confirms the inappropriateness of her sexuality happens after the surgery when Molly begins to show sexual interest in her brother. She asks him what a "blow job" is and that she would "like to wake up next to you in the morning and feel the stubble on your chin." Buck quickly tells Molly that brothers and sisters cannot get married and can only be friends. Molly's seemingly inappropriate sexual advances are redirected away from her brother toward Sam (Thomas Jane), another individual with an intellectual disability, while Buck enters into a sexual relationship with the physician who operates on Molly, Susan Brookes (Jill Hennessy). The threat of sibling sexuality is resolved with the introduction of more suitable partners—one disabled, the other not a sibling. Buck has sexual intercourse with Susan while Molly and Sam only kiss. The problem of Molly's sexuality is resolved with a largely adolescent courtship that is interrupted when the effects of her surgery wear off and her intellectual impairment returns. Her sexuality is replaced with a meaningful relationship with her brother. The end of the movie finds Molly and Buck living together as Buck recreates in his home the décor from Molly's room at the institution. Once again the character with an intellectual disability helps to reunite estranged family members and inspire heterosexual relationships. It appears that suitable partners for these female characters are men with intellectual disabilities. The potential for a relationship between a woman with an intellectual disability and someone without, male or female, is not explored.[44]

These films effectively deny the sexual capability of characters with intellectual disabilities. Even when characters explicitly engage in sexual relations *(The Other Sister)*, the sexual relationship is largely guarded and almost immediately results in marriage. Marriage sanctions the continuing sexual relationship. Sexuality for the sake of pleasure becomes unattainable for characters with intellectual disabilities. While more contemporary representations withhold the characterization of intellectual disability and sexual threat to others, characters largely remain lacking sexual agency.

Public Mocking: "Do You Know What Actual Sex Is?"

The Howard Stern Show is an American satellite radio program heard on Sirius XM Radio by over a million listeners a week. The show is also broadcast on digital television. Howard Stern regularly initiates sexist conversations on his program, often using derogatory terminology such as "whore" and "slut" to refer to women who appear on his show. Stern, along with a regular cadre of other personalities, uses the show as a platform largely to malign female sexuality and anatomy. Sexist jokes about women as sexual objects that men utilize for their own pleasure provide much of the "comic" element in his show, although guests like Sandra Bernhard prevent a simplistic rendering of the show as antifeminist or thoroughly misogynist, even if the success of such an intervention by Bernhard and others can be debated.

Stern has a regular group of guests called the "Wack Pack," which includes two individuals with intellectual disabilities, "Gary the Retard" and "Wendy the Retard," deliberately exploiting the derogatory connotation of the term. Gary lives in Oregon and usually calls into the show instead of appearing live in the studio. As with any type of talk radio program, there is an element of character building that takes on a fictional element. Much of the "humor" in the show depends on formulaic assessments of intellectual disability. These characters are often used to facilitate a type of politically incorrect humor that promotes heterosexual male pleasure, often at the expense of women.

Gary and Wendy both have social media accounts and websites that host electronic recordings and videos of their segments, helping to fuel additional online mocking of the characterization of their sexuality and sexual knowledge.[45] In his book *Disability Hate Crimes,* Mark Sherry documents the widespread nature of disability hate speech on the Internet that "contribute[s] to a social climate in which disability hatred is a regular occurrence."[46] Sherry points out that disability hate speech on the Internet uses hyper-violent and -sexual imagery to "convey disrespect and bodily domination."[47] Sherry reminds us that "hate crimes often reflect the fears and anxieties of the haters" and that disability hate speech can be used for a "wider political agenda" that espouses racist, sexist, transphobic, and classist ideologies.[48] Spending a brief amount of time on Wendy and Gary's Facebook pages and similar fan sites will illuminate Sherry's point; the postings on the walls for both reveal violently sexist, racist, and homophobic language and imagery, which I will not reproduce here. Goodley and Runswick-Cole's article exploring violence and disablism, particularly directed at disabled children, argues "that the violence of disablism becomes a cultural norm because disabled people come to occupy a figure invested as a disavowed libidinal object of both love and hate; fascination and disgust."[49] Ableism (or disablism in Goodley and Runswick-Cole's usage) and hatred of disabled people provides comedic material that certain segments of the population find humorous.

In one of the segments of the show,[50] Gary tells Stern about his girlfriend. Gary started a new relationship with a woman without an intellectual disability, who recently was released from jail. During the course of the segment, Stern and his regular co-host, Robin Quivers, and former colleague Artie Lange question Gary about his relationship and sexual knowledge. They want to know if Gary "knows what actual sex is." Although Gary confirms that he does regularly participate in vaginal and oral intercourse, the hosts fail to believe Gary. Instead they posit that Gary's girlfriend must have some sort of fetish or be a sex worker. The implication is that no one who is not disabled or without a fetish would willingly have sex with Gary without financial compensation, explicitly denying his sexual self-determination and attractiveness. During the course of the phone call, Gary gets increasingly impatient as the radio hosts continue to deny Gary's sexual experiences. Before the segment ends, the hosts question if Gary's girlfriend is actually a man or a "retarded tranny," reflecting the convergence between transphobia and disability hatred. As a whole, Gary's sexual experiences and his responses to the hosts' inquiries provide much of the piece's "comic" element. Gary becomes someone to be laughed at precisely because he is intellectually disabled *and* sexually active. The association with sex workers, homosexuality, and transsexuals adds to the apparent amusing quality of the segment, the connotation being that Gary's sexual experiences would be more understandable and probable if he did have sex with a sex worker or a man rather than an able-bodied woman. The association among homosexuality, sex work, disabled sexuality, and transsexuals illustrates how patriarchy, heteronormativity, and able-bodiedness depend on maligning nondominant sexuality and gender nonconformity to maintain their domination. Scholars have traced the connection between reinforcing hegemonic masculinity and homophobia.[51] As Michael Kimmel remarks, "Homophobia is a central organizing principle of our cultural definition of manhood . . . Homophobia is the fear that other men will unmask us, emasculate us, reveal to us and the world that we do not measure up, that we are not real men."[52] The assumed stability of masculinity depends on distancing from traditionally perceived feminine aspects of masculinity and sexuality. C. J. Pascoe argues, "Homophobia is indeed a central mechanism in the making of contemporary American adolescent masculinity."[53] Adolescent and young-adult males, which make up the majority of Stern's listenership, use terms like "fag" to malign nondominant sexuality, while reinforcing a certain expression of (white) masculinity.[54] *The Howard Stern Show* operates within this equation, where able-bodied heterosexual male promiscuity acts as an endorsed norm for listeners while continuing to discredit alternate sexuality, including that of disability. Sexual ableism operates to deny the sexual agency of Gary, simultaneously maligning other sexual expressions outside a narrowly defined articulation of sex as able-bodied, heterosexual, and male-focused. Sexual ableism labels sexual behavior, desires, and activities, including those of sex workers, people with various fetishes, the elderly, and nonheterosexuals, as deviant, immoral, and/or in need of regulation.

In another segment, Gary receives a phone call from Blue Iris, a sixty-nine-year-old woman who was a regular character on *The Howard Stern Show* until her death. Blue Iris engages in a sexually explicit conversation with Gary, telling him that she "took out her teeth" and is ready to engage in oral sex. The remaining portion of the phone call is quite pornographic, as Blue Iris instructs Gary to masturbate while she describes his genitals in graphic detail for the listeners to hear. This segment again uses the identity of the two callers—Gary, a sexually active and assumed to be innocent disabled man, and Blue Iris, an elderly, sexually provocative, predatory woman—to create even more comic appeal. Howard Stern's comedic efforts reinforce assumptions about sexuality in the elderly and disabled people not by highlighting each individual's sexual potential, but rather by illustrating the apparent foolishness of the pairing. This brand of misogyny has helped Stern become "an iconic figure in certain parts of male culture" as a "preeminent role model" for male listeners.[55] Gary's participation on the show confirms how hegemonic masculinity coalesces around maligning identities, practices, and desires that seek to challenge—or render less influential—a system of power that facilitates domination. More directly, the attention on criticizing disabled, queer, gender-diverse, and elderly sexualities illuminates how heterosexual masculinity is easily challenged.

Stern also hosts Wendy on his show to foster comic attention. Similar to Gary, Wendy is often queried on her knowledge of sexuality—as if listeners find it simultaneously shocking and crude that Gary, Wendy, and by extension all people with intellectual disabilities know about reproduction and sexuality. Wendy is also the subject of misogynistic mockery, particularly when jokes are made about her sexual organs. Although the show is not a fair forum for self-representation by Gary and Wendy, they do make strong efforts to voice their sexuality that cannot be removed even by the deleterious nature of the program. Individuals advocating for their own sexual agency directly confront the tired rhetoric of eugenics, protectionism, and disability-drag-based representations that deny individuals the opportunity and right to be sexual beings. Individuals with intellectual disabilities are active agents of their sexual and nonsexual lives seeking out their pleasures.

The Idiots and Sexual Pleasure

Lars von Trier's film *The Idiots* (1998) tells the story of a group of individuals who express their "inner-idiot, " a type of "disability drag" referred to in the film as "spassing," by acting as if they have intellectual disabilities in a variety of settings.[56] The rationale is that they are merely expressing what every person tries to suppress, effectively universalizing idiocy as being part of everyone's inner self. Part of the appeal of the film is its lifelike feel in both the filming and social situations, based loosely on a written script. *The Idiots* is made in compliance with the Dogme 95 Manifesto, which compels films to be made in an anti-Hollywood fashion that prohibits the use of special effects, postproduction modification, and other film technologies. As such, *The Idiots* is filmed on a handheld camera, and all sound is diegetic. The voyeuristic quality of the film helps to blur the boundaries between documentary and fiction, creating "cinema verité live documentary aesthetics, where camera movement and (im)balance suggest an immediate attachment to events which unfold truthfully in front of the camera."[57] Siebers remarks that the film "shows less investment in the character development of its protagonists as disabled and greater interest in how society reacts to disability and how the characters use the masquerade to manage their emotional and interpersonal problems."[58]

One of the more controversial scenes in the film involves group sex that occurs when some of the characters are "spassing" while the others are not. The scene is not simulated; intercourse is shown, providing a certain pornographic element. Viewers see people, some pretending to be intellectually disabled, having "real" sex. The realness of the sex helped to give the film a restrictive rating, and this sex scene was redacted in some theatrical releases.[59] Film and media studies scholar Anne Jerslev argues that the "gang bang" scene, as well as the one where the character Stoffer (Jens Albinus) has an erection, show how "character and actor intertwine most disturbingly" because "the character's desire is shown most literally."[60] Stoffer's erect penis becomes a sign of desire and helps to highlight its apparent inappropriateness in the almost entirely female space, while it becomes appropriate and normative in the "gang bang" scene.[61] Although it is quite clear that the characters in the film are not actually individuals with intellectual disabilities, the overt sexual nature of the scene is unlike any type of representation offered on intellectual disability and sexuality. It is this transgressive potential, where actors are having sex that is not simulated, while pretending to be intellectually disabled, that upsets assumptions about reality, performance, and intellectual disability.

The film deserves more attention than I give it here for its representational potential of intellectual disability, but the effect of the sex scene gives us pause to consider its implications. Unlike the representations described above, wherein characters with intellectual disabilities are largely seen as facilitating family unification, able to participate in guarded sexual relationships, or deserving of ableist scorn, *The Idiots* challenges us to rethink the boundaries of intellect and sexuality. Even though the viewer knows that the characters on the screen are faking intellectual disability, playing as intellectually disabled allows them to become sexual with one another while challenging expectations of sexual deviance and capacity. This representation also contributes to the problematic association of hypersexuality with intellectually disabled individuals. Let me be clear that the "spassing" of individuals with and without intellectual disabilities engaging in intercourse is not necessarily the type of representation that ultimately affords individuals with intellectual disabilities to be considered active agents in their own sexual development. However, this scene complicates the eugenic and paternalistic narratives alluded to above by providing an example of sexuality. *The Idiots* challenges us to consider the representational implications of a certain type of heterosexual spontaneous sexuality for individuals with intellectual disabilities. At the very least, this sexuality is hopeful in the rendering of sexual pleasure as an outcome for characters desiring intellectual disabilities. In the same light, however, this representation of desire can potentially reinforce sexually ableist interventions where intellectual disability is too easily equated with hypersexual, animalistic activity. It is already assumed that "idiocy" frees up individuals for excessive sexual expression, and *The Idiots* can reaffirm these assumptions for viewers.

This chapter has resisted the temptation to code certain images as "positive" and "negative." Segments of the disability rights movement challenge the stereotypical and paternalistic representations of disability in film and television in order to facilitate realistic plots and representations as a type of political action. When it comes to representations of intellectual disability and sexuality, there is no doubt that a certain static trajectory remains.[62] Insomuch as these representations benefit from formulaic conceptions of disability, the effect conveys an understanding of intellectual disability and sexuality that denies individual agency (and pleasure) at the expense of family unification. These representations as a whole illustrate that people with intellectual disabilities can be subjected to scorn and protectionism because of their sexuality. Spontaneity in sexuality becomes the apparent unattainable characteristic of sexual encounters. Aside from spontaneity, it would appear, based on these representations, that individuals with intellectual disabilities are largely unable to live sexually fulfilling lives. The plot in *The Other Sister* is exceptional in that it offers a compelling narrative of two individuals with intellectual disabilities participating in an apparently sexually satisfying relationship, but even this story is limiting—its class- and race-based exclusions are covered over by the promise of liberal acceptance.

In the next chapter, I explore an emerging type of representation, the reality show *The Specials,* which offers a fresh perspective on relationships and individuals with intellectual disabilities. Read together, these chapters help to illustrate the representational potential of new media for intellectual disability, as contrasted with more traditional modes of representation. As such, the diversity of images offers compelling narratives that challenge entrenched sexually ableist assumptions of lives lacking enjoyment, pleasure, and feelings of worthiness.

1 Smashing Disability

Sexual Transgression and the Lady Boys of Bangkok

While reality shows are not new, a reality show choosing to broadcast on the web the everyday lives of a group of individuals with intellectual disabilities is part of an emerging trend in complicating traditional representations of disability. Specifically, in contrast to the messages of sexuality analyzed in the previous chapter, this chapter explores patterns of gender and sexual transgression in *The Specials,* a web-based reality show that *The Guardian* describes as a "docusoap."[1] *The Specials* follows five white young adults with intellectual disabilities, Hilly, Lewis, Lucy, Megan, and Sam, living together in Brighton, England. Imagined as *The Real World* meets *Friends,* it offers up selections of everyday events in these young adults' lives that are deemed worthy of circulation and consumption.[2] *The Specials* was originally conceived as a traditional television broadcast reality show, but after the pilot was created, the broadcaster decided not to pursue the series.[3] Despite the lack of institutional funding and support, producer/director Katy Lock and web developer Daniel May continued the series as a web-based reality program in 2009. My analysis of *The Specials* is informed by the critical premise that, as Marc Andrejevic states, reality television operates with a "promise of interactivity" that "functions increasingly as a form of productive surveillance."[4] *The Specials* uses "the promise of the internet" not only in allowing the housemates to gain celebrity status by having their lives documented and broadcast, but also by "gain[ing] greater participation in and control over the mediated version of reality in which they are immersed."[5]

More specifically, this chapter engages with Margrit Shildrick's observation that "the interweaving of disability, subjectivity, and sexuality constitutes a dangerous mix" in light of both the reality genre and new media.[6] Here, I explore the productive potential of that "dangerous mix" while simultaneously considering how gender and sexualized desires are reified in the process of being exhibited online. Intellectually disabled heterosexuality enables a queer critique of sexual ableism, effectively challenging assumptions of sexual desire and capability tied to impairment status. At various moments in the series, Sam, one of the housemates, expresses his attraction to and love of women, often within earshot of the object of his desire. Sam also transgresses expected patterns of relationships by actively courting women without intellectual disabilities, albeit unsuccessfully. For example, in the first episode of the series, Sam and his housemates go out drinking and singing karaoke. While in the pub, Sam actively flirts with but unsuccessfully courts a woman, Pippa. One of the overarching themes of the series is the desire of the housemates, including Sam, to date and find romantic partners. Yet the sexual desire of men with intellectual disabilities is often constructed as deviant if not potentially threatening, and though Sam tries quite hard to live up to traditionally masculine norms of gender and sexuality, he is often shown failing to do so, which could be read as negating any potential threat associated with men with intellectual disabilities.[7] Quite literally, Sam's sexual desire as recorded by the camera and broadcast online illustrates how sexual ableism can operate in the lives of those labeled as intellectually disabled. How are sexual desire and gender trouble—crafted through Sam's gendered identity and his repeated expressions of desire—politicized through intellectual disability in this web-based serial? How does the show valorize the gender transgressing performance of "The Lady Boys of Bangkok"—a cabaret of Thai *kathoey* drag performers featured in the episode on which I focus—as it is perceived by these young adults with intellectual disabilities who are, in turn, navigating their own sexualized desires? By addressing these questions, I discuss the crip and queer limitations and possibilities of this series in expanding an articulation of intellectual disability, sexuality, gender, and desire.

My analysis focuses on the portrayal of sexuality in the third episode of the first season of *The Specials,* in which the housemates attend a show by the Lady Boys, a traveling, U.K.-based performance group. Here, Sam is particularly vocal about his excitement to see the "sexy ladies" perform. During the show, one of the performers sings Frank Sinatra's "My Way" while removing a wig and all makeup. At the end of the song, the camera closes in on Sam's face as he appears at the very least surprised, if not disappointed or shocked, at the transformation he has just witnessed on stage. Of particular interest is the contrast, visually constructed through intercutting camera shots, between Sam's reaction to the performers' comment on the mutability of gender and other audience members' presumed understanding and endorsement of the event, as indicated by their applause. This momentary gender trouble is quickly resolved for Sam as new performers dressed in feminine clothing take the stage and the spectacle of the show continues, leaving him to believe that they are indeed Thai women. C. J. Pascoe writes, "People are supposed to act in ways that line up with their presumed sex. That is, we expect people we think are females to act like women and males to act like men. People hold other people accountable for 'doing gender' correctly."[8] Pascoe highlights the persistent and particular tensions attendant on gender and performance. Outside of drag shows, there appears to be very little cultural room for ambiguity around gendered performances, especially in a reality show in which male participants are portrayed as intellectually disabled and sexually normative.

The draw of the Lady Boys depends on a deployment of the colonial gaze—that is, on a type of ethnicized imagination. Edward Said reminds us that "the relationship between Occident and Orient is a relationship of power, of domination, of varying degrees of a complex hegemony."[9] And Anne McClintock updates Said by remarking that imperialism has to be understood through the interconnectedness of race, class, gender, and sexuality.[10] Peter A. Jackson traces the autonomous development of gay cultures in Japan and Thailand to complicate the dominant narrative of the "West" imposing queerness on the "East."[11] Taken together, these three positions help me to explore the messages contained in the representation of *The Specials* and on the stage at the Lady Boy of Bangkok performance. To what extent does Sam's and his housemates' readings of the genders of the performers depend on a Western binary model of sex/gender that fails to embrace diversity, ambiguity, and self-identification? How is intellectual disability read through a celebration of Thai queerness? The analysis below traces the interlocking representational and relational implications of the Lady Boys' performance as well as Sam's gendered desire for the performers. It is questionable whether, within the bounds of ethnicized entertainment for an audience presumed to be white, drag and a playful parody of gender provide sufficient theoretical ground to illuminate the transformative potential of intellectual disability and sexual desire.

Drag, the Lady Boys, and a Reification of Otherness?

In their ethnographic examination of drag queens at the 801 Cabaret, a popular tourist attraction in Key West, Florida, Leila Rupp and Verta Taylor remark that "drag embodies ambiguity and ambivalence. When straight women exclaim that they are attracted to the girls and they aren't even lesbians, when straight men are aroused by gay men in dresses, when lesbians find it erotic to see two drag queens doing the lesbian number 'Take Me or Leave Me' from the Broadway show *Rent*, the conventional divisions between female and male, straight and gay, become almost meaningless."[12] For Rupp and Taylor, the ambiguity around gender binaries and labels of sexual identity, desire, and orientation that the drag show offers—to performers and audience members alike—creates a type of "protest" not only against traditional gender and sexual scripts, but also against bodily expectations, a "subtle questioning of the meaning of gender and sexuality as we normally understand them. It is in that sense that the drag queens 'perform protest.'"[13] This protest against gender norms and hegemonic power has the potential to highlight the artificiality of presumed continuities between genitalia, desire, and sexuality.[14] On-stage ambiguity and ambivalence are intensified when Western intellectual disability and non-Western eroticization complicate visibility and attraction through the mode of a reality show. Jackson writes, "In Thailand the antiquity of the term *kathoey* has masked the modernity of the identities now labeled by this word. Capitalism has also had a role in the emergence of this and other modern Asian MTF transgender cultures."[15] Certainly a system of exotic queer entertainment for a white Western audience is enabled through a transnational capitalism that decontextualizes history (and self-narrative) for a sustainable and successful stage show.

On the website advertising the Lady Boys' 2010 *Fantasy and Feather* traveling performance, the description of the performance foregrounds ethnic difference interlaced with gender and sexual diversity:

> It's non-stop entertainment all the way . . . In a flamboyant extravaganza combining the heady spice of Bangkok's exotic night-

life with the glamorous showgirl appeal of Las Vegas . . . Performed
by 16 of the world's most beautiful show-girls (who just happen to
be men!) . . . The fantasy starts as soon as you enter the fully carpeted Sabai Pavilion. You have left behind your daily existence and
are transported to Bangkok's exotic nightlife. Inhale the aroma of
freshly prepared Thai food—then choose from a range of mouth-
watering dishes . . . Direct from the heart of Bangkok's exotic
nightlife, you will be entertained—like no one has entertained you
before!—by 16 of the world's most stunningly beautiful represen-
tatives of the Third Sex (Kathoey)—the sensational Lady Boys of
Bangkok. It's the best party night in town![16]

From Vegas to Bangkok, from Thai food to showgirls, the *Fantasy and
Feather* performance is advertised as a night to remember. Audience
members are invited to consume a constructed version of Thailand
mediated through costuming and cuisine. Echoing the imperial display, eroticization, and consumption of ethnological wonders, the show
promises a narrative of tourism through food and costume while simultaneously exalting (and fetishizing) difference.[17] Significantly, this
representation of Thailand completely avoids any mention of the sociopolitical and economic conditions in twenty-first-century Thailand. The
recent coup d'état by a military junta and ongoing violent (and often
deadly) struggles for power are noticeably absent from the fantasy and
feathers. The representation of Thailand is sanitized for the Western
audience, and entertaining performances gloss over any discomfort
that could be caused by addressing political instability.

Though it erases a certain type of political difference, the show
does advertise an education in the limits of dichotomous gendered
thinking, or, rather, hints at the limits of this type of thinking with
the mention of *kathoey*, a type of "third gender" within Thailand.[18]
Kathoey refers to a male-to-female transgendered person or an effeminate gay man, although no one of these categories necessarily maps
out completely onto the individuals who embrace one or another of
them. Han ten Brummelhuis argues that *kathoey* have to be seen as
women, regardless of genitalia, and that definitions of *kathoey* remain
fluid because there is not one universally accepted definition.[19] One
Thai saying describes *kathoey* as a person born physiologically male
but possessing a "female heart."[20] Nevertheless, the category of *kathoey*

most often connotes an alignment with femininity through dress, mannerisms, or body modifications such as breast enhancement surgery or hormone-induced alterations. In English, *kathoey* is most often translated as "lady boy," and thus the gendered mix of the Lady Boys of Bangkok is embedded in the title of the group as well as the advertisement of the event.[21] Jackson remarks on the importance of tracing how the market has allowed *kathoey, bakla, waria,* and other transgender identities to "form around the commodification of modern forms of feminine beauty."[22] Here we see how the success of the Lady Boys of Bangkok is enabled through transnational capitalism that balances feminine notions of beauty and a discourse of local culture, tastes, and experiences. Market forces have enabled a "proliferation of queer cultures and identities."[23] To what extent have drag shows anticipated the reception of performers like the Lady Boys of Bangkok? And how does the dominant two-gender system allow for a celebration of *kathoey* as feminine?

The Lady Boys of Bangkok are a well-traveled group, often performing on multiple dates in each of the cities they visit and catering to groups and "hen parties." A BBC article describing the Lady Boys at the 2010 Edinburgh Fringe Festival reports that the ratio of men to women in the audience was forty to sixty, and that 75 percent of the audience is made up of individuals not specifically attending the Fringe Festival.[24] These demographics indicate that the mainstream appeal of the Lady Boys is well established; the narratives of travel, entertainment, and excitement are well received. How do mainstream audiences encounter the intersecting gender, sexual, racial, and ethnic differences that structure the Lady Boys' performances? And, with respect to my focus in this chapter, how do disability and desire complicate such encounters? Can Sam's sexualized desire destabilize and queer assumptions of appropriateness and competency?

In *The Feeling of Kinship: Queer Liberalism and the Racialization of Intimacy,* David Eng explores queer liberalism and the emergence of a queer agenda that "works to oppose a politics of intersectionality, resisting any acknowledgment of the ways in which sexuality and race are constituted in relation to one another, each often serving to articulate, subsume, and frame the other's legibility in the social domain."[25] Eng's analysis of queer liberalism allows me to problematize the Lady Boy performance as a seemingly progressive location where gender performativity automatically challenges dichotomous gendered thinking. Accordingly, as Jackson contends, "global queering can be seen as the sum of many local transformations that have emerged from the intersecting influences of both national and transnational forms of capitalism."[26] Interactions between the largely white European audience and the Thai performers might complicate notions of sexuality and desire in ways that depend on constructions of ethnicity and exoticness. The Lady Boys of Bangkok put on an entertaining show to attract an audience. The reliance on costuming, lighting, pop music, and Thai food that caters to an English palate, along with a simultaneous decontextualization of the economic, social, and political realities of Thailand, most likely does not challenge many of the previously held perceptions of audience members. In the next section, though, as I explore the episode in question from *The Specials,* I will be proposing that Sam's reading of the Lady Boys as women potentially has the ability to challenge gendered scripts and expectations of sexualized desire for men with intellectual disabilities. More explicitly, his articulations, very much grounded in a heterosexual masculine space, can open up a critical crip/queer epistemology that challenges sexual ableism, even though these articulations are actively stifled and constructed as naïve. Additionally, borrowing from Eng's formulation of queer diasporas as a response to queer liberalism that "offers a critique of modernity and its forgetting of race that calls attention to unauthorized subjects and to unacknowledged structures of feeling beyond an empirical tradition of liberal rights and representation," I theorize the unruly patterns of affect, kinship, and desire that the interaction between the housemates and the Lady Boys generates.[27]

Gender, Sexuality, and Desire in *The Specials*

In the third episode of *The Specials,* Sam and his housemate Lewis are discussing the upcoming Lady Boy show with their support-staff member, Robbie. Sam and Lewis are, respectively, twenty-two- and nineteen-year-old white males. Robbie is also white, and is older than both housemates. At the beginning of the scene, Robbie remarks to Sam and Lewis, "You do realize, and you, Lewis, that what we are going to watch tonight—the show—the Lady Boys of Bangkok are not actually girls, they're boys pretending." Sam emphatically responds, "I already told you! They are real girls. Trust me." Robbie again tells Sam that the Lady Boys are good performers, are very pretty, and do good impressions, but are not actually girls. Sam, in a moment of dramatic desperation, gets down on one knee and says, "Please, I beg you. They are just real girls." The exchange concerning the "realness" of the performers' sex—boys or girls—becomes an anatomy lesson when Robbie tells Sam that the Lady Boys have "willies." In a last-ditch effort to convince Robbie that he is in fact mistaken, Sam says, "Well, A: They've got a vagina. B: They are real girls." Sam's emphatic insistence that the Lady Boys are women centers partially on his assertion that the performers have vaginas, presumably as opposed to "willies." It would appear that gender, as imagined by these two men, is debated purely through the presence or absence of particular genitals, which, in turn, is assumed based on gender expressions they observe. Both individuals are making assumptions of genitals based on gender expression, which regrettably reinforces a linking of sex to gender. Both Sam and Robbie are asserting their understandings of "truth" in relation to the performers. Sam is quite vocal during this episode about the sexy ladies he is going to see. To help explain his desire to see these performers as women, he has to categorically deny Robbie's reading of the performers as boys—a reading that, I would speculate, is shared by the majority of those attending the Lady Boys' shows. Lewis, sensing Robbie and Sam's inability to come to an agreement, suggests that they ask the performers themselves. His suggestion, a motion to a type of standpoint epistemology around gender, embodiment, and self-identification, prioritizes the experiences and self-knowledge of the Lady Boys in this discussion of sex and anatomy. Unfortunately, the experiences of the performers are not shared in the episode.[28]

In her foundational work on the topic of drag, Judith Butler remarks that "the impossibility of reading means that the artifice works, the approximation of realness appears to be achieved, the body performing and the ideal performed appear indistinguishable."[29] Quite possibly, Sam's vocal desire to see the performers as women against the dominant narrative that they are not points to his own ambiguity and in-betweenness.

In his discussion of *kathoey,* Brummelhuis comments that since "sexual excitement is about images, the presence or absence of a penis can be bargained about or accommodated."[30] Brummelhuis is interested in explaining how European men, who do not necessarily identify as gay or queer, find *kathoey* sexually attractive and enter into sexual relationships with them, either as customers in a sex work arrangement or as long-term dating partners. Part of the success of *kathoey* working in European locations, especially in sex work, centers on what Brummelhuis considers as "the impression that *[kathoey]* attraction works best in Western environments because of the heavily dominated two-gender system."[31] Because of the rigid gender system in which bodies "ought" to be coded as male or female, the outward appearance of femininity can confirm gender identity for a Westernized audience that is not willing to accept or entertain ambiguity.[32] While the Lady Boys of Bangkok blur the borders of gender in their stage show, the discussion between Sam and Robbie attempts to reify gender borders. As evidenced by the gender-based debate, however, assumed borders of gender are not as tangible as they appear. Even as the discussion about whether the performers are "real" women reinscribes normative binary gender categories, the conversation also registers varied expressions of desire, regardless of biological genitalia and disability status, that reflect the ambiguity of gender and sexual desire. According to Butler, "The phallus functions as a synecdoche, for insofar as it is a figure for the penis, it constitutes an idealization and isolation of a body part and, further, the investment of that part with the force of symbolic law."[33]

In representing young men labeled as intellectually disabled having discussions about desire, *The Specials* challenges gender normative declarations of attraction. Additionally, this type of representation has the potential to shift audience perceptions of the relationship between masculinity, heterosexuality, and queerness. In their study of images and how participants labeled genders, Suzanne Kessler and Wendy McKenna note that if the image had a penis, participants identified the images as male 96 percent of the time, regardless of other characteristics, including breasts and long hair. The presence of a vulva resulted in the figure being labeled female only 64 percent of the time.[34] They comment that "penis equals male but vagina does not equal female . . . gender attribution is, for the most part, genital attribution; and genital attribution is essentially penis attribution."[35] Kessler and McKenna continue, "The cultural genital is the one which is assumed to exist and which, it is believed, should be there. As evidence of the 'natural sexuality,' the cultural genital is a legitimate possession. Even if the genital is not present in a physical sense, it exists in a cultural sense if the person feels entitled to it and/or is assumed to have it."[36] Sam's affectively motivated reading of the Lady Boys as female secures them as objects of heterosexual desire and himself as a desiring subject, and Sam's reasoning to Robbie is based on a linking of femaleness to what he calls "vaginas." Sam's desire to see the "sexy ladies" can be considered queer in that it validates the Lady Boys' temporary and performative self-expressions of gender, a type of disidentification.[37] Sam's insistence on femaleness, in the term's both sexed and gendered meanings, enables the Lady Boys' self-identification process to rewrite the narrative of gender within the reading of their bodies as "boy." Both Sam's reading of gender and the Lady Boys' gendered presentations challenge normative social identities "bound to a hegemonic structure of whiteness" that are "circumscribed by a homosexual prohibition bound to a racialized position."[38] The minoritarian subject positions of the Lady Boys and Sam illuminate the limits of recognizing desire solely within normative constructions tied to dominant racial, ethnic, sexual, gendered, and disability identities.

In an interview with *.net,* an Internet magazine for web designers, Katy Lock, producer and director of *The Specials,* comments that part of the reason the broadcaster withdrew support for the series was because of the uncertainty about the show's success given the content: "To be honest, *The Specials* does make for challenging viewing at times, such as when Sam falls in love with the ladyboys of Bangkok or Lucy sings an ear-splitting karaoke version of "Greased Lightning." Scenes like these can be confusing for the viewer. Is it okay to laugh or not? But we thought it was important to show the guys' lives as honestly as possible. Like anyone else, they have good times and bad times and sometimes the joke's on them! However, maybe these kinds of scenes made the broadcasters nervous."[39] By her own admission, Lock considers Sam's expressions of love (or temporary sexual attraction and arousal) for the Lady Boys challenging. Her comment raises the question, To what extent does the dynamic of surveillance inherent to the reality genre render Sam's sexualized desire and the Lady Boys' gendered self-expression unthinkable or inappropriate—and perhaps deviant? Does Sam's sexualized desire reinscribe or confront sexually ableist assumptions regarding the appropriateness of individuals labeled as intellectually disabled? Overall, these scenes create a sense of ambiguity and nervousness, especially around intellectual disability, sexuality, and gender queerness. Even so, the apparent "honesty" of representation challenges the narratives of intellectual disability pervasive in television and Hollywood cinema, particularly those explored in the previous chapter. *The Specials* carefully documents the varied intricacies of these young adults with intellectual disabilities navigating a desire to enter into long-term relationships. As an example, the most sustainable relationship involves Lucy and her boyfriend, Nick. Lucy and Nick display all the markers of a successful heterosexual relationship: public displays of affection, dinner dates, expressions of love, and intimacy. Hilly, another of the housemates, meets someone, Robert, in episode 4, but later finds out that Robert already has a girlfriend. Later, Hilly meets an available partner, Owen. One of the assets of the series is its willingness not to gloss over the heartaches and successes of the housemates in finding love and companionship. For example, mirroring the legacy of reality show confessionals, a few times in the series Sam is interviewed alone, at night, after drinking, dancing, and unsuccessfully courting a woman. In these emotional confessionals, Sam expresses his strong desire to find a girlfriend. In episode 6, Lewis and Megan end their relationship and the housemates struggle to work through this rupture in the collective life of their house, especially after Sam and Megan separately express that they like each other in later episodes. Part of an emerging genre of reality television programs that address disability, *The Specials* presents a certain type of narrative that changes the landscape of intellectual disability and sexual desire. It becomes important to interrogate how such images can be used as "raw materials for representing a disempowered politics or positionality that has been rendered unthinkable by the dominant culture."[40] The interaction between disability and non-Westernness, with inflections of the erotic and desire, complicates the commodification of a certain type of gendered representation for consumers that capitalizes on a sense of otherness, if not freakishness.

Geographies of Desire: Otherness on Display?

Now let me connect the categorization of the Lady Boys and Sam's queer desire to Anne Anlin Cheng's contention that, "with phenomena such as segregation and colonialism, the racial question is an issue of *place* (the literalization of Freudian melancholic suspension) rather than of full relinquishment. Segregation and colonialism are internally fraught institutions not because they have eliminated the other but because they need the very thing they hate or fear."[41] The Lady Boys' performance depends on a construction of *place*—a place of ethnographic promise that constructs the performers' bodies and Thai culture as consumable goods. Jacqui Alexander, in exploring the contours of gay-themed tourism, wonders, "What kinds of geographies of desire and pleasure are possible, and necessary, in light of the conflation of the erotic and the exotic?"[42] Alexander is particularly concerned with the ways in which a "queer fetishized native" gets commodified through the development and promotion of gay cruises, queer-friendly airlines, travel-themed credit card offers, gay-themed guide books, and travel specifically marketed toward gay men and lesbians—all of which promote a narrative of orientalized fetishes that, in essence, recolonizes tourist destinations through the promotion of "friendly" natives for the largely white Western travelers.[43] Along with Cheng's point about *place,* Alexander's questions about constructing solidarity communities and geographies of desire and pleasure help me to tease out post-colonial, feminist, queer, and critical disability studies approaches to the representation work at play in *The Specials,* especially given the promise of tourism and travel foregrounded in the advertisements for the Lady Boys. Moreover, Eng complements Alexander by wondering if queer diasporas can attend to a "retheorization of family and kinship relations."[44] The *place* of the Lady Boy performance on English soil, *mediated through* reality television, points to the potentiality of affective kinship—outside of normative constructions of family—as geographies of desire.

After the above-mentioned discussion between Sam, Lewis, and Robbie, this episode of *The Specials* shows but a brief glimpse of the Lady Boys' performance. In a quick succession of shots, the camera captures the housemates entering the performance tent. Once inside, it cuts from shots of Sam dancing as he takes his seat to large banners hanging on the walls, depicting various Lady Boys. Next, we see the stage as the curtain opens. A voice announces, "Welcome, to the Lady Boys of Bangkok!" The Lady Boys are shown on stage, enveloped in fog and pink stage lights. Almost immediately, we see a group of performers on stage dancing to the Pussycat Dolls' song, "Don't Cha," the lyrics of which add an element of irony to the performance: "Don't cha wish your girlfriend was hot like me? Don't cha wish your girlfriend was a freak like me? Don't cha?" In the middle of the performance, Sam comments to the camera, "The girls are sexy!" Although the rest of the housemates are clearly enjoying the show, Sam is particularly vocal about his pleasure, both in direct dialogue with the camera and through his active participation.

Sam's dialogue about the sexiness of the performers functions as a kind of "inside joke" for viewers. Most viewers "know" that the Lady Boys are not "girls" in a biological sense; that is, they "know" the truth of gender and sex, while Sam does not. Katy Lock's suggestion that the joke, at times, is "on" the housemates is clearly at work in this episode, illustrating Andrejevic's claims about the connection between reality television and surveillance.[45] Robbie interprets Sam's apparent unwillingness to read the Lady Boys as men as naïveté, and the scene prepares viewers to reach the same conclusion. Yet such a dismissive reading depends on denying both Sam's and, perhaps, the Lady Boys' own understandings of gender. In addition, it troublingly presents one version of gender as the truth, while other readings (or epistemologies) are read as not quite right, or even false.

Social scientists have demonstrated that intellectual disability is often associated with naïveté and acquiescence to suggestion, and, at face value, Sam's vocal expressions of desire within the space of a drag performance by a group of Thai nationals certainly has the potential to invoke anxiety about his credulity.[46] Yet Shildrick's comment that, "if any coming together of bodies, and more specifically the intercorporeality of much sexuality, is encompassed with an implicit anxiety about the loss of self-definition, then that body of the other already breaches normative standards of embodiment," allows me to fashion a critical reading of spectatorial anxiety.[47] Sam's repeated denials of Robbie's reading of the Lady Boys as men also entail the possibility that, at some point in the near future, and perhaps off camera, Sam will "get it." And when he does "get it," he will be ashamed and disappointed—perhaps embarrassed.[48] Anxiety is not only the property or problem of the spectators, then, for Sam's potential loss of self-definition is also at stake.

Homophobia and ableism often work together not only to deny the disabled subject the ability to express sexual agency and desire, but also to actively redirect queer sexual desire. Considering Sam as inappropriately sexual and unable to comprehend gender and desire constructs his intellectual disability as a force of negation. This construction in turn upholds sexual ableism. In this context, what I particularly emphasize is that the gendered exoticism of the Lady Boys, combined with Sam's disability status, conflates contentious images—images that are simultaneously problematic and violent as well as transgressive to dominant narratives of gender, ethnicity, disability, and the "intelligibility of sex."[49] The non-Western, gender-queer bodies of the Lady Boys become the occasion for a meaning-making process that generates multiple identifications as well as multiple anxieties.

Regardless of what "we" might assume to "know" about the bodies (and, more specifically, the genitalia) of the Lady Boys, their embodiment is mitigated through self-presentation. What theater audiences, as well as audiences tuning in to the web broadcast of *The Specials,* see on the stage is a constructed version of the Lady Boys' bodies as well as their nationality. The offer of traditional Thai food in the fully carpeted pavilion has the potential, in Alexander's terms, to recolonize individuals through native fetishes.[50] Cheng's point about *place* and racial melancholy illustrates how racial and ethnic stereotypes contain subjects in order to sustain "the exclusion-yet-retention of racialized others."[51] The Lady Boys and Sam are contained in the episode through the upholding of stereotypical understandings of ethnicity, gender, sexuality, and disability. The internal anxiety of misreading gender interacts with the recolonizing of Thai bodies, customs, and food for a Western audience. Both Sam and the performers are linked through the narrative in the episode of desire reducing both to their embodiment.

In turn, reading Sam's sexuality through his embodiment of "disability" creates a disavowal. It is important to note that the sexuality (or sexual appeal) of the Lady Boys is clearly on display in the episode through brief clips of the performers dancing in bikinis to pop music; on one level, then, Sam's desire is visually corroborated. Yet, despite the transgressive potential of validating the queer desires of a disabled man, Sam's sexual expression is renounced as an ostensibly inappropriate object choice based on incorrect understandings of nonnormative embodiment. Sam's sexual desire is seen not only as comical, but also as inherently "inappropriate" and queerer, reinforcing sexual ableism. Shildrick considers that to deny sexuality for those "whose embodiment is non-normative" is to "damage the very possibility of human becoming," and Sam's encounter with the Lady Boys shows that there is a certain amount of rhetorical (and actual) violence in denying the sexual agency of individuals with intellectual disabilities.[52] Sam's apparent naïveté has the potential to justify the need to protect those with certain disabilities from becoming sexually active because of concerns about manipulation and abuse.

Tellingly, the segment in the episode about the Lady Boys is bookended by another narrative of romance, desire, and sexuality, one that both sutures people with disabilities into heteronormativity and negates their ability to inhabit its norms. Two of the housemates, Lewis and Megan, are in a long-term relationship. We learn that their relationship is one of guarded physical interaction, no kissing, and strained communication. In the first episode, Dafydd, Hilly's father and owner, with his wife, Carol, of the house where the housemates live, teases Lewis that he is the worst boyfriend in the whole world. In a typical Lewis fashion, he replies, "Thank you." In the second episode of the season, Megan moves into the house where Lewis and Sam live, along with their other housemates, Hilly and Lucy. During the third episode, as a way to reconnect and move beyond their strained and awkward interactions, Lewis and Megan go out on a dinner date.[53] Commenting on the interactions between Lewis and Megan, Lucy remarks, "I think he's a bit shy, I think. Because Megan moved in. Because they're not talking to each other." Lewis admits to not talking much to Megan either, although he wishes that this were not the case. This lack of communication between people in a relationship who are expressly not fighting seemingly illustrates the tentative nature of that relationship.

Sam and Lewis's expressions of heterosexuality and masculinity—grounded in longing for intimacy with Megan or sexual attraction for the Lady Boys—illustrate for the viewers of *The Specials* that men with intellectual disabilities are capable of clear articulation of desires. As the focus is primarily on Sam and his desire to see the performance, the desires of Hilly and Lucy are not as fully represented. After the performance, Hilly and Lucy respond that they enjoyed the performance and want to come again. Their desire is also represented, but their desire is mitigated, however, through a focus on Sam's rowdy masculine desire and Lewis's efforts at reconnecting through a dinner date. Even though both Hilly and Lucy at times participate in heterosexual relationships in the series, Sam's vocal desires are given more screen time. As Lewis and Megan get ready for their date, the camera shows Lewis putting product in his hair and gargling with mouthwash. Sam's voice-over tells the viewer that tonight could mark the first kiss between Megan and Lewis. Megan, meanwhile, waits patiently, dressed up, coat on, purse in hand at the bottom of the stairs. The camera, in a low-angle shot, shows the empty staircase. We hear Lewis gargling and spitting off-screen. As he finally appears, walking down the stairs, he proclaims, "That mouthwash was awful!" Despite having taken the conventionally held steps to ensure a good date, including dressing up and freshening his breath, as Lewis walks down the stairs he walks right by Megan and proceeds to search for a house key, even though Megan announces that she has one. This constructed version of a "dinner date" stands in direct contrast with Sam's portrayal as a "typical," rowdy heterosexual man, even though both instances show men trying to inhabit normative heterosexual masculinity. One important difference between their expressions of masculinity and sexuality is that Sam believes and insists that he is succeeding and that his expression is authentic. In comparison, as a couple, Megan and Lewis do not seem to be communicating on multiple levels, and the strained and uncomfortable interaction between the two anticipates the dissolution of their relationship.[54] Later, after an extremely quiet dinner in which Lewis appears to be most interested in getting the last drops of soda from his can, Megan and Lewis are walking back home. Lewis audibly says to himself, "Go for it!" The camera then shows Megan and Lewis holding hands. Lewis questions aloud, "Is she holding my hand? I'm not minding that!" We have no idea if Megan is enjoying this expression of physical contact, although at different times in the series she mentions a desire to become more physically connected to Lewis. As Megan and Lewis walk back home with the camera behind them, the episode ends. At least temporarily, they have reconnected through physical contact. The two plots of this episode work together to indicate a range of sexual desires and expressions while, at the same time, putting either housemate's ability to attain "real" heterosexual masculinity into doubt. Lewis has a fair amount of ambivalence about kissing Megan, and this ambivalence ultimately renders their relationship unsustainable. Megan's desire for intimacy—in particular a kiss—is at odds with Lewis's desire.

As a whole, then, the episode seems to comment on the appropriateness of certain types of interactions between people with intellectual disabilities. Given that *The Specials* is one of the first reality shows to feature participants with intellectual disabilities, the nonsexual nature of Lewis and Megan's relationship does not necessarily concern the viewer in the same ways that Sam's expression of desire for the Lady Boys might. Lewis and Megan are seemingly living up to societal standards for their sexuality—as is Sam, as long as he does not actually begin dating a Lady Boy. Shildrick remarks that those outside the corporeal mainstream (those who are transgendered, HIV positive, disabled) have a choice between "apparent asexuality that comforts normative expectations in its very powerlessness to challenge or an expression of desire that will be necessarily exploratory and transformative."[55] The transformative potential of a certain type of sexuality—one that fundamentally challenges heteronormative and ableist norms rather than reconfirming paternalism—can ultimately queer normative expectations of embodiment and desire. However, this potential is not actualized within a representational formula and a spectator dynamic that tends toward the recovery of the norm.

Drag, Desire, and Disability

As a way to conclude, I want to look closely at a brief moment during the performance, referred to at the beginning of this chapter, when one of the Lady Boy performers sings "My Way" while gradually removing makeup, eyelashes, and a wig. This moment directly contrast the other brief glimpses of the Lady Boy show, when Sam is a visibly engaged audience member. When the Lady Boy performer transitions from the female costume, the audience, with the exception of Sam, applaud the Lady Boy's playful mocking of the limits and enactment of the fluidity of gender. Sam, however, is directly confronted with the reality that the performer he previously saw as sexy and feminine does not seem to be so any longer. Only after a few dramatic moments in which Sam has a look of wonder on his face does he gradually clap his hands in a show of support for the performer. After this moment of gender trouble, a new group of Lady Boys takes the stage in bikinis, dancing to the lyrics, "I can't wait for the weekend to begin." Sam shifts into the mode of an engaged audience member once again as he dances along to the music and claps his hands, with an enormous smile on his face.

At the end of the Lady Boy performance, in an interview with Katy Lock that is part of the episode, Sam declares his wish to see the sexy ladies again. His housemates, Hilly and Lucy, again repeat the declaration that the Lady Boys are not women but lady *boys*. Their pleasure in reading the performers as boys confirms that they, too, have active desires, even if the episode does not explicitly present them to the viewer. Sam's apparent unwillingness to accept his roommates' readings of the performers highlights a rigid reading of the sex/gender system on both sides. A more playful reading is that Sam is purposefully negating his roommates' readings of the Lady Boys in order to illustrate the absurdity of such a desire to label and classify. The Lady Boy doing "My Way" is performing a gendered commentary on the queer potentiality of drag as much as performing a type of disguisability of "real" identity, and Sam could be reading the transition of the Lady Boy into male costume as another type of drag, a particular interpretation on the mutability of masculinity. If drag performers can be understood as "educat[ing] their audiences about the performativity of gender . . . sending different messages about what queer genders and sexualities look like," then, no matter his intention, Sam, in this episode, does as much as the Lady Boys to dismantle rigid articulations of dichotomous gender.[56] His affective desire enabled through a crip/queer critique helps to reshape assumptions regarding intellectual disability and sexual agency.

Conclusion

Dismantling Ableist Assumptions

In my introduction to gender, women's, and sexuality studies courses, when I first discuss sexuality with the students in the class, I preface the discussion with the following caveat: "If you aren't more confused, at the end of class today, than you are now, at the beginning of class, I haven't done my job." Usually I get a few confused stares, maybe a giggle or two, but in general my statement about the need for confusion is met with general uncertainty. Isn't my job as a professor to make things clearer? Shouldn't I be unlocking the "secrets" of sexuality?

In class, I follow up the statement about purposeful confusion with a statement of clarification of intent. I want my students to begin to challenge their own hypotheses regarding the assumed relationship between gender assignment, gender identity, gender performance, and sexual orientation. For example, particularly in the United States, there are many sexual scripts and myths around virginity, sexual desire, and sexual pleasure. As an illustration, ask a room of first- and second-year college students what makes someone a virgin, and you will find a wide diversity of ideas on the legitimacy or fiction of the concept, not to mention the various types of activities that confirm or take away the status. In an effort to momentarily withhold assumed relationships between topics, practices, and identities, I encourage my students to think critically about the relationship between activities, desires, labels of orientation, and identity. I ask them why we claim our sexual identities based on what we do and not what we don't. I ask my students about the relationship, if any, between frequency and identity claims. How many sexual encounters or vivid dreams, unarticulated desires, fantasies are needed before one can be "authentically" straight, or queer? I encourage my students to contemplate how white supremacy, heteronormativity, classism, ableism—among other systems of oppression—influence their own assumptions about which bodies are able to be sexual, without oversight, and which bodies seem to warrant intrusion. Taking my cue from scholars like Kimberly Springer, I ask my students to queer their assumptions of sexuality. I encourage an exploration of how somewhat vague concepts of access, or privacy, agency, or competence, influence the sexual lives of their colleagues, friends, and family members. I want my students to resist a simple narrative of sexuality in order to think through what they desire in their own sexual lives—and how these desires come into being.

I have tried to strike a similar note in this book. Although purposeful confusion might be less forgivable in this venue, I have attempted to resist simple narratives in the exploration of sexuality, reproduction, and intellectual disability. One such narrative, that disabled individuals are constructed as asexual, covers over the reality that some disabled individuals identify as asexual, or don't desire sexual relationships. Of course, there are active efforts of desexualization, and what has been called the "myth of asexuality" has persisted in ableist denials of sexual pleasure and reproductive desires. Certainly sexual ableism operates by linking ableist assumptions about intellect and rationality to justify sterilization procedures, invasive birth control prescriptions, or residential segregation practices. The growing visibility and legacy of eugenic sterilization practices in the United States, including in North Carolina and Virginia, bears witness to how various individuals' sexual and reproductive lives were stolen by state legislatures, guardians, medical practitioners, social workers, and wealthy businessmen, among others. The links between these practices and contemporary efforts of regulation are perhaps less clear, but to claim eugenics as only a historical practice fails to recognize how discourses of fitness and competency still define the sexual and reproductive lives of individuals, including those with labels of intellectual disabilities.

As such, I have resisted endorsing competency as a construct or qualification to be sexual. There are many assessments of competence available, but these tools can reinforce assumptions of the relationship *between* intellectual disability and *inability* to consent. In upholding competence as a defining characteristic or regulatory mechanism, we risk further limiting the sexual and reproductive lives of individuals based on assumptions that can shift, or are never valid to begin with. If some individuals are competent, then others are deemed incompetent. One manifestation of ableism, which lays out assumptions that those who are disabled are categorically unable to complete certain tasks, seems to demand an articulation that those abelist assumptions are incorrect. Expansion of rights for some means that others are unable to meet the qualifications embedded in these rights claims. It is for this reason that I have focused on desire, to parent, to participate or not in sexual activities, as a valid mechanism for expression of sexual self-determination. I have also advocated that individual sexual pleasure be recognized as authentic. I firmly believe that when individuals are enabled to seek out sexual pleasure on their own terms, and feel empowered to claim this pleasure, sexually ableist practices are challenged. My use of sexual agency is less about thinking that some are able to be sexual beings, but rather that some maintain active sexual lives and desires, despite sexually ableist efforts of restriction. Individuals are "already doing it" in the midst of limited sex education, discourses of risk, and active efforts of desexualization. Uncovering, or claiming, or even acknowledging that intellectually disabled individuals have sexual desires highlights the naïveté of the individual doing the uncovering and claiming, not that of the disabled person. Much like the process I undertake with the students in my intro classes, what needs to be challenged, or forgotten, denied, or ignored, in discussions of intellectual disability, sexuality, and reproduction? What narratives of disabled sexuality can be challenged to make possible less sexually ableist futures?

When I first started the initial research for this project almost a decade ago, I grew increasingly frustrated with the discourse of protectionism, seemingly taken for granted, in the majority of the literature authored by various academics, researchers, and professionals from applied health sciences and special education disciplines. I longed for radical critiques of the discourses of protectionism. I imagined feminist theorists taking intellectual disability as their subject of analysis. I desired disability studies and queer theory articulations of the relationship between constructs of intelligence, agency, and sexuality. I imagined deeper connections between reproductive justice and disability justice. And I envisioned a future where disabled individuals and their sexual and reproductive lives are not constructed as "special" or in need of regulation. These imaginations and longings propelled me as I wrote, revised, and again revised this book.

I imagine my work as a provocation and challenge. The provocation comes from my insistence that professional able-bodied authority connected to paternalism and harm reduction of sexuality, including my past practices, as I explore in the preface, is a key component in upholding the primacy of sexual ableism. When we assume to know what is best for others, this knowledge can often actively hide or deny individual sexual self-determination. The challenge is to continue to forward sexual pleasure and desire in sex education materials, to continue partnerships with disability justice and reproductive justice, to advocate for and believe in coalitions that enable equitable and accessible futures. My hope is that my work will serve as a catalyst, a document to work with, against, and ultimately to move beyond. I dream of disabled futures, of spaces, places, and lives, where constructs of intellect, ability, and competence are no longer used to justify sexually ableist interventions. I long for futures not where disability is rendered illegible or absent, but rather where disability and impairment are perceived to enhance, not spoil, life, including conceptions of sexuality and reproduction. Or, to paraphrase the hip-hop duo Salt-n-Pepa, we can talk about how sex is, how it could be, how it was, and more important how it should be.

Acknowledgments

I am incredibly grateful to an ever-expansive group of individuals who listened to, loved and supported, challenged, and believed in me during the process of writing this book. In what follows, I will attempt to publicly acknowledge their influence in this work and my life. Although I can never repay the support and encouragement I received during this process, it is my hope that these individuals and various readers find this research and writing worthwhile and thought provoking.

This project has its origins in a dissertation written during my time at the University of Illinois at Chicago. Collectively, I have had the privilege of working with six amazing professors, all leading scholars in their respective fields. I am a better scholar because of the guidance and mentoring I received from Lennard Davis, Judith Kegan Gardiner, Sarah Parker Harris, Mark Sherry, Tobin Siebers, and Virginia Wright Wexman. Each of them provided invaluable feedback on my progress. I am indebted to their commitment and generosity to my project and academic development. In addition, I thank Sharon Snyder and David Mitchell, who mentored me throughout my graduate education.

I am grateful to the following individuals who generously read drafts of chapters and offered their thoughts, encouragement, responses, and constructive criticisms: Alexis Boylan, Sarah Brophy, Alyson Cole, Martha Cutter, Anna Mae Duane, Janice Hladki, Alison Kafer, Kathy Knapp, Nicole Markotić, Judy Rohrer, Shawn Salvant, and Cynthia Wu. Robert McRuer read the entire manuscript and offered excellent suggestions for revision and much-needed encouragement. I have been truly lucky to receive their responses to drafts, and I hope to repay their kindness in the future.

Portions of this text were presented at various academic conferences. I am grateful for the audience members and panelists who generously listened and could imagine my arguments as more fully developed and nuanced. The conferences where earlier portions of this text were presented include the annual meetings of the Society for Disability Studies in Seattle (2007), New York (2008), Philadelphia (2010), and Denver (2012). I presented portions of the text at the National Women's Studies Association annual meetings in Denver (2010) and Atlanta (2011), and the American Men's Studies Association conferences in Atlanta (2010) and Minneapolis (2012). I presented portions of the text at the conference "Health, Embodiment, and Visual Culture" in Hamilton, Ontario (2010) and the American Studies Association conference in Washington, D.C. (2013). I presented various chapters at the University of Connecticut as part of the "Spotlight Series" in the Women's, Gender, and Sexuality Studies Program, the "Out to Lunch" series in the Rainbow Center, and as part of the Human Rights Institute–funded workshop I organized with Cathy Schlund-Vials, "Disability, Human Rights, and the Limits of Humanitarianism." The Gender and Women's Studies Program at the University of Illinois at Chicago, the Women's, Gender, and Sexuality Studies Program at the University of Connecticut, and Grinnell College all generously supported my travel to these conferences. I thank the librarians at these institutions who generously helped me obtain copies of obscure texts and materials.

My academic career thus far has been marked by contract positions at the University of Connecticut and Grinnell College. I am appreciative to the many colleagues and friends I met at these institutions, including Alexis Boylan, Jason Oliver Chang, Manisha Desai, Karla Erickson, Barbara Gurr, Sharon Harris, Astrid Henry, Carolyn Herbst Lewis, Lakesia Johnson, Micki McElya, Kimberly McKee, Nancy Naples, Judy Rohrer, Ralph Savarese, Cathy Schlund-Vials, Coleen Spurlock, Heather Turcotte, and Chris Vials. I have had the privilege of teaching students at the University of Illinois at Chicago, the University of Connecticut, the University of Wisconsin–Madison, and Grinnell College. I most feel the impact of my work when I teach, and each class has given me their time, effort, and scholarly thoughts. To my former, current, and future students, thank you for trusting me to facilitate the classroom discussion and allowing me the opportunity to learn from you.

Richard Morrison, formerly at the University of Minnesota Press, was a wonderfully encouraging editor. Thank you, Richard, for believing in my project, offering your support and expertise, cheering me on, and knowing just the right time to check on my progress. I offer sincere thanks to Erin Warholm-Wohlenhaus, Mike Stoffel, Doug Armato, and the rest of the team at the University of Minnesota Press. It was an absolute delight to work with you, and I consider myself lucky to join the ranks of Minnesota authors. I also thank Michael Needham of Humanities First for his skill in transforming my manuscript, and I appreciate Nicholas Taylor's copyediting skill. Cathy Schlund-Vials was an early believer in the importance of my work and I value her friendship and support. I am grateful to Mark Sherry for his mentoring, friendship, and general encouragement. Thank you to Nancy Pastor for granting permission to reprint two photographs from her collection "Jasmine's World" and for being generous with her time as I sought further clarification and updates. I appreciate the help I received from Elena Gutiérrez, Katy Lock, and Rickie Solinger. I am grateful to Stephen Lance for generously mailing me a copy of his film *Yolk* that I discuss in chapter 2. Katie Watson graciously shared the amicus curiae brief I discuss in chapter 4.

I am lucky to have an amazing group of friends who appreciate, understand, and support the work I do. Disability studies and gender studies communities are vibrant, generative spaces, and I consider myself blessed to be a part of them. Thank you to DL Adams, Cynthia Barounis, Liat Ben-Moshe, Laurie Belzer, Alexis Boylan, Sally Chivers, John D'Emilio, Finn Enke, Nirmala Erevelles, Jim Ferris, Ann Fox, Michele Friedner, Rosemarie Garland-Thomson, Pernille Ipsen, Catherine Jacquet, Michelle Jarman, Jenell Johnson, Alison Kafer, Eunjung Kim, Petra Kuppers, Liam Lair, Riva Lehrer, Keisha Lindsay, Simi Linton, Corinne Louw, Maureen Madden, Nicole Markotić, Micki McElya, Robert McRuer, Rod Michalko, Colleen Norton, Susan Nussbaum, Kelly Parrey-Munger, Ryan Parrey-Munger, Julie Passanante Elman, Suzanne Poirier, Diane Price Herndl, Gayatri Reddy, Kimberly Rorie, Ellen Samuels, Carrie Sandahl, Cathy Schlund-Vials, Neslihan Sen, Janet Settle, Mark Sherry, Jill Siebers, Tobin Siebers, Bethany Stevens, Sandy Sufian, Terri Thrower, Tanya Titchkosky, Shelley Tremain, Sara Vogt, Cindy Wu, and Sandie Yi. Any list is of course incomplete and I have inadvertently left individuals off; first, my apologies for this oversight, and second, please know I appreciate the support and encouragement you offer. To all my friends and colleagues—whom I know on- and offline—thank you for encouraging me to be a better scholar, teacher, and person.

My family has been incredibly supportive of my progress, from entering graduate school to finishing this project. The support, love, and encouragement you all have given me has sustained me through my academic journey: my parents, Steve and Jan Gill; my sister, Molly Cook, and her husband, Kevin, and daughter, Zoe; my brother, Marcus Gill, and his wife, Lila, and children, Galveston and Róisín; my aunt, Nancy Buergel; Kyoung-jin Kim; Hong Haesook and Ahn Joong Bae; Hyunjung, Hardy, Jonah, and Haeil Kim; and Kimo Kim. A special note of gratitude goes to my partner, Eunjung Kim. Thank you, Eunjung, for supporting me unconditionally, reading many, many drafts of this project, sitting beside me in coffee shops in the United States and in Korea as we struggle to write, offering your excellent thoughts, disagreements, and ideas, knowing just the right thing to say or do when I wanted to give up, and not judging me when I just want to binge on television. I am blessed to have you in my life.

Notes

Preface

1. A sheltered workshop is a location that offers employment services for intellectually and developmentally disabled individuals in a segregated setting where employees receive sub–minimum wage remuneration.

2. http://www.ted.com/talks/chimamanda_adichie_the_danger_of_a_single_story.html.

3. Ibid.

4. Perhaps more controversial, I wonder why individuals with intellectual or cognitive disability are not allowed to participate in self-harm. Are efforts of behavior redirection in the name of avoiding harm ableist?

5. Home site staff work where individuals with intellectual and developmental disabilities live. Often these staff members are nondisabled. They are also usually paid barely above minimum wage, resulting in a high level of staff turnaround. Home site staff have no affiliation or relation to the sheltered workshop. At the workshop there was one executive director, one job developer, a workshop supervisor, a woodshop manager, and direct support staff. I was one of the direct support staff.

6. In an attempt to ensure confidentiality, I have changed the names of people here and elsewhere in the book.

7. The 2007 documentary film *Doin' It: Sex, Disability, and Videotape* by the Empowered Fe Fes, in conjunction with Beyondmedia and Salome Chasnoff, narrates how a group of disabled young women from the Chicago area explore their sexual lives (and desires) affected by experiences of disability informed by race, ethnicity, and class. The title of my book is inspired by the Fe Fes video exploring diverse sexual cultures and experiences.

8. Examples include Paul Cambridge and Bryan Mellan, "Reconstructing the Sexuality of Men with Learning Disabilities: Empirical Evidence and Theoretical Interpretations of Need," *Disability and Society* 15, no. 2 (2000): 293–311; LeeAnn Christian, Jennifer Stinson, and Lori Ann Dotson, "Staff Values Regarding the Sexual Expression of Women with Developmental Disabilities," *Sexuality and Disability* 19, no. 4 (2001): 283–91; E. M. Coleman and W. D. Murphy, "A Survey of Sexual Attitudes and Sex Education Programs

among Facilities for the Mentally Retarded," *Applied Research in Mental Retardation* 1, nos. 3–4 (1980): 269–76; Monica Cuskelly and Rachel Bryde, "Attitudes towards the Sexuality of Adults with an Intellectual Disability: Parents, Support Staff, and a Community Sample," *Journal of Intellectual and Developmental Disability* 29, no. 3 (2004): 255–64; Lori Dotson, Jennifer Stinson, and LeeAnn Christian, "'People Tell Me I Can't Have Sex': Women with Disabilities Share Their Personal Perspectives on Health Care, Sexuality, and Reproductive Rights," *Women and Therapy* 26, nos. 3–4 (2003): 195–209; Jennifer Galea et al., "The Assessment of Sexual Knowledge in People with Intellectual Disability," *Journal of Intellectual and Developmental Disability* 29, no. 4 (2004): 350–65; Bob Heyman and Sarah Huckle, "Sexuality as a Perceived Hazard in the Lives of Adults with Learning Difficulties," *Disability and Society* 10, no. 2 (1995): 139–56; Delores D. Walcott, "Family Life Education for Persons with Developmental Disabilities," *Sexuality and Disability* 15, no. 2 (1997): 91–98; Pamela S. Wolfe, "The Influence of Personal Values on Issues of Sexuality and Disability," *Sexuality and Disability* 15, no. 2 (1997): 69–90. These represent just a small sample of the massive literature on sexuality and intellectual disability in journals in the social and applied health sciences.

Introduction

1. The Honorable Justice Mostyn, "England and Wales High Court (Court of Protection) Decisions," January 28, 2011, http://www.bailii.org/ew/cases/EWHC/COP/2011/101.html.

2. Ibid. The judge writes that Alan doesn't understand about reproduction or the mechanics of vaginal/penile sex. Additionally, he was unable to correctly put a condom on a model penis.

3. A final determination of Alan's ability to participate in sexual activity has not been made. He is still receiving sex education.

4. Jane Fae, "Disabled Man Banned from Having Sex with Male Partner," *Pink News,* February 8, 2011, http://www.pinknews.co.uk/2011/02/08/disabled-man-banned-from-having-sex-with-male-partner/.

5. Ibid.

6. Tobin Siebers, *Disability Theory* (Ann Arbor: University of Michigan Press, 2008), 8. He argues that this preference for nondisability is connected to "the baseline by which humanness is determined, setting the measure of body and mind that gives or denies human status to individual persons. It affects nearly all our judgments, definitions, and values about human beings, but because it is discriminatory and exclusionary, it creates social locations outside of and critical of its purview, most notably in this case, the perspective of disability."

7. Rod Michalko, *The Difference That Disability Makes* (Philadelphia: Temple University Press, 2002), 14.

8. Roderick A. Ferguson, *Aberrations in Black: Toward a Queer of Color Critique* (Minneapolis: University of Minnesota Press, 2004), 4.

9. Ibid., 26. Ferguson utilizes Muñoz's ideas of disidentification as central to a queer of color critique. José Esteban Muñoz, *Disidentifications: Queers of Color and the Performance of Politics* (Minneapolis: University of Minnesota Press, 1999).

10. Robert McRuer, *Crip Theory: Cultural Signs of Queerness and Disability* (New York: New York University Press, 2006).

11. Robert McRuer, "Critical Investments: AIDS, Christopher Reeve, and Queer/Disability Studies," *Journal of Medical Humanities* 23, no. 3 (2002): 236.

12. Michel Desjardins, "The Sexualized Body of the Child: Parents and the Politics of 'Voluntary' Sterilization of People Labeled Intellectually Disabled," in *Sex and Disability*, ed. Robert McRuer and Anna Mollow (Durham: Duke University Press, 2012), 74.

13. Ibid., 78.

14. Desjardins mentions that the parents interviewed were somewhat open to their children participating in same-sex sexual activity, but the primary reason for sterilization is to prevent reproduction while allowing sexual activity, presumably conceived as heterosexual and penetrative.

15. Desjardins, "The Sexualized Body of the Child," 79. In Quebec, the disabled individual has to fill out a petition to seek sterilization, so the conversion process involves the parents communicating their desire to their children, having their children change their desire from reproduction to infertility, and then communicating that desire to a bioethics committee.

16. Siebers, *Disability Theory*, 148.

17. Tom Shakespeare, Kath Gillespie-Sells, and Dominic Davies, *The Sexual Politics of Disability: Untold Desires* (New York: Cassell, 1996), 131.

18. Siebers, *Disability Theory*, 142.

19. Ibid., 148.

20. Ibid., 152.

21. Tom Shakespeare, *Disability Rights and Wrongs* (New York: Routledge, 2006), 168.

22. Mark Sherry, *Disability and Diversity: A Sociological Perspective* (New York: Nova Science Publishers, 2008), 1.

23. Lennard J. Davis, *Enforcing Normalcy: Disability, Deafness, and the Body* (New York: Verso, 1995); Rosemarie Garland-Thomson, *Extraordinary Bodies: Figuring Physical Disability in American Culture and Literature* (New York: Columbia University Press, 1997).

24. Garland-Thomson, *Extraordinary Bodies*, 8.

25. Paul K. Longmore, *Why I Burned My Book, and Other Essays on Disability* (Philadelphia: Temple University Press, 2003), 3–5.

26. Michael Oliver, *The Politics of Disablement: A Sociological Approach* (New York: St. Martin's Press, 1990), xiv.

27. Dan Goodley, *Self-Advocacy in the Lives of People with Learning Difficulties: The Politics of Resilience* (Philadelphia: Open University Press, 2000); Bill Hughes and Kevin Paterson, "The Social Model of Disability and the Disappearing Body: Towards a Sociology of Impairment," *Disability and Society* 12, no. 3 (1997): 325–40; Tom Shakespeare and Nicholas Watson, "The Social Model of Disability: An Outdated Ideology?" in *Research in Social Science and Disability, Volume 2: Exploring Theories and Expanding Methodologies,* ed. Sharon Barnartt and Barbara Altman (Oxford: Elsevier Science, 2001), 9–28.

28. Shelley Tremain, "Foucault, Governmentality, and Critical Disability Theory: An Introduction," in *Foucault and the Government of Disability,* ed. Shelley Tremain (Ann Arbor: University of Michigan Press, 2005), 10.

29. I do, however, discuss definitions of intellectual disability, especially as they relate to notions of competence in chapter 1.

30. Mark Rapley, *The Social Construction of Intellectual Disability* (New York: Cambridge University Press, 2004).

31. Petra Kuppers refers to this process of scanning bodies to determine impairment as the "diagnostic gaze." Kuppers, *Disability and Contemporary Performance: Bodies on Edge* (New York: Routledge, 2003), 15, 39.

32. Tanya Titchkosky, *Disability, Self, and Society* (Toronto: University of Toronto Press, 2003).

33. For example, in each of the last five years, over a thousand articles about intellectual disability have appeared in U.S. newspapers. As a comparison, during 1990 to 1995, the total number of articles was around six hundred.

34. Jane Gross, "Learning to Savor a Full Life, Love Life Included," *New York Times,* April 20, 2006.

35. Dennis Altman, *Global Sex* (Chicago: University of Chicago Press, 2001), 86–105.

36. Sharon L. Snyder and David T. Mitchell, *Cultural Locations of Disability* (Chicago: University of Chicago Press, 2006).

37. Winifred Kempton and Emily Kahn, "Sexuality and People with Intellectual Disabilities: A Historical Perspective," *Sexuality and Disability* 9, no. 2 (1991): 93–94.

38. Dave Reynolds, "The Eugenic Apologies: How a Pair of Disability Rights Advocates Score the First State Apology for Eugenics, and What They Have Planned Next," *Ragged Edge Magazine,* November–December 2003. It is estimated that at least sixty thousand intellectually disabled adults were forcibly sterilized against their will during the early-to-mid twentieth century

(Kempton and Emily Kahn, "Sexuality and People with Intellectual Disabilities," 96). Thirty-three U.S. states had eugenics sterilization laws (Reynolds, "The Eugenic Apologies").

39. See V. V. Anderson for an example of this historical eugenic rhetoric: "Feeble-minded persons are especially prolific and reproduce their kind with greater frequency than normal persons, and through such reproduction provide a legitimate outlet for the exercise of charitable impulses in each generation, and an endless stream of defective progeny, which are a serious drain on the resources of the nation." Georgia Commission on Feeblemindedness, V. V. Anderson, and National Committee for Mental Hygiene, *Mental Defect in a Southern State: Report of the Georgia Commission on Feeblemindedness and the Survey of the National Committee for Mental Hygiene* (New York: National Committee for Mental Hygiene, 1919).

40. Jennifer Nelson, *Women of Color and the Reproductive Rights Movement* (New York: New York University Press, 2003); Elena R. Gutiérrez, *Fertile Matters: The Politics of Mexican-Origin Women's Reproduction* (Austin: University of Texas Press, 2008).

41. David J. Rothman and Sheila M. Rothman, *The Willowbrook Wars: Bringing the Mentally Disabled into the Community* (New Brunswick, N.J.: Aldine Transaction, 2005).

42. Michael Gill, "The Myth of Transition: Contractualizing Disability in the Sheltered Workshop," *Disability and Society* 20, no. 6 (2005): 613–23.

43. Jack Levinson, *Making Life Work: Freedom and Disability in a Community Group Home* (Minneapolis: University of Minnesota Press, 2010), 19–56.

44. Joe Caldwell, "Experiences of Families with Relatives with Intellectual and Developmental Disabilities in a Consumer-Directed Support Program," *Disability and Society* 22, no. 6 (2007): 549–62; Allison C. Carey, *On the Margins of Citizenship: Intellectual Disability and Civil Rights in Twentieth-Century America* (Philadelphia: Temple University Press, 2009); Sheryl A. Larson and K. Charlie Lakin, "Parent Attitudes about Residential Placement before and after Deinstitutionalization: A Research Synthesis," *Journal of the Association for Persons with Severe Handicaps* 16, no. 1 (1991): 25–38; Steven Noll and James W. Trent, *Mental Retardation in America: A Historical Reader* (New York: New York University Press, 2004); James W. Trent, *Inventing the Feeble Mind: A History of Mental Retardation in the United States* (Berkeley: University of California Press, 1994); David L. Braddock et al., *The State of the States in Developmental Disabilities* (Washington, D.C.: American Association on Intellectual and Developmental Disabilities, 2008); K. Johnson et al., *Deinstitutionalization and People with Intellectual Disabilities: In and Out of Institutions* (Philadelphia: Jessica Kingsley Publishers, 2005).

45. Quoted in Shakespeare, Gillespie-Sells, and Davies, *The Sexual Politics of Disability*, 5–6.

46. Eunjung Kim, "Asexuality in Disability Narratives," *Sexualities* 14, no. 4 (2011): 479–93.

47. Nathan J. Wilson et al., "Conditionally Sexual: Men and Teenage Boys with Moderate to Profound Intellectual Disability," *Sexuality and Disability* 29, no. 3 (2011): 279.

48. Ibid., 279–85.

49. Ibid., 286.

50. Cynthia H. Enloe, *Globalization and Militarism: Feminists Make the Link* (Lanham, Md.: Rowman and Littlefield, 2007).

1. Questions of Consent

1. Sherene Razack, *Looking White People in the Eye: Gender, Race, and Culture in Courtrooms and Classrooms* (Toronto: University of Toronto Press, 1998), 51.

2. Glenn Beck, "Transcript of Glenn Beck Show: July 27th, 2006," CNN, http://transcripts.cnn.com/TRANSCRIPTS/0607/27/gb.01.html. On his show Beck criticizes the rhetoric of Kalie McArthur as enjoying abuse with the following: "Well, this district is amazing, because they have said in this particular sexual abuse case that Kalie enjoyed the experience of the sexual abuse, and it's phenomenal to me. The reason why I'm staying on this story, Mike [Michael Cook, attorney], is because I have yet to talk to anyone, anyone in charge of the school district, of the town, of anything that has any power." I discuss the case of Kalie McArthur in this chapter.

3. Anne Fausto-Sterling, *Sexing the Body: Gender Politics and the Construction of Sexuality* (New York: Basic Books, 2000); Razack, *Looking White People in the Eye.*

4. Cynthia H. Enloe, *Maneuvers: The International Politics of Militarizing Women's Lives* (Berkeley: University of California Press, 2000).

5. Mark Sherry discusses the relationship between poverty and intellectual disability. There is a class-based element to an individual's socially perceived "vulnerability," especially if a lack of resources and a diagnosis of disability are mutually constructed. Mark Sherry, *Disability and Diversity: A Sociological Perspective* (New York: Nova Science, 2008).

6. The American Association on Intellectual and Developmental Disabilities defines intellectual disability as "a disability characterized by significant limitations both in intellectual functioning and in adaptive behavior, which covers many everyday social and practical skills." American Association on Intellectual and Developmental Disabilities, "Definition of Intellectual Disability," http://aaidd.org/intellectual-disability/definition. Later in this chapter, I explore how intellectual disability is defined and how this definition limits individual agency and choice, perhaps leading to an increase of sexual abuse.

7. There is a historical tradition that calls on white men to "defend" virginal white women's bodies from predators. This problematic view of gender and race relations is replayed below, where McArthur's purity "requires" defense from the threat that her attacker represents. Of course, the notion of defense contributes to her perceived vulnerability. McArthur's whiteness is not remarked on in the journalistic accounts of the case. I argue, however, that others see her abuse as more "horrific" because she is a white woman. Whiteness creates an inconsistent response to experiences of sexual abuse.

8. Razack, *Looking White People in the Eye.*

9. Glenn Beck, "Transcript of Glenn Beck Show: June 30th, 2006," CNN, http://transcripts.cnn.com/TRANSCRIPTS/0606/30/gb.01.html.

10. Ibid.

11. Where else would individuals be forced to clean the school except in a special education class? I discuss this issue in another publication. See Michael Gill, "The Myth of Transition: Contractualizing Disability in the Sheltered Workshop," *Disability and Society* 20, no. 6 (2005): 613–23.

12. Jeffrey Weeks, "Court Brief on Behalf of Kalie McArthur," Weeks and Luchetta Law Firm, http://www.wrightslaw.com/law/pleadings/mcarthur.academy.complaint.pdf.

13. Ibid.

14. Brian Newsome, "Entire Family Affected by What Teen Calls a Lapse of Judgment," *The Gazette,* January 15, 2008.

15. Ibid.

16. Deborah Frazier, "Lawyer Sees School Hush-Up: Girl's Parents Sue over Alleged Assault by Young Caretaker," *Rocky Mountain News,* June 13, 2006.

17. Razack, *Looking White People in the Eye.*

18. Newsome, "Entire Family Affected by What Teen Calls a Lapse of Judgment."

19. Frazier, "Lawyer Sees School Hush-Up"; Associated Press, "Parents: Expert Says Attack Pleasurable," *Associated Press,* June 13, 2006; Glenn Beck, "Transcript of Glenn Beck Show: June 28th, 2006," CNN, http://transcripts.cnn.com/TRANSCRIPTS/0606/28/gb.01.html; Newsome, "Entire Family Affected by What Teen Calls a Lapse of Judgment."

20. Weeks, "Court Brief on Behalf of Kalie McArthur."

21. Newsome, "Entire Family Affected by What Teen Calls a Lapse of Judgment."

22. Ibid.

23. Ibid.

24. Ibid.

25. Ibid.

26. Brian Newsome, "Innocence Undone," *The Gazette,* January 12, 2008.

27. Ibid.

28. The age of consent in Colorado is seventeen, however, there are "close-in-age exceptions."

29. Weeks, "Court Brief on Behalf of Kalie McArthur," 18.

30. Peter Laufer, *A Question of Consent: Innocence and Complicity in the Glen Ridge Rape Case* (San Francisco: Mercury House, 1994); Bernard Lefkowitz, *Our Guys: The Glen Ridge Rape and the Secret Life of the Perfect Suburb* (Berkeley: University of California Press, 1997).

31. Weeks, "Court Brief on Behalf of Kalie McArthur."

32. Frazier, "Lawyer Sees School Hush-Up."

33. Ibid.; Associated Press, "Parents"; Beck, "Transcript of Glenn Beck Show: June 30th, 2006"; Weeks, "Court Brief on Behalf of Kalie McArthur."

34. Robert McRuer, *Crip Theory: Cultural Signs of Queerness and Disability* (New York: New York University Press, 2006).

35. Ibid.

36. Rosemarie Garland-Thomson, "Integrating Disability, Transforming Feminist Theory," *NWSA Journal* 14, no. 3 (2002): 1–33; Razack, *Looking White People in the Eye*; Sharon L. Snyder and David T. Mitchell, *Cultural Locations of Disability* (Chicago: University of Chicago Press, 2006); Pamela Block, "Sexuality, Fertility, and Danger: Twentieth-Century Images of Women with Cognitive Disabilities," *Sexuality and Disability* 18, no. 4 (2000): 239–54.

37. Fregoso describes how the feminicide in Juarez, Mexico, has been explained as the result of the murdered women's double lives as sex workers. The moral discourse around the murders in Juarez places the blame on women for supposedly being sex workers instead of addressing systematic discrimination and oppression that allows these murders to continue. See Rosa-Linda Fregoso, "Voices without Echo: The Global Gendered Apartheid," *Emergencies: Journal for the Study of Media and Composite Cultures* 10, no. 1 (2000): 137–55.

38. Razack, *Looking White People in the Eye*.

39. Doezema discusses how commentators and legislative interventions frame sex workers within the "forced/free" and "virgin/whore" dichotomies. See Jo Doezema, "Forced to Choose: Beyond the Voluntary vs. Forced Prostitution Dichotomy," in *Global Sex Workers: Rights, Resistance, and Redefinition,* ed. Kamala Kempadoo and Jo Doezema (New York: Routledge, 1998), 34–50.

40. Kamala Kempadoo, "From Moral Panic to Global Justice: Changing Perspectives on Trafficking," in *Trafficking and Prostitution Reconsidered: New Perspectives on Migration, Sex Work, and Human Rights,* ed. Kamala Kempadoo, Jyoti Sanghera, and Bandana Pattanaik (Boulder: Paradigm, 2005), xxiv.

41. Bette L. Bottoms et al., "Jurors' Perceptions of Adolescent Sexual Assault Victims Who Have Intellectual Disabilities," *Law and Human Behavior* 27, no. 2 (2003): 205–27.

42. Mark R. Kebbell and Chris Hatton, "People with Mental Retardation as Witnesses in Court: A Review," *Mental Retardation* 37, no. 3 (1999): 179–87; Mark R. Kebbell, Christopher Hatton, and Shane D. Johnson, "Witnesses with Intellectual Disabilities in Court: What Questions Are Asked and What Influence Do They Have?" *Legal and Criminological Psychology* 9, no. 1 (2004): 23–35; Denise C. Valenti-Hein and Linda D. Schwartz, "Witness Competency in People with Mental Retardation: Implications for Prosecution of Sexual Abuse," *Sexuality and Disability* 11, no. 4 (1993): 287–94.

43. Lesley Chenoweth, "Violence and Women with Disabilities," *Violence against Women* 2, no. 4 (1996): 391–411; Mark Sherry, *If I Only Had a Brain: Deconstructing Brain Injury* (New York: Routledge, 2006).

44. Catharine A. MacKinnon, *Feminism Unmodified: Discourses on Life and Law* (Cambridge: Harvard University Press, 1987).

45. Carole S. Vance, *Pleasure and Danger: Exploring Female Sexuality* (Boston: Routledge and K. Paul, 1984).

46. MacKinnon, *Feminism Unmodified*, 14.

47. Michelle McCarthy and David Thompson, "Sexual Abuse by Design: An Examination of the Issues in Learning Disability Services," *Disability and Society* 11, no. 2 (1996): 205–18.

48. Hilary Brown and Vicky Turk, "Defining Sexual Abuse as It Affects Adults with Learning Disabilities," *Journal of the British Institute of Mental Handicap* 20, no. 2 (1992): 44–55.

49. Michelle McCarthy, "Sexual Experiences of Women with Learning Difficulties in Long-Stay Hospitals," *Sexuality and Disability* 11, no. 4 (1993): 277–86.

50. H. Matthews, "What Staff Needs to Know" (paper presented at the Sexual Abuse and Learning Disability Conference Proceedings, London, 1994).

51. McCarthy and Thompson, "Sexual Abuse by Design," 206.

52. Richard Sobsey, *Violence and Abuse in the Lives of People with Disabilities: The End of Silent Acceptance?* (Baltimore: P. H. Brooks, 1994).

53. Marklyn Champagne, "Helping Individuals Recover from Sexual Abuse: One Therapist's Model," in *Facts of Life and More: Sexuality and Intimacy for People with Intellectual Disabilities*, ed. Leslie Walker-Hirsch (Baltimore: Paul H. Brookes, 2007), 247–64; Lydia Fegan and Anne Rauch, *Sexuality and People with Intellectual Disability* (Baltimore: Paul H. Brookes, 1993).

54. Brown and Turk, "Defining Sexual Abuse as It Affects Adults with Learning Disabilities"; Michelle McCarthy, "The Sexual Support Needs of People with Learning Disabilities: A Profile of Those Referred for Sex Education," *Sexuality and Disability* 14, no. 4 (1996): 265–79.

55. Jenny A. Keeling and John L. Rose, "Relapse Prevention with Intellectually Disabled Sexual Offenders," *Sexual Abuse: A Journal of Research and Treatment* 17, no. 4 (2005): 407–23; Andrew J. R. Harris and Susan Tough,

"Should Actuarial Risk Assessments Be Used with Sex Offenders Who Are Intellectually Disabled?" *Journal of Applied Research in Intellectual Disabilities* 17, no. 4 (2004): 275–83.

56. John Rose et al., "A Group Treatment for Men with Intellectual Disabilities Who Sexually Offend or Abuse," *Journal of Applied Research in Intellectual Disabilities* 15, no. 2 (2002): 138–50.

57. Biza Stenfert Kroese and Gail Thomas, "Treating Chronic Nightmares of Sexual Assault Survivors with an Intellectual Disability: Two Descriptive Case Studies," *Journal of Applied Research in Intellectual Disabilities* 19, no. 1 (2006): 75–80.

58. R. Balogh et al., "Sexual Abuse in Children and Adolescents with Intellectual Disability," *Journal of Intellectual Disability Research* 45, no. 3 (2001): 194–201.

59. McCarthy and Thompson, "Sexual Abuse by Design."

60. Sobsey, *Violence and Abuse in the Lives of People with Disabilities.*

61. Wolf Wolfensberger, "Social Role Valorization: A Proposed New Term for the Principle of Normalization," *Mental Retardation* 21, no. 6 (1983): 234–39; Wolf Wolfensberger, "A Reconceptualization of Normalization as Social Role Valorization," *Mental Retardation* 34, no. 7 (1984): 22–26.

62. Champagne, "Helping Individuals Recover from Sexual Abuse," 249.

63. Mark Sherry, *Disability Hate Crimes: Does Anyone Really Hate Disabled People?* (Burlington, Vt.: Ashgate, 2010).

64. Michel Foucault, *Madness and Civilization: A History of Insanity in the Age of Reason* (New York: Pantheon, 1965).

65. Mark Rapley, *The Social Construction of Intellectual Disability* (New York: Cambridge University Press, 2004), 36.

66. Richard Jenkins, *Questions of Competence: Culture, Classification and Intellectual Disability* (New York: Cambridge University Press, 1998).

67. Robert B. Edgerton, *The Cloak of Competence* (Berkeley: University of California Press, 1993).

68. Licia Carlson, "Cognitive Ableism and Disability Studies: Feminist Reflections on the History of Mental Retardation," *Hypatia* 16, no. 4 (2001): 140.

69. Clare Graydon, Guy Hall, and Angela O'Brien-Malone, "The Concept of Sexual Exploitation in Legislation Relating to Persons with Intellectual Disability," *Murdoch University Electronic Journal of Law* 13, no. 1 (2006): 150–74; A. C. O'Callaghan and G. H. Murphy, "Sexual Relationships in Adults with Intellectual Disabilities: Understanding the Law," *Journal of Intellectual Disability Research* 51, no. 3 (2007): 197–206; Ruth Luckasson and Leslie Walker-Hirsch, "Consent to Sexual Activity: Legal and Clinical Considerations," in *Facts of Life and More: Sexuality and Intimacy for People with Intellectual Disabilities,* ed. Leslie Walker-Hirsch (Baltimore: Paul H. Brookes, 2007), 179–92; Martin Lyden, "Assessment of Sexual Consent Capacity," *Sexuality*

and Disability 25, no. 1 (2007): 3–20; Julia L. Wacker, Susan L. Parish, and Rebecca J. Macy, "Sexual Assault and Women with Cognitive Disabilities," *Journal of Disability Policy Studies* 19, no. 2 (2008): 86–94.

70. Lyden, "Assessment of Sexual Consent Capacity."

71. O'Callaghan and Murphy, "Sexual Relationships in Adults with Intellectual Disabilities."

72. Luckasson and Walker-Hirsch, "Consent to Sexual Activity."

73. O'Callaghan and Murphy, "Sexual Relationships in Adults with Intellectual Disabilities."

74. Graydon, Hall, and O'Brien-Malone, "The Concept of Sexual Exploitation in Legislation Relating to Persons with Intellectual Disability," 169.

75. Ibid.; Wacker, Parish, and Macy, "Sexual Assault and Women with Cognitive Disabilities."

76. Lyden and Stavis and Walker-Hirsch are two examples of these scales to determine consent. See Lyden, "Assessment of Sexual Consent Capacity"; Paul F. Stavis and Leslie Walker-Hirsch, "Consent to Sexual Activity," in *A Guide to Consent*, ed. Robert D. Dinerstein, Stanley S. Herr, and Joan L. O'Sullivan (Washington, D.C.: American Association on Mental Retardation, 1999), 57–68. Both scales are to be used by service providers, parents, and guardians to determine if an individual understands and is able to consent to sexual activity.

77. Lyden, "Assessment of Sexual Consent Capacity."

78. Stavis and Walker-Hirsch, "Consent to Sexual Activity."

79. Ibid.; Luckasson and Walker-Hirsch, "Consent to Sexual Activity."

80. Stavis and Walker-Hirsch, "Consent to Sexual Activity."

81. In the Introduction, I discuss a court case where the judge determined that "Alan," an individual with a label of intellectual disability, did not comprehend mechanics of sexuality and, as such, could not consent to sexual activities.

82. Fred Kaeser, "Can People with Severe Mental Retardation Consent to Mutual Sex?" *Sexuality and Disability* 10, no. 1 (1992): 33–42.

83. Champagne, "Helping Individuals Recover from Sexual Abuse."

84. Rapley, *The Social Construction of Intellectual Disability*, 202.

85. Tobin Siebers, *Disability Theory* (Ann Arbor: University of Michigan Press, 2008); Tom Shakespeare, Kath Gillespie-Sells, and Dominic Davies, *The Sexual Politics of Disability: Untold Desires* (New York: Cassell, 1996); Robert McRuer and Anna Mollow, *Sex and Disability* (Durham: Duke University Press, 2012).

86. Luckasson and Walker-Hirsch, "Consent to Sexual Activity."

87. Davina Cooper, *Challenging Diversity: Rethinking Equality and the Value of Difference* (New York: Cambridge University Press, 2004), 73.

88. McRuer, *Crip Theory*, 1.

89. Ibid., 31.

90. Margrit Shildrick, *Dangerous Discourses of Disability, Subjectivity, and Sexuality* (New York: Palgrave Macmillan, 2009).

91. Sherry, *If I Only Had a Brain*, 87.

92. Abby Wilkerson furthers discussions of sexual citizenship in her pieces on "sexual radicalism" and "normate sex." I engage with Wilkerson's concepts in Chapters 3 and 4. See Abby Wilkerson, "Disability, Sex Radicalism, and Political Agency," *NWSA Journal* 14, no. 3 (2002): 33–57; Abby Wilkerson, "Normate Sex and Its Discontents," in *Sex and Disability*, ed. Robert McRuer and Anna Mollow (Durham: Duke University Press, 2012), 183–207.

93. Carrie Sandahl, "Queering the Crip or Cripping the Queer? Intersections of Queer and Crip Identities in Solo Autobiographical Performance," *GLQ: A Journal of Lesbian and Gay Studies* 9, no. 1 (2003): 42. "Piss on Pity" is a slogan that disabled people wear on T-shirts, shout at protests, and theorize at conferences. The slogan captures the idea that pity (and to some degree compassion) is experienced by disabled people as an assessment by those without disabilities of the unfortunate circumstances of disability—in other words, that being disabled is a "pitiful" existence. Some disabled people resist this type of emotional response as unfairly characterizing their lives as well as not meaningfully challenging the circumstances that create discrimination and oppression.

94. Sherene Razack, "From Consent to Responsibility, from Pity to Respect: Subtexts in Cases of Sexual Violence Involving Girls and Women with Developmental Disabilities," *Law and Social Inquiry* 19, no. 4 (1994): 891–922.

95. Razack, *Looking White People in the Eye*, 152.

96. I am using Paul Farmer's articulation of structural violence to theorize the ways in which service delivery structures facilitate sexual abuses. See Paul Farmer, "Women, Poverty, and AIDS," in *Women, Poverty, and AIDS: Sex, Drugs, and Structural Violence*, ed. Paul Farmer, Margaret Conners, and Janie Simmons (Monroe, Maine: Common Courage Press, 2007), 3–38.

97. Laufer, *A Question of Consent*, 36.

98. McRuer, *Crip Theory*, 71–72.

2. Pleasure Principles

1. Stephen Lance, *Yolk* (Head Pictures, 2007). Actress Audrey O'Conner stars as Lena. She is part of an emerging group of actors with intellectual disabilities landing substantial roles in television and film. O'Conner is active in the Don't DIS my ABILITY campaign in New South Wales.

2. Teenage boys and adult men often hide pornography under beds.

3. Lena shares a room with at least one of her sisters, so the bathroom provides much-needed privacy.

4. Masturbation can be interpreted as "stunted" or "immature" sexual expression. Her desire to be with Daniel then could mark her entry into "adulthood" or "mature" sexuality.

5. Fiction films appear more open to this type of pairing. Justin Lerner's film *Girlfriend* (Wayne/Lauren Film Company, 2011) and Antonio Naharro and Alvaro Pastor's *Yo, tambien* (Olive Films, 2009) both show male characters with disabilities entering into romantic relationships with nondisabled women.

6. I have no proprietary interest in any of the sex educational materials analyzed in this chapter.

7. Janice M. Irvine, *Talk about Sex: The Battles over Sex Education in the United States* (Berkeley: University of California Press, 2002), 3.

8. Ibid., 17–34.

9. Jessica Fields, *Risky Lessons: Sex Education and Social Inequality* (New Brunswick: Rutgers University Press, 2008); Irvine, *Talk about Sex*; Mitchell S. Tepper, "Sexuality and Disability: The Missing Discourse of Pleasure," *Sexuality and Disability* 18, no. 4 (2000): 283–90.

10. Julie Askew, "Breaking the Taboo: An Exploration of Female University Students' Experiences of Attending a Feminist-Informed Sex Education Course," *Sex Education: Sexuality, Society, and Learning* 7, no. 3 (2007): 251–64.

11. Marklyn P. Champagne et al., CIRCLES®: *Safer Ways* (Santa Barbara, Calif.: James Stanfield Publishing, 1988); James Stanfield et al., CIRCLES®: *Level 2, Intimacy and Relationships* (Santa Barbara, Calif.: James Stanfield Publishing, 2006); James Stanfield et al., CIRCLES®: *First Step Introduction, Special Needs, Level 1, Intimacy and Relationships* (Santa Barbara, Calif.: James Stanfield Publishing, 2000).

12. There have already been studies conducted to determine the educational effectiveness of sex education materials. These include Monique Garwood and Marita P. McCabe, "Impact of Sex Education Programs on Sexual Knowledge and Feelings of Men with a Mild Intellectual Disability," *Education and Training in Mental Retardation and Developmental Disabilities* 35, no. 3 (2000): 269–83; Marita P. McCabe, "Sexual Knowledge, Experience, and Feelings among People with Disability," *Sexuality and Disability* 17, no. 2 (1999): 157–70; Michele A. Whitehouse and Marita P. McCabe, "Sex Education Programs for People with Intellectual Disability: How Effective Are They?" *Education and Training in Mental Retardation and Developmental Disabilities* 32, no. 3 (1997): 229–40.

13. I am unsure how often these particular sex education materials are used. The publisher for CIRCLES® advertises that its materials are used in over ten thousand facilities across the United States. The other materials are representative of the typical content of sex education materials for people with intellectual disabilities.

14. Abby Wilkerson, "Disability, Sex Radicalism, and Political Agency," *NWSA Journal* 14, no. 3 (2002): 41.

15. Tim Dean, *Unlimited Intimacy: Reflections on the Subculture of Bare-backing* (Chicago: University of Chicago Press), 24.

16. Ibid., 24.

17. Ibid., 45.

18. I appreciate Robert McRuer's assistance in thinking through the discourses of risk and sexuality in this chapter.

19. Fields, *Risky Lessons*, 171.

20. Winifred Kempton and Emily Kahn, "Sexuality and People with Intellectual Disabilities: A Historical Perspective," *Sexuality and Disability* 9, no. 2 (1991): 98.

21. Ibid., 98–99.

22. Patrick White, "Sex Education; or, How the Blind Became Heterosexual," *GLQ: A Journal of Lesbian and Gay Studies* 9, nos. 1–2 (2003): 133–47.

23. Ibid., 133.

24. Michael John Craft and Ann Craft, *Sex and the Mentally Handicapped: Guide for Parents and Carers* (Boston: Routledge and Kegan Paul, 1982); Ann Craft and Michael John Craft, *Sex Education and Counseling for Mentally Handicapped People* (Baltimore: University Park Press, 1983); Warren Johnson, "Sex Education of the Mentally Retarded," in *Human Sexuality and the Mentally Retarded,* ed. Felix F. de la Cruz and Gerald D. LaVeck (New York: Brunner/Mazel, 1973), 57–66; Warren Russell Johnson, *Sex Education and Counseling of Special Groups: The Mentally and Physically Handicapped, Ill and Elderly* (Springfield, Ill.: Thomas, 1975); Wendy and Lydia Fegan McCarthy, *Sex Education and the Intellectually Handicapped: A Guide for Parents of Caregivers* (Balgowlah, N.S.W.: ADIS Health Science Press, 1984); Lydia Fegan and Anne Rauch, *Sexuality and People with Intellectual Disability* (Baltimore: P. H. Brookes, 1993).

25. Felix de la Cruz, "Preface," in *Human Sexuality and the Mentally Retarded,* ed. Felix F. de la Cruz and Gerald D. LaVeck (New York: Brunner/Mazel, 1973), xvi.

26. Jeannette Rockefeller, "Greetings from the President's Committee on Mental Retardation," in *Human Sexuality and the Mentally Retarded,* ed. Felix F. de la Cruz and Gerald D. LaVeck (New York: Brunner/Mazel, 1973), xvii–xviii.

27. Johnson also challenged the utility of using "mental retardation" as a diagnostic characteristic: "Labels like 'mentally retarded' tend both to create and to conceal *individuals* under them. It is, therefore, hazardous to suppose that such a label necessarily provides any useful information with dealing with any given person, either with regard to his capacity to learn or his interest in sex" (Johnson, "Sex Education of the Mentally Retarded," 58). Chal-

lenging the usefulness of "mental retardation" points to the problems associated with the diagnosis—intellectual disability means one thing to a group
of professionals, educators, and physicians, and something else to the general
public; and in reality the limitations in intellect and functioning associated
with the impairment might not apply to individuals. Or put another way, "the
fact that someone is mentally retarded tells us little about the sexuality of that
person" (McCarthy, *Sex Education and the Intellectually Handicapped*, 1).

28. Kempton and Kahn, "Sexuality and People with Intellectual Disabilities," 95.

29. Johnson, "Sex Education of the Mentally Retarded," 62.

30. Irvine, *Talk about Sex*. Irvine explains how the success of groups like
Jerry Falwell's Moral Majority and the John Birch Society depended in part
on attacking the SIECUS and advocates of comprehensive sex education as
corrupting the traditional values and morals of U.S. society. Ibid., 63–68. "In
historically unprecedented coalitions, conservative Catholics, conservative
Jews, along with Christian evangelicals, fundamentalists, Pentecostals, and
even some Muslim allies abrogated denominational loyalties to fight for 'traditional values'—a move which united opponents of sex education" (ibid., 65).
While Johnson and the other members of this conference appear sheltered
from these debates because of the professional and specific focus of their efforts, discussions of morality and traditional values provide important background to the endeavors made to expand sex education materials for people
with intellectual disabilities. This connection between morality and education becomes especially revealing later in the chapter when an analysis of
CIRCLES® highlights connections between neoconservative morals and a view
of nonreproductive, heterosexual activity promoted in the materials.

31. Johnson, "Sex Education of the Mentally Retarded," 65.

32. Joe Osburn, "An Overview of Social Role Valorization Theory," *SRV
Journal* 1, no. 1 (2006): 4–13; Wolf Wolfensberger, "Social Role Valorization: A
Proposed New Term for the Principle of Normalization," *Mental Retardation*
21, no. 6 (1983): 234–39. As an example, Fields traces the relationship between
individual morality and sex education curriculum development in North
Carolina. See Fields, *Risky Lessons*.

33. Abby Wilkerson, "Normate Sex and Its Discontents," in *Sex and Disability*, ed. Robert McRuer and Anna Mollow (Durham: Duke University
Press, 2012), 183–207.

34. Ibid., 184–85.

35. Johnson, *Sex Education and Counseling of Special Groups*, 7–8; McCarthy,
Sex Education and the Intellectually Handicapped, 2–3.

36. Johnson, *Sex Education and Counseling of Special Groups*, 48.

37. Ibid., 49. The process of sterilization continues today, under different
legislative and political frameworks. Currently, it operates in a context where

eugenic tendencies operate at the individual, rather than state, level. Effectively, eugenic practices have been privatized. See Anne Kerr and Tom Shakespeare, *Genetic Politics: From Eugenics to Genome* (Cheltenham: New Clarion Press, 2002).

38. Johnson, *Sex Education and Counseling of Special Groups*, 51.

39. Others often consider people with disabilities asexual. Shakespeare, Gillespie-Sells, and Davies assert that "stereotypes of disability often focus on asexuality, of lack of sexual potential or potency. Disabled people are subject to infantilization, especially disabled people who are perceived as being 'dependent.' Just as children are assumed to have no sexuality, so disabled people are similarly denied the capacity for sexual feeling. Where disabled people are seen as sexual, this is in terms of deviant sexuality, for example inappropriate sexual display or masturbation." Tom Shakespeare, Kath Gillespie-Sells, and Dominic Davies, *The Sexual Politics of Disability: Untold Desires* (New York: Cassell, 1996), 10. There is a tension between being labeled as asexual and actively choosing an asexual lifestyle. Celibacy and temporary asexuality also complicate this tension. The Asexuality Visibility and Education Network is largely an online forum where people across the globe discuss asexual identity and orientation. See Eunjung Kim, "Asexuality in Disability Narratives," *Sexualities* 14, no. 4 (2011): 334–47.

40. Johnson, *Sex Education and Counseling of Special Groups,* 53.

41. Examples include Paul Cambridge and Bryan Mellan, "Reconstructing the Sexuality of Men with Learning Disabilities: Empirical Evidence and Theoretical Interpretations of Need," *Disability and Society* 15, no. 2 (2000): 293–311; LeeAnn Christian, Jennifer Stinson, and Lori Ann Dotson, "Staff Values Regarding the Sexual Expression of Women with Developmental Disabilities," *Sexuality and Disability* 19, no. 4 (2001): 283–91; E. M. Coleman and W. D. Murphy, "A Survey of Sexual Attitudes and Sex Education Programs among Facilities for the Mentally Retarded," *Applied Research in Mental Retardation* 1, nos. 3–4 (1980): 269–76; Monica Cuskelly and Rachel Bryde, "Attitudes towards the Sexuality of Adults with an Intellectual Disability: Parents, Support Staff, and a Community Sample," *Journal of Intellectual and Developmental Disability* 29, no. 3 (2004): 255–64; Lori Dotson, Jennifer Stinson, and LeeAnn Christian, "'People Tell Me I Can't Have Sex': Women with Disabilities Share Their Personal Perspectives on Health Care, Sexuality, and Reproductive Rights," *Women and Therapy* 26, nos. 3–4 (2003): 195–209; Jennifer Galea et al., "The Assessment of Sexual Knowledge in People with Intellectual Disability," *Journal of Intellectual and Developmental Disability* 29, no. 4 (2004): 350–65; Bob Heyman and Sarah Huckle, "Sexuality as a Perceived Hazard in the Lives of Adults with Learning Difficulties," *Disability and Society* 10, no. 2 (1995): 139–55; Delores D. Walcott, "Family Life Education for Persons with Developmental Disabilities," *Sexuality and Disability*

15, no. 2 (1997): 91–98; Pamela S. Wolfe, "The Influence of Personal Values on Issues of Sexuality and Disability," *Sexuality and Disability* 15, no. 2 (1997): 69–90.

42. For an example Galea and colleagues conclude that "the results suggest that participants, generally, were limited in their sexual knowledge . . . Participants scored poorly in relation to other areas on the sections assessing knowledge of puberty, menstruation, menopause, safer sexual practices, sexual health, sexually transmitted infections, legal issues and contraception" ("The Assessment of Sexual Knowledge in People with Intellectual Disability," 362.)

43. Alain Giami et al., "Sex Education in Schools Is Insufficient to Support Adolescents in the 21st Century," *Sexual and Relationship Therapy* 21, no. 4 (2006): 485–90.

44. Heather Weaver, Gary Smith, and Susan Kippax, "School-Based Sex Education Policies and Indicators of Sexual Health among Young People: A Comparison of the Netherlands, France, Australia, and the United States," *Sex Education: Sexuality, Society, and Learning* 5, no. 2 (2005): 171–88.

45. Cuskelly and Bryde, "Attitudes towards the Sexuality of Adults with an Intellectual Disability," 261.

46. Cambridge and Mellan, "Reconstructing the Sexuality of Men with Learning Disabilities."

47. Craft and Craft, *Sex Education and Counseling for Mentally Handicapped People.*

48. Christian, Stinson, and Dotson, "Staff Values Regarding the Sexual Expression of Women with Developmental Disabilities," 284.

49. Ibid., 290.

50. Craft and Craft, *Sex Education and Counseling for Mentally Handicapped People,* 46–48. Institutionalization places people into living situations often without their consent. Lack of choice in living situations is another violation of rights for individuals with intellectual disabilities.

51. White, "Sex Education," 139.

52. John D. Allen and Group Rainbow Support, *Gay, Lesbian, Bisexual, and Transgender People with Developmental Disabilities and Mental Retardation: Stories of the Rainbow Support Group* (New York: Harrington Park Press, 2003).

53. Tess Vo and ReachOUT Program, *Our Compass* (North York, Ont.: Griffin Centre, 2009).

54. McCarthy, *Sex Education and the Intellectually Handicapped,* 11.

55. Johnson, "Sex Education of the Mentally Retarded," 59.

56. Rosalyn Kramer Monat-Haller, *Sexuality and the Mentally Retarded: A Clinical and Therapeutic Guidebook* (San Diego: College-Hill Press, 1982), 31. In the sex education session during my fifth-grade year, all the male students

repeatedly asked questions about oral sex because we wanted our teacher to use words like "blow job." He refused to do so, and instead of expanding our understanding about things related to sex and sexuality, our class was generally stalled in our comprehension of sex education and fascinated by the apparent taboos around oral sex and the terminology associated with that activity.

57. Johnson, "Sex Education of the Mentally Retarded."

58. Johnson and Kempton, *Sex Education and Counseling of Special Groups*, 125–31.

59. Lise Shapiro Sanders, "The Failures of the Romance: Boredom, Class, and Desire in George Gissing's *The Odd Women* and W. Somerset Maugham's *Of Human Bondage*," *Modern Fiction Studies* 47, no. 1 (2001): 192.

60. If one of the major goals for sex education activities for people with intellectual disabilities is to facilitate understanding and comprehension of sexuality, then the educator can be encouraged to be more comfortable with the use of idiomatic phrases for terms such as intercourse and fellatio. But a focus on using certain terms to make the education apparently easier to understand is as much about educator ease as it is about educating learners.

61. Fields, *Risky Lessons*, 72.

62. Didier Eribon and Michael Lucey, *Insult and the Making of the Gay Self* (Durham: Duke University Press, 2004); C. J. Pascoe, *Dude, You're a Fag: Masculinity and Sexuality in High School* (Berkeley: University of California Press, 2007).

63. Institute for the Study of Mental Retardation and Related Disabilities and University of Michigan, *What's Dirty in a Word?* (Ann Arbor: University of Michigan Media Resources Center, 1980).

64. *Let My People Come* was an off-Broadway musical that debuted in 1974. It ran until 1980, ending with a brief and ultimately unsuccessful run on Broadway and showings in London, Philadelphia, and Toronto. The title of *What's Dirty in a Word?* comes from a song in the musical, "Dirty Words."

65. In the next chapter I discuss a similar scene from the film *The ABC of Sex Education for Trainables*. See Matt Brecher, *The ABC of Sex Education for Trainables* (Hallmark Films, 1975).

66. John D'Emilio and Estelle B. Freedman, *Intimate Matters: A History of Sexuality in America* (Chicago: University of Chicago Press, 1997), 343–45.

67. Irvine, *Talk about Sex*, 81–90.

68. Henry L. Fischer, Marilyn J. Krajicek, and William A. Borthick, *Sex Education for the Developmentally Disabled: A Guide for Parents, Teachers, and Professionals* (Baltimore: University Park Press, 1973), 1.

69. Ibid., 1.

70. Fields, *Risky Lessons*, 102.

71. Ibid., 103.

72. Rosemarie Garland-Thomson, "Integrating Disability, Transforming Feminist Theory," *NWSA Journal* 14, no. 3 (2002): 1–33; Sherene Razack, *Looking White People in the Eye: Gender, Race, and Culture in Courtrooms and Classrooms* (Toronto: University of Toronto Press, 1998); Sharon L. Snyder and David T. Mitchell, *Cultural Locations of Disability* (Chicago: University of Chicago Press, 2006).

73. Michelle McCarthy, "Sexual Experiences of Women with Learning Difficulties in Long-Stay Hospitals," *Sexuality and Disability* 11, no. 4 (1993): 277–86.

74. White, "Sex Education," 141–42.

75. Ibid., 141.

76. Ibid., 139. The entire quote from White reads, "Ultimately, sex education is about the assimilation of the blind into the heterosexual matrix." While White is speaking about only blind individuals, a similar assessment could be made about how sex education for those with intellectual disabilities is *primarily* a tool that teaches the apparent infallibility and permanence of the categories of male and female and the belief that sexuality ought to be heterosexual and reproductive.

77. Anne Fausto-Sterling, *Sexing the Body: Gender Politics and the Construction of Sexuality* (New York: Basic Books, 2000), 75–76.

78. Nicholas Addison, "The Doll and Pedagogic Mediation: Teaching Children to Fear the 'Other,'" *Sex Education: Sexuality, Society, and Learning* 8, no. 3 (2008): 274.

79. Ibid., 273.

80. Judith Halberstam, *In a Queer Time and Place: Transgender Bodies, Subcultural Lives* (New York: New York University Press, 2005).

81. Leslie Walker-Hirsch, "Six Key Components of a Meaningful Comprehensive Sexuality Education," in *The Facts of Life . . . and More: Sexuality and Intimacy for People with Intellectual Disabilities,* ed. Leslie Walker-Hirsch (Baltimore: Paul H. Brookes, 2007), 45.

82. Mary E. Mohr, "The CIRCLES® Program: Is It Effective in Teaching Social Distance Skills to Mild, Moderate, and Severely Mentally Retarded Adults?" (Ph.D. diss., Shippensburg University, 1991), 8.

83. Walker-Hirsch, "Six Key Components of a Meaningful Comprehensive Sexuality Education," 45–46.

84. Champagne et al., CIRCLES®: *Safer Ways,* 8.

85. Walker-Hirsch, "Six Key Components of a Meaningful Comprehensive Sexuality Education," 45.

86. Ibid.

87. Champagne et al., CIRCLES®: *Safer Ways,* 44–45.

88. Ibid., 3.

89. Kempton and Kahn, "Sexuality and People with Intellectual Disabilities," 108.

90. Champagne et al., CIRCLES®: *Safer Ways*, 3.

91. I appreciate Cynthia Wu helping me think through the limits of directed intimacy and physical contact.

92. Champagne et al., CIRCLES®: *Safer Ways*, 3.

93. Walker-Hirsch, "Six Key Components of a Meaningful Comprehensive Sexuality Education," 46.

94. Ibid.

95. Ibid.; Champagne et al., CIRCLES®: *Safer Ways*, 3.

96. Champagne et al., CIRCLES®: *Safer Ways*, 3.

97. Walker-Hirsch, "Six Key Components of a Meaningful Comprehensive Sexuality Education," 46.

98. Ibid.

99. Champagne et al., CIRCLES®: *Safer Ways*, 3.

100. In the curriculum, gay men are presented, but in ways that do not promote inclusion and diversity. Rather, gay men are seen as promiscuous deviants that transmit HIV. Lesbian sexuality is not represented at all. The particular scene where male same-sex sexuality is addressed is discussed at length later in the chapter.

101. Tim Dean, *Unlimited Intimacy* (Chicago: University of Chicago Press, 2009), 63.

102. Champagne et al., CIRCLES®: *Safer Ways*, 5.

103. Ibid.

104. The irony is that by storing the condom in his wallet, Sam is compromising its effectiveness.

105. Jan Zita Grover, "AIDS: Keywords," *October* 43 (1987): 27.

106. Champagne et al., CIRCLES®: *Safer Ways*, 38.

107. Ibid., 44.

108. Tobin Siebers, *Disability Theory* (Ann Arbor: University of Michigan Press, 2008), 136.

109. Champagne et al., CIRCLES®: *Safer Ways*, 45.

110. Ibid., 47.

111. Ibid., 49.

112. Ibid., 47.

113. Ibid.

114. Grover, "AIDS," 24.

115. Ibid., 28.

116. Champagne et al., CIRCLES®: *Safer Ways*, 49.

117. An earlier story in *Safer Ways*, "Baseball Cards," tells the story of two grade-school-age best friends, Tony and Paul. We learn that Tony was infected

with HIV while receiving a blood transfusion as a baby. This tale teaches the students that casual contact, such as trading baseball cards and using the same restroom, does not place one individual at risk to contract HIV. In "Baseball Cards," Roger continually educates his classmates that it is safe to trade baseball cards and use the same restroom, thus reinforcing, even subtly, that Tony cannot speak for himself and needs a "healthy" spokesperson to educate his peers about HIV/AIDS and what is called "casual contact" (ibid., 26). Unlike Phil and Dan in "Fitness Fever," however, Tony "deserves" our sympathy because he contracted HIV unwillingly, not because of "high-risk activity."

118. Ibid., 49.

119. Ibid., 47.

120. Ibid., 49.

121. Grover, "AIDS," 19–20.

122. Champagne et al., CIRCLES®: *Safer Ways,* 35.

123. The gendered image of a "dangerous, loose woman" has a long cultural history.

124. In Mary Mohr's unpublished thesis about the efficacy of CIRCLES®, in teaching the CIRCLES® program, the author told the intellectually disabled students which person belonged in each of their circles. If the student put an individual in a level that was deemed inappropriate by the author, she corrected them. Mohr, "The CIRCLES® Program," 25–26.

125. As seen in chapter 1, the majority of those who abuse individuals with intellectual disabilities are not strangers, but rather would populate the inner levels of an individual's circle. Partitioning of relationships based on closeness does not always provide protection against abuse and manipulation.

126. Weaver, Smith, and Kippax, "School-Based Sex Education Policies and Indicators of Sexual Health among Young People."

127. Ibid.; Giami et al., "Sex Education in Schools Is Insufficient to Support Adolescents in the 21st Century."

128. Michelle Fine, "Sexuality, Schooling, and Adolescent Females: The Missing Discourse of Desire," *Harvard Educational Review* 58, no. 1 (1988): 33.

129. Susan Sprecher, Gardenia Harris, and Adena Meyers, "Perceptions of Sources of Sex Education and Targets of Sex Communication: Sociodemographic and Cohort Effects," *Journal of Sex Research* 45, no. 1 (2008): 17–26.

130. Fields, *Risky Lessons,* 160.

131. Askew, "Breaking the Taboo."

132. Roger Ingham, "'We Didn't Cover That at School': Education against Pleasure or Education for Pleasure?" *Sex Education* 5, no. 4 (2005): 375–88.

133. Ibid., 381.

134. Fine, "Sexuality, Schooling, and Adolescent Females," 33.

135. Catherine Donovan and Marianne Hester, "'Because She Was My First Girlfriend, I Didn't Know Any Different': Making the Case for Mainstreaming Same-Sex Sex/Relationship Education," *Sex Education: Sexuality, Society, and Learning* 8, no. 3 (2008): 277–87.

3. Sex Can Wait, Masturbate

1. Elissa Down et al., *The Black Balloon* (NeoClassic Films, 2010).
2. L-plates are signs placed inside the front and rear of a car marking that the driver is a "learner." In the film, Thomas is quite keen on learning how to drive, and the birthday present of these signs marks that his parents are recognizing his transition out of childhood and into a period of increased responsibility and potential freedom.
3. Eve Sedgwick, "Jane Austen and the Masturbating Girl," in *Tendencies* (Durham: Duke University Press, 1993), 117–18.
4. Michel Foucault et al., *Abnormal: Lectures at the College de France, 1974–1975* (New York: Picador, 2003), 59.
5. Matt Brecher, *The ABC of Sex Education for Trainables* (Hallmark Films, 1975).
6. Sandra R. Leiblum and Raymond Rosen, *Sexual Desire Disorders* (New York: Guilford, 1988), 1.
7. Dorothy E. Roberts, *Killing the Black Body: Race, Reproduction, and the Meaning of Liberty* (New York: Vintage Books, 1999); Jennifer Nelson, *Women of Color and the Reproductive Rights Movement* (New York: New York University Press, 2003).
8. John D'Emilio and Estelle B. Freedman, *Intimate Matters: A History of Sexuality in America* (Chicago: University of Chicago Press, 1997), 324.
9. Ibid., 327–28.
10. Allison C. Carey, *On the Margins of Citizenship: Intellectual Disability and Civil Rights in Twentieth-Century America* (Philadelphia: Temple University Press, 2009), 134–59.
11. J. William Cook et al., "Use of Contingent Lemon Juice to Eliminate Public Masturbation by a Severely Retarded Boy," *Behaviour Research and Therapy* 16, no. 2 (1978): 131–34; Balázs Tarnai, "Review of Effective Interventions for Socially Inappropriate Masturbation in Persons with Cognitive Disabilities," *Sexuality and Disability* 24, no. 3 (2006): 153.
12. Cook et al., "Use of Contingent Lemon Juice to Eliminate Public Masturbation by a Severely Retarded Boy," 132.
13. Abby Wilkerson, "Disability, Sex Radicalism, and Political Agency," *NWSA Journal* 14, no. 3 (2002): 33–34. Wilkerson quotes Lydia Fegan and Anne Rauch, *Sexuality and People with Intellectual Disability* (Baltimore: P. H. Brookes, 1993), 9.
14. Sedgwick, "Jane Austen and the Masturbating Girl," 112.

15. Arthur Hoerl et al., *Reefer Madness* (20th Century Fox Home Entertainment, 2004). For example, the user-posted comments on the Google Video site for *ABC* include the following: "This *[sic]* people should not reproduce. If possible parents should be able to neutralize *[sic]* them at birth. As soon as they find out the baby is retarded" and "They're teaching them to breed. Good Lord, they must be stopped." Accessed March 2, 2010, at http://video.google.com/videoplay?docid=-2987243478639579087. The comment and link have since been deleted. Other hosted video sites of the film, including on YouTube, have similar ableist comments.

16. Dennis Altman, *Global Sex* (Chicago: University of Chicago Press, 2001).

17. Georgia L. Stevens, Cohen Whiteford, and Video Press, University of Maryland at Baltimore, *Dealing with Sexually Inappropriate Behavior: Masturbation and Sexually Provocative Behavior* (Video Press, University of Maryland, School of Medicine, 1996).

18. Michael Bauer, "Their Only Privacy Is between Their Sheets: Privacy and the Sexuality of Elderly Nursing Home Residents," *Journal of Gerontological Nursing* 25, no. 8 (1999): 37–41; Bonnie L. Walker and Paul H. Ephross, "Knowledge and Attitudes toward Sexuality of a Group of Elderly," *Journal of Gerontological Social Work* 31, nos. 1–2 (1999): 85–107; Thomas Walz, "Crones, Dirty Old Men, Sexy Seniors: Representations of the Sexuality of Older Persons," *Journal of Aging and Identity* 7, no. 2 (2002): 380–84.

19. Bauer, "Their Only Privacy Is between Their Sheets"; Michael Bauer, Rhonda Nay, and Linda McAuliffe, "Catering to Love, Sex, and Intimacy in Residential Aged Care: What Information is Provided to Consumers?," *Sexuality and Disability* 27, no. 1 (2009): 3–9.

20. Rosemarie Garland-Thomson, "Integrating Disability, Transforming Feminist Theory," *NWSA Journal* 14, no. 3 (2002): 1–32; Sherene Razack, *Looking White People in the Eye: Gender, Race, and Culture in Courtrooms and Classrooms* (Toronto: University of Toronto Press, 1998); David Mitchell and Sharon Snyder, "The Eugenic Atlantic: Race, Disability, and the Making of an International Eugenic Science, 1800–1945," *Disability and Society* 18, no. 7 (2003): 843–64; Michael A. Rembis, *Defining Deviance: Sex, Science, and Delinquent Girls, 1890–1960* (Urbana: University of Illinois Press, 2011).

21. Tobin Siebers, *Disability Theory* (Ann Arbor: University of Michigan Press, 2008), 145. Wilkerson also discusses how privacy affects an individual's ability to express his or her sexuality. Abby Wilkerson, "Normate Sex and Its Discontents," in *Sex and Disability*, ed. Robert McRuer and Anna Mollow (Durham: Duke University Press, 2012), 186–87.

22. Examples include Lester Dearborn, "Masturbation," in *Human Autoerotic Practices*, ed. Manfried DeMartino (New York: Human Sciences Press, 1979), 36–53; Frederick E. Kaeser, *Masturbation and the Quality of Life, Health, and Sexual Expression of People with Profound Mental Retardation:*

A Philosophical Study (New York: New York University, School of Education, 1995); Frederick Kaeser, "Developing a Philosophy of Masturbation Training for Persons with Severe or Profound Mental Retardation," *Sexuality and Disability* 14, no. 4 (1996): 295–308; Frederick Kaeser and John O'Neill, "Task Analyzed Masturbation Instruction for a Profoundly Mentally Retarded Adult Male: A Data Based Case Study," *Sexuality and Disability* 8, no. 1 (1987): 17–24; Suzanne Sarnoff and Irving Sarnoff, *Masturbation and Adult Sexuality* (New York: M. Evans, 1979).

23. Foucault et al., *Abnormal,* 55–80.

24. Ibid., 241.

25. Ibid.

26. Havelock Ellis, *Studies in the Psychology of Sex* (New York: Random House, 1940); Denna McGaughey and Richard Tewksbury, "Masturbation," in *Prison Sex: Practice and Policy,* ed. Christopher Hensley (Boulder, Colo.: Lynne Rienner, 2002), 138–39.

27. Brian Zamboni and Isiaah Crawford, "Using Masturbation in Sex Therapy: Relationships Between Masturbation, Sexual Desire, and Sexual Fantasy," in *Masturbation as a Means of Achieving Sexual Health,* ed. Walter Bockting and Eli Coleman (New York: Haworth Press, 2002), 124–25, 138–39.

28. Ibid., 125.

29. Thomas Walter Laqueur, *Solitary Sex: A Cultural History of Masturbation* (New York: Zone Books, 2003), 16.

30. Ibid.

31. Alfred C. Kinsey, Wardell Baxter Pomeroy, and Clyde E. Martin, *Sexual Behavior in the Human Male* (Philadelphia: W. B. Saunders, 1948); Alfred C. Kinsey and Institute for Sex Research, *Sexual Behavior in the Human Female* (Philadelphia: W. B. Saunders, 1953).

32. Shere Hite, *The Hite Report: A Nationwide Study on Female Sexuality* (New York: Macmillan, 1976); Sam Janus and Cynthia L. Janus, *The Janus Report on Sexual Behavior* (New York: Wiley, 1993).

33. Robert T. Michael et al., *Sex in America: A Definite Survey* (New York: Little, Brown, 1994).

34. Alan Soble, *Sexual Investigations* (New York: New York University Press, 1996). Quoted from McGaughey and Tewksbury, "Masturbation," 60.

35. Margrit Shildrick, "Contested Pleasures: The Sociopolitical Economy of Disability and Sexuality," *Sexuality Research and Social Policy* 4, no. 1 (2007): 56.

36. Ibid., 57, 64.

37. Ibid., 64.

38. David Batty, "Prisoner Found Guilty of Masturbating in His Cell," *The Guardian,* July 26, 2007, http://www.guardian.co.uk/world/2007/jul/26/usa.davidbatty6.

39. Christopher Hensley, Richard Tewksbury, and Jeremy Wright, "Exploring the Dynamics of Masturbation and Consensual Same-Sex Activity within a Male Maximum Security Prison," *Journal of Men's Studies* 10, no. 1 (2001): 66.

40. Ibid., 68–69.

41. Ibid., 69–70.

42. Christopher Hensley, Richard Tewksbury, and Mary Koscheski, "Masturbation Uncovered: Autoeroticism in a Female Prison," *Prison Journal* 81, no. 4 (2001): 496, 499.

43. Ibid., 499.

44. Ibid.

45. There is a significant amount of research done on sexuality and sexual practices in prison. Hopper traces out a program that allows conjugal visits between married couples. See Columbus B. Hopper, *Sex in Prison: The Mississippi Experiment with Conjugal Visiting* (Baton Rouge: Louisiana State University Press, 1969). The rationale for the program is that inmates who have opportunities for conjugal visits have lower rates of recidivism than those who are not. Opportunity for sex supposedly reduces problem behaviors; a similar rationale is expressed regarding teaching some individuals with intellectual disabilities how to masturbate in order to reduce behavioral issues. Conjugal visits, however, are not widely adopted throughout the United States, due in part to expanding prison populations and the prison industrial complex. Mary Bosworth makes the argument that female prisoners participate in lesbian sexual relationships even if they do not identify as lesbians outside the walls of the prison: "Lesbian and homosexual relations in prison can be understood as strategies of resistance not only to the pains of imprisonment as traditional sociologists would have us believe, but also to constructions of gender put forward by the institutions themselves." Mary Bosworth, "Gender, Race, and Sexuality in Prison," in *Women in Prison: Gender and Social Control,* ed. Barbara Zaitzow and Jim Thomas (Boulder, Colo.: Lynne Rienner, 2003), 150. Scholars argue that the institutional nature of the prison restricts and encourages different expressions of sexuality based on notions of gender and appropriateness. Early research on sexuality, including work done by sexologist Havelock Ellis and researcher Joseph Fulling Fishman, took on an alarmist tone when predicting the number of homosexuals in prison. While Ellis estimates that 20 percent of male prisoners are in homosexual relationships, even if not entirely physical, Fishman estimates the number at close to 80 percent. Ellis, *Studies in the Psychology of Sex*; Joseph Fulling Fishman, *Sex in Prison: Revealing Sex Conditions in American Prisons* (New York: National Library Press, 1934). Fishman even goes on to study individuals who came to the prison already identifying as gay and those who "became gay" while in prison, thus further pointing to

the ways in which certain types of sexuality are feared for the inmates. Currently only four states allow conjugal visits for their prisoners in the United States. Christopher Hensley, "What We Learned from Studying Prison Sex," *Humanity and Society* 24, no. 4 (2000): 348–60. California and New York allow conjugal visits for same-sex partners that are married or in registered domestic partnerships.

46. When it comes to individuals with intellectual disability, Kaeser reports that masturbation is the most common form of sexual expression, despite being a behavior generally not approved of by staff members. Kaeser, "Developing a Philosophy of Masturbation Training for Persons with Severe or Profound Mental Retardation," 295. Fegan and Rauch contend that masturbation is harmless and potentially beneficial for people with intellectual disabilities. Fegan and Rauch, *Sexuality and People with Intellectual Disability,* 23.

47. Anthony Walsh, "Improve and Care: Responding to Inappropriate Masturbation in People with Severe Intellectual Disabilities," *Sexuality and Disability* 18, no. 1 (2000): 27–39.

48. Paul Cambridge, Steven Carnaby, and Michelle McCarthy, "Responding to Masturbation in Supporting Sexuality and Challenging Behaviour in Services for People with Learning Disabilities," *Journal of Learning Disabilities* 7, no. 3 (2003): 252.

49. Kaeser and O'Neill, "Task Analyzed Masturbation Instruction for a Profoundly Mentally Retarded Adult Male"; Tarnai, "Review of Effective Interventions for Socially Inappropriate Masturbation in Persons with Cognitive Disabilities."

50. McGaughey and Tewksbury, "Masturbation," 135.

51. D'Emilio and Freedman, *Intimate Matters,* 356.

52. McGaughey and Tewksbury, "Masturbation," 133, 139. In the reductive framework, sexual activities regardless of the type are considered to spread disease.

53. Jean Stengers and Anne van Neck, *Masturbation: The History of a Great Terror* (New York: Palgrave, 2001).

54. There is limited research on the rate of sexually transmitted infection for people with intellectual disabilities. Henny M. J. van Schrojenstein Lantman-De Valk et al., in "Health Problems in People with Intellectual Disability in General Practice: A Comparative Study," *Family Practice* 17, no. 5 (2000): 405–7, report a higher than average rate of sexually transmitted infections for men with intellectual disabilities in their research cohort, linking the lack of sexual hygiene as the reason for the increase. There is a clear need for prevalence studies on HIV and other sexually transmitted infections in the intellectually disabled community.

55. Cambridge, Carnaby, and McCarthy, "Responding to Masturbation in

Supporting Sexuality and Challenging Behaviour in Services for People with Learning Disabilities," 261.

56. Beatrice "Bean" E. Robinson, Walter O. Bockting, and Teresa Harrell, "Masturbation and Sexual Health: An Exploratory Study of Low Income African American Women," in *Masturbation as a Means of Achieving Sexual Health*, ed. Walter Bockting and Eli Coleman (New York: Haworth Press, 2002), 85–102; Steven D. Pinkerton et al., "Factors Associated with Masturbation in a Collegiate Sample," in *Masturbation as a Means for Achieving Sexual Health*, ed. Walter Bockting and Eli Coleman (New York: Haworth Press, 2002), 103–22.

57. Robinson, Bockting, and Harrell, "Masturbation and Sexual Health," 97. Masturbation promotion can be used to "cure" hypoactive sexual desire disorder, but too much masturbation might place an individual at risk of HIV, where masturbation is constructed to increase sexual drive, which in turn is assumed to lead to more "unsafe" sexual practices—a complicated equation of sexuality and safety indeed.

58. Ibid., 97; Y. J. Choi et al., "Masturbation and Its Relationship to Sexual Activities of Young Males in Korean Military Service," *Yonsei Medical Journal* 41, no. 2 (2000): 205–8; J. Kenneth Davidson, "Autoeroticism, Sexual Satisfaction, and Sexual Adjustment Among University Females: Past and Current Patterns," *Deviant Behavior* 5, nos. 1–4 (1984): 121–40; J. Kenneth Davidson and Nelwyn B. Moore, "Masturbation and Premarital Sexual Intercourse among College Women: Making Choices for Sexual Fulfillment," *Journal of Sex and Marital Therapy* 20 no. 3 (1994): 178–99.

59. Davidson and Moore, "Masturbation and Premarital Sexual Intercourse among College Women"; Robinson, Bockting, and Harrell, "Masturbation and Sexual Health," 97.

60. Pinkerton et al., "Factors Associated with Masturbation in a Collegiate Sample," 118.

61. Ibid.

62. Zamboni and Crawford, "Using Masturbation in Sex Therapy."

63. Lonnie Garfield Barbach, *For Yourself: The Fulfillment of Female Sexuality* (New York: Anchor Press/Doubleday, 1976); Eli Coleman, "Masturbation as a Means of Achieving Sexual Health," in *Masturbation as a Means of Achieving Sexual Health*, ed. Walter Bockting and Eli Coleman (New York: Haworth Press, 2002), 5–16; Betty Dodson, *Sex for One: The Joy of Selfloving* (New York: Crown, 1987); World Association for Sexology, "Declaration of Sexual Rights," http://www.worldsexology.org/resources.

64. In the words of Surgeon General of the United States Joycelyn Elders in 1994, "Masturbation is part of human sexuality, and it's a part of something that perhaps should be taught. But we have not even taught our children the basics. And I feel that we have tried ignorance for a long time and its time we

try education." Joycelyn Elders, "Address to the World AIDS Day Conference at the United Nations," ACT UP New York, http://www.actupny.org/reports/elders.html. Cited in Coleman, "Masturbation as a Means of Achieving Sexual Health," 13. The background of Elders's words is that masturbation could be an effective way to reduce HIV/AIDS while still expressing human sexuality. Her comments in front of the United Nations resulted in almost immediate disapproval from the Clinton administration and ultimately caused her removal from the position of Surgeon General because the Clinton administration disagreed with her views on the utility of masturbation as well as other issues. On an episode of the television program *Penn & Teller: Bullshit!* Elders remarked, "I am against abstinence programs because I consider abstinence only to be child abuse." Star Prince, Scott Firestone, and Chip Selby, "Abstinence," in *Penn & Teller: Bullshit!* (2006).

65. Of course pornography shows both men and women masturbating in front of the camera, both individually and in groups. Additionally, pornography is used as a tool to facilitate masturbation. The association between masturbation and pornography is perhaps one reason why masturbation is not discussed in the United States.

66. Laqueur, *Solitary Sex,* 413.

67. Nelson, *Women of Color and the Reproductive Rights Movement.*

68. Ibid., 113–32.

69. Kaeser, "Developing a Philosophy of Masturbation Training for Persons with Severe or Profound Mental Retardation."

70. Siebers, *Disability Theory,* 162.

71. Ibid., 162–63.

72. Cambridge, Carnaby, and McCarthy, "Responding to Masturbation in Supporting Sexuality and Challenging Behaviour in Services for People with Learning Disabilities," 261.

73. Loree Erickson's short film *Want* (Femmegimp, 2005) provocatively explores the relationship between personal assistance and facilitated sexuality. The documentary *Scarlet Road* describes sex worker Rachel Wotton and her work specifically for disabled individuals. Catherine Scott et al., *Scarlet Road* (Women Make Movies, 2011). These films can assist dialogue around important issues related to sexuality, disability, agency, and care.

74. Margrit Shildrick, *Dangerous Discourses of Disability, Subjectivity, and Sexuality* (New York: Palgrave Macmillan, 2009), 70–71.

75. Fegan and Rauch, *Sexuality and People with Intellectual Disability,* 26–30.

76. Cambridge, Carnaby, and McCarthy, "Responding to Masturbation in Supporting Sexuality and Challenging Behaviour in Services for People with Learning Disabilities," 259.

77. Fegan and Rauch, *Sexuality and People with Intellectual Disability,* 28.

78. Siebers, *Disability Theory,* 163.

79. New South Wales Family Planning, *About Masturbation: For People with an Intellectual Disability: For Males* (Ashfield, N.S.W.: Family Planning N.S.W., 2007); Neil Smith and New South Wales Family Planning, *About Masturbation: For People with an Intellectual Disability: For Females* (Ashfield, N.S.W.: Family Planning N.S.W., 2011).

4. Reproductive Intrusions

1. Katie Watson, "Cut to the Chase: Should Kristen Johnson Be Allowed to Have Kids?" *Chicago Sun-Times,* August 21, 2005.

2. Ibid.

3. *Estate of K.E.J., a Disabled Person,* Judge Joseph Gordon (2008), 2.

4. Ibid., 2, 5.

5. Ibid., 29.

6. Ibid., 28.

7. Ibid., 9.

8. Michael Higgins, "Court Denies Bid to Sterilize Mentally Disabled Woman," *Chicago Tribune,* April 19, 2008.

9. *Estate of K.E.J., a Disabled Person,* 28.

10. I appreciate Alison Kafer and Robert McRuer helping me think through these complex issues here and in other places in the chapter.

11. Katie Watson, "Brief of Amici Curiae Bioethicists in Support of Respondent Appellant K.E.J.," Medical Humanities and Bioethics Program (Chicago: Northwestern University, 2007), 1.

12. Ibid., 2.

13. Ibid.

14. Ibid. "Best interest standard" refers to surrogate decision making, where an individuals' desires or wishes are unknown or where that individual is deemed incompetent, thus requiring another person to make a decision "in their best interests."

15. *Skinner v. Oklahoma* ruled that compulsory sterilization could not be imposed as a punishment for a crime.

16. *Estate of K.E.J., a Disabled Person,* 14.

17. Ibid., 14.

18. Watson, "Cut to the Chase."

19. AmberFRIDA, "Disability Presence at the Johnson Ruling Thursday, January 5," http://fridanow.blogspot.com/2006/01/disability-presence-at-johnson-ruling.html#links.

20. Michael Higgins, "Guardian Sues to Sterilize Her Niece: A Mentally Disabled 26-Year-Old Wins Stay on Forced Surgery," *Chicago Tribune,* August 12, 2005.

21. Ibid.

22. Tim Booth and Wendy Booth, *Parenting under Pressure: Mothers and Fathers with Learning Difficulties* (Philadelphia: Open University Press, 1994); Tim Booth and Wendy Booth, "Self-Advocacy and Supported Learning for Mothers with Learning Difficulties," *Journal of Learning Disabilities* 7, no. 2 (2003): 471–85; Tim Booth and Wendy Booth, "Parents with Learning Difficulties in the Child Protection System," *Journal of Intellectual Disabilities* 9, no. 2 (2005): 109–29; Tim Booth and Wendy Booth, "Men in the Lives of Mothers with Intellectual Disabilities," *Journal of Applied Research in Intellectual Disabilities* 15, no. 3 (2002): 187–99; Susan Collings and Gwynnyth Llewellyn, "Children of Parents with Intellectual Disability: Facing Poor Outcomes or Faring Okay?" *Journal of Intellectual and Developmental Disability* 37, no. 1 (2012): 65–82; Rachel Mayes and Gwynnyth Llewellyn, "Mothering Differently: Narratives of Mothers with Intellectual Disability Whose Children Have Been Compulsorily Removed," *Journal of Intellectual and Developmental Disability* 37, no. 2 (2012): 121–30; Gwynnyth Llewellyn, "People with Intellectual Disability as Parents: Perspectives from the Professional Literature," *Journal of Intellectual and Developmental Disability* 16, no. 4 (1990): 369–80; Gwynnyth Llewellyn, "Talking with Parents with Intellectual Disability," in *Does This Child Need Help? Identification and Early Intervention,* ed. Christine Johnson (Sydney: Australian Early Intervention Association, 1993), 162–69; Barbara Y. Whitman, Betty Graves, and Pasquale J. Accardo, "Training in Parenting Skills for Adults with Mental Retardation," *Social Work* 34, no. 5 (1989): 431–34; Linda Dowdney and David Skuse, "Parenting Provided by Adults with Mental Retardation," *Journal of Child Psychology and Psychiatry* 34, no. 1 (1993): 25–47.

23. Margrit Shildrick, *Dangerous Discourses of Disability, Subjectivity, and Sexuality* (New York: Palgrave Macmillan, 2009), 64.

24. The use of "retarded persons" reflects a historical moment before the widespread use of "intellectual disability," "developmental disability," and other less ableist terms. I have reproduced the title of the declaration but am aware of, and support, efforts to ban the "R word." Spread the Word to End the Word is a campaign to encourage people to stop using "retarded," removing the term from laws and official documents, and raise awareness of the hurtful and hateful effects of its usage.

25. United Nations General Assembly, "Declaration on the Rights of Mentally Retarded Persons," Office of the United Nations High Commissioner for Human Rights Website, http://www.ohchr.org/EN/ProfessionalInterest/Pages/RightsOfMentallyRetardedPersons.aspx.

26. Ibid.

27. Ibid.

28. National Council on Disability, "White Paper: Understanding the Role

of an International Convention on the Human Rights of People with Disabilities" (Washington, D.C.: National Council on Disability, 2002), 25–26.

29. United Nations General Assembly, "Declaration on the Rights of Disabled Persons," Office of the United Nations High Commissioner for Human Rights, http://www.ohchr.org/EN/ProfessionalInterest/Pages/RightsOfDisabled Persons.aspx.

30. Allison C. Carey, *On the Margins of Citizenship: Intellectual Disability and Civil Rights in Twentieth-Century America* (Philadelphia: Temple University Press, 2009), 134–59.

31. Janet Lord, "Disability Rights and the Human Rights Mainstream: Reluctant Gate-Crashers?" in *The International Struggle for New Human Rights,* ed. Bob Clifford (Philadelphia: University of Pennsylvania Press, 2009), 86.

32. Lee was one of the original drafters of the 1971 UN declaration. It becomes clear that the language of limiting rights set forth in the 1971 declaration is carried forth in his later statement on sexuality and reproduction.

33. George Lee, "An International Point of View," in George William Lee and Gregor Katz, *Sexual Rights of the Retarded: Two Papers Reflecting the International Point of View* (London: National Society for Mentally Handicapped Children, 1974), 8.

34. Ibid.

35. Some examples include David May and Murray K. Simpson, "The Parent Trap: Marriage, Parenthood, and Adulthood for People with Intellectual Disabilities," *Critical Social Policy* 23, no. 1 (2003): 25–43; Susan Parish, "Parenting," in *Health of Women with Intellectual Disabilities,* ed. Patricia Noonan Walsh and Tamar Heller (Oxford: Blackwell, 2002), 103–20; Wendy Booth and Tim Booth, "A Family at Risk: Multiple Perspectives on Parenting and Child Protection," *British Journal of Learning Disabilities* 32, no. 1 (2004): 9–15; Booth and Booth, *Parenting under Pressure*; Catherine Wade, Gwynnyth Llewellyn, and Jan Matthews, "Review of Parent Training Interventions for Parents with Intellectual Disability," *Journal of Applied Research in Intellectual Disabilities* 21, no. 4 (2008): 351–66; David McConnell and Gwynnyth Llewellyn, "Stereotypes, Parents with Intellectual Disability and Child Protection," *Journal of Social Welfare and Family Law* 24, no. 3 (2002): 1–21.

36. Lord, "Disability Rights and the Human Rights Mainstream," 91.

37. United Nations General Assembly, "Convention on the Rights of Persons with Disabilities," United Nations Enable, http://www.un.org/disabilities/documents/convention/convoptprot-e.pdf.

38. Ibid.

39. Including the important work of Adrienne Asch, "Prenatal Diagnosis and Selective Abortion: A Challenge to Practice and Policy," *American Journal of Public Health* 89, no. 11 (1999): 1649–57; Anne Finger, *Past Due: A Story*

of Disability, Pregnancy, and Birth (Seattle: Seal Press, 1990); Erik Parens and Adrienne Asch, *Prenatal Testing and Disability Rights* (Washington, D.C.: Georgetown University Press, 2000); Erik Parens and Adrienne Asch, "Special Supplement: The Disability Rights Critique of Prenatal Genetic Testing Reflections and Recommendations," *Hastings Center Report* 29, no. 5 (1999): S1–S22; Marsha Saxton, "Why Members of the Disability Community Oppose Prenatal Diagnosis and Selective Abortion," in *Prenatal Testing and Disability Rights*, ed. Erik Parens and Adrienne Asch (Washington, D.C.: Georgetown University Press, 2000), 147–64; Shelley Tremain, "Reproductive Freedom, Self-Regulation, and the Government of Impairment in Utero," *Hypatia* 21, no. 1 (2006): 35–43; Dorothy Roberts, "Race, Gender, and Genetic Technologies: A New Reproductive Dystopia?" *Signs* 34, no. 4 (2009): 783–804; Dorothy Roberts, *Killing the Black Body* (New York: Vintage Books, 1999).

40. Carey, *On the Margins of Citizenship*, 217.

41. Ibid., 219.

42. Ibid., 33.

43. Ibid.

44. Ibid.

45. Licia Carlson, "Cognitive Ableism and Disability Studies: Feminist Reflections on the History of Mental Retardation," *Hypatia* 16, no. 4 (2001): 124–46.

46. Parish, "Parenting," 113.

47. Ibid.

48. National Council on Disability, "Rocking the Cradle: Ensuring the Rights of Parents with Disabilities and Their Children" (Washington, D.C.: National Council on Disability, 2012).

49. See http://www.lookingglass.org/. The mission of the organization reads, "To create, demonstrate, and encourage non-pathological and empowering resources and model early intervention services for families with disability issues in parent or child which integrate expertise derived from personal disability experience and disability culture."

50. Parish, "Parenting," 113. See Robert L. Hayman Jr., "Presumptions of Justice: Law, Politics, and the Mentally Retarded Parent," *Harvard Law Review* 103, no. 6 (1990): 1207–72.

51. Michael Noonan and Rebecca Richardson, *Unlikely Travellers* (Accent Film Entertainment, 2008). His PhD thesis included a feature-length film, *Down Under Mystery Tour*. In the film, a television director with an intellectual disability, Malcolm (Malcolm Bebb), who is more interested in sexually objectifying women, is forced to use two actors with intellectual disabilities, Darren (Darren Magee) and James (James Bradley). Malcolm attempts to force Darren and James off his set. The film was co-written by Noonan and the three actors with intellectual disabilities. The controversy around

the film was about whether Noonan objectified disabled individuals or participated with them in collaboration. Assumptions about naïveté, morality, and intellectual disability were used in the allegations against Noonan. All three actors featured in *Down Under Mystery Tour* also appear in *Unlikely Travellers,* thus illustrating Noonan's long-term relationship with these men. Noonan has written about the controversy in an article. See Michael Noonan, "Managing Manipulation: Tools and Challenges in Creative Collaborations with Intellectually Disabled People," *Disability and Society* 27, no. 7 (2012): 997–1009.

52. Noonan and Rebecca Richardson, *Unlikely Travellers.*

53. In the narrative of the film, it is unclear how often Stanley is able to visit his children. While being interviewed in his apartment, Stanley shows the camera a toy car he purchased for his son, Andy. Also, all the pictures of his children are from when they were quite young, further indicating that Stanley has not had frequent interactions with his children or received any recent pictures of them.

54. While Natasha doesn't want to rush into a physical relationship, Stanley seems quite adamant that their relationship develop into one. At one point in the documentary, the camera shows, in a long shot, Stanley and Natasha in an embrace signifying their increasingly physical relationship. John Hart, the director of the agency that organized the trip, says that he is worried Natasha and Stanley's relationship will become sexual. This coupling is in contrast with another budding relationship between two other travelers, Darren and Carla. While Carla and Darren's nonsexual relationship is presented as naïve and cute, Stanley's sexual desire seems to threaten the cohesiveness of the group.

55. Even though Stanley's lack of welcome is the exception at the airport, many individuals with intellectual disabilities are isolated or estranged from their birth parents and siblings, often because of placement in institutions, group homes, or other residential facilities.

56. Booth and Booth, "Men in the Lives of Mothers with Intellectual Disabilities," 188.

57. Ibid.

58. Llewellyn, "People with Intellectual Disability as Parents," 376.

59. Booth and Booth, "Men in the Lives of Mothers with Intellectual Disabilities," 197–98. They write, "These skills were many and varied—literacy and numeracy, street savvy, the ability to drive, do-it-yourself expertise, the confidence to deal with public officials, money management, another pair of hands with the children, and so on. Where partners brought complementary skills to the relationship—skills that supplemented rather than duplicated those already possessed by the mother—the resultant net addition to human capital increase the adaptive capacity of the family" (197).

60. Tanya Titchkosky, *The Question of Access: Disability, Space, Meaning* (Toronto: University of Toronto Press, 2011), 15.

61. Ibid., 16.

62. Ibid., 16–17.

63. Ibid., 17. Titchkosky writes, "Under modern conditions of global capitalism, where disability is consistently regarded as a problem, a politics of wonder can help dissuade us from a tyranny of containment that is achieved by current domination knowledge regimes and through which devastating control is held" (18).

64. Bryan S. Turner, *Vulnerability and Human Rights* (University Park: Pennsylvania State University Press, 2006), 105–6.

65. Tobin Siebers, *Disability Theory* (Ann Arbor: University of Michigan Press, 2008). Wilkerson makes a similar observation. Abby Wilkerson, "Disability, Sex Radicalism, and Political Agency," *NWSA Journal* 14, no. 3 (2002): 33–57.

66. David L. Eng, *The Feeling of Kinship: Queer Liberalism and the Racialization of Intimacy* (Durham: Duke University Press, 2010), 47. I do not know how K.E.J. racially self-identifies. Stanley is white. Others interpret both Stanley's and K.E.J.'s disabilities, including professional staff, as allowing intervention and intrusion of privacy.

67. Ibid.

68. Ibid., 101.

69. Judith Halberstam, *The Queer Art of Failure* (Durham: Duke University Press, 2011), 71.

70. Watson, "Cut to the Chase."

5. Not Just an Able-Bodied Privilege

1. Rickie Solinger, "Is Motherhood a Class Privilege in America?" http://www.mothersmovement.org/features/solinger/solinger_p1.htm.

2. Ibid.

3. As I explain below, "Jasmine's World" is primarily focused on Jasmine's experiences of having two disabled parents. In addition, within the "Beggars and Choosers" space there are other representations of disabled parenting, including mothers who use wheelchairs.

4. Rosemarie Garland-Thomson, "Misfits: A Feminist Materialist Disability Concept," *Hypatia* 26, no. 3 (2011): 592. Garland-Thomson writes that the potential to misfit "emphasizes the peculiarity of varying lived embodiments" as a "shifting spatial and perpetually temporal relationship [that] confers agency and value on disabled subjects at risk of social devaluation by highlighting adaptability, resourcefulness, and subjugated knowledge as potential effects of misfitting."

5. The letter is a response to a series of events. The 2010 Nobel Prize in

Medicine recipient, Dr. Robert Edwards, promotes the use of reproductive assistive technologies to prevent the birth of disabled children. British journalist Virginia Ironside commented that giving birth to a disabled child was "cruel" and a disabled child should be euthanized as a sign of compassion. Generations Ahead, "Robert Edwards, Virginia Ironside, and the Unnecessary Opposition of Rights," http://www.generations-ahead.org/resources/the-unnecessary-opposition-of-rights.

6. Ibid.

7. Alison Kafer, *Feminist, Queer, Crip* (Bloomington: Indiana University Press, 2013), 167.

8. Ibid., 167–68.

9. Men with intellectual disabilities are largely excluded from the category of "appropriate parent," but most often women with intellectual disabilities are targeted as not being able to reproduce and parent. Eugenic histories of forced sterilization and institutionalization are a significant part of this trend. In this chapter, I am specifically referring to women with intellectual disabilities, but an analysis that excludes men with intellectual disabilities can further segment and jeopardize coalitional politics.

10. See, for example, Lee Edelman, *No Future: Queer Theory and the Death Drive* (Durham: Duke University Press, 2004). Edelman critiques the move to secure family and reproductive rights for LGBT individuals as too normative or distancing from the potential of queerness. "Indeed, at the heart of my polemical engagement with the cultural text of politics and the politics of cultural texts lies a simple provocation: that *queerness* names the side of those *not* 'fighting for the children,' the side outside the consensus by which all politics confirms the absolute value of reproductive futurism. The ups and downs of political fortune may measure the social order's pulse, but *queerness,* by contrast, figures, outside and beyond its political symptoms, the place of the social order's death drive: a place, to be sure, of abjection expressed in the stigma, sometimes fatal, that follows from reading that figure literally, and hence a place from which liberal politics strives—and strives quite reasonably, given its unlimited faith in reason—to disassociate the queer" (3). Anna Mollow has begun the important work of a critical disability studies theory reading of Edelman's work. See Mollow, "Is Sex Disability? Queer Theory and the Disability Drive," in *Sex and Disability,* ed. Robert McRuer and Anna Mollow (Durham: Duke University Press, 2012), 285–312. Mollow writes, "I therefore read *No Future* not as advocating that goals such as gay marriage or accessible workplaces be surrendered, but rather as insisting that the work of queer theory—and, I propose here, of disability theory—is also to unsettle the assumptions that underlie these goals. *No Future* issues a troubling challenge: can we envision a politics not framed in terms of futurism or a futurity not grounded in reproductive (or, I ask here, rehabilitative) ideology? Insofar

as reproductive (and perhaps also rehabilitative) futurism seem invariably to give shape to 'the only politics we're permitted to know,' Edelman's refusal of the political cannot easily be dismissed" (291).

11. José Esteban Muñoz, *Cruising Utopia: The Then and There of Queer Futurity* (New York: New York University Press, 2009), 11.

12. I appreciate Alison Kafer's assistance and encouragement in thinking through these issues.

13. Reproductive justice work might only make passing reference to disability; likewise, disability studies might not adequately consider the racial, ethnic, or class-based experiences of disablement or ableism. Queer theory might not attend to the disabled subject as a queer one, while some disability theories might distance themselves from their partners in queer theory. Finally, the claims of reproductive justice seem to be at odds with those of some segments of queer theory, especially regarding the centrality (or not) of reproduction. Kafer writes, "In fact, I think reproductive justice frameworks offer the possibility not only of cross-movement analysis that fully integrate disability, but also of fuller *cross-disability* analyses. Physical disabilities and intellectual disabilities are often construed differently in debates over prenatal testing and selective abortion, and disability movements need to acknowledge (even as we interrogate) those distinctions" (*Feminist, Queer, Crip*, 162). My intent is to foster these analyses by forwarding intellectual disability as a subjectivity that often gets overlooked in the aforementioned theoretical subjectivities.

14. Dorothy E. Roberts, *Killing the Black Body: Race, Reproduction, and the Meaning of Liberty* (New York: Vintage Books, 1999), 69.

15. David Mitchell and Sharon Snyder, "The Eugenic Atlantic: Race, Disability, and the Making of an International Eugenic Science, 1800–1945," *Disability and Society* 18, no. 7 (2003): 843–64; Roberts, *Killing the Black Body*; Michael A. Rembis, *Defining Deviance: Sex, Science, and Delinquent Girls, 1890–1960* (Urbana: University of Illinois Press, 2011).

16. Roberts, *Killing the Black Body*, 69.

17. See Jennifer Nelson, *Women of Color and the Reproductive Rights Movement* (New York: New York University Press, 2003); Elena R. Gutiérrez, *Fertile Matters: The Politics of Mexican-Origin Women's Reproduction* (Austin: University of Texas Press, 2008); Roberts, *Killing the Black Body*; Jael Miriam, Fried Silliman, Marlene Gerber Fried, Loretta Ross, and Elena Gutiérrez, *Undivided Rights: Women of Color Organize for Reproductive Justice* (Cambridge, Mass.: South End Press, 2004).

18. See Michelle McCarthy, "Whose Body Is It Anyway? Pressures and Control for Women with Learning Disabilities," *Disability and Society* 13, no. 4 (1998): 557–74; Winifred Kempton and Emily Kahn, "Sexuality and People with Intellectual Disabilities: A Historical Perspective," *Sexuality*

and Disability 9, no. 2 (1991): 93–111; Susan Parish, "Parenting," in *Health of Women with Intellectual Disabilities,* ed. Patricia Noonan Walsh and Tamar Heller (Oxford: Blackwell, 2002).

19. Charis Thompson, *Making Parents: The Ontological Choreography of Reproductive Technologies* (Cambridge: MIT Press, 2005).

20. These children are often disabled as well. There are long-standing critiques of transnational adoption, which can replay colonial narratives by using the whiteness (and citizenship status) of the parents. Racial, ethnic, class, and disability status are deployed to label certain children as needing "saving." See Laura Briggs, *Somebody's Children: The Politics of Transnational and Transracial Adoption* (Durham: Duke University Press, 2012); Laura Briggs and Diana Marre, *International Adoption: Global Inequalities and the Circulation of Children* (New York: New York University Press, 2009); Twila L. Perry, "The Transracial Adoption Controversy: An Analysis of Discourse and Subordination," *NYU Review of Law and Social Change* 21 (1993): 33–108; Twila L. Perry, "Transracial and International Adoption: Mothers, Hierarchy, Race, and Feminist Legal Theory," *Yale Journal of Law and Feminism* 10 (1998): 101–45; Dorothy Roberts, "Feminism, Race, and Adoption Policy," in *Color of Violence: The INCITE! Anthology,* ed. INCITE! Women of Color against Violence (Cambridge, Mass.: South End Press, 2006), 42–52.

21. Rickie Solinger, "Beggars and Choosers: Motherhood Is Not a Class Privilege in America," *Labor History* 43, no. 4 (2002): 413.

22. Rayna Rapp, *Testing Women, Testing the Fetus: The Social Impact of Amniocentesis in America* (New York: Routledge, 1999).

23. Dorothy Roberts, "Race, Gender, and Genetic Technologies: A New Reproductive Dystopia?" *Signs* 34, no. 4 (2009): 785.

24. Ibid., 799.

25. Ruby C. Tapia, "Race, Class, and the Photopolitics of Maternal Revision in Rickie Solinger's 'Beggars and Choosers,'" *Feminist Studies* 36, no. 2 (2010): 386.

26. Suleman, who came to international attention when she gave birth to octuplets in January 2009, is also known colloquially by the offensive moniker "Octomom."

27. See http://www.nancypastor.com/, accessed June 30, 2012. Notice the language of "normalcy" and "extraordinary" in the description by Pastor. Rosemarie Garland-Thomson, in *Extraordinary Bodies: Figuring Physical Disability in American Culture and Literature* (New York: Columbia University Press, 1997), explores how concepts like "normalcy" and "extraordinary" mark disabled bodies as seemingly freakish and deviant. While Pastor is not invoking the history of the freak show in her comment, Jasmine is still positioned against an environment labeled "abnormal" and "extraordinary." In framing the series about Jasmine and not her parents, Pastor is clearly

demarcating intellectually disabled parenting as potentially disruptive and *disabling* to Jasmine. This is the narrative I am trying to interrupt in this chapter.

28. In an e-mail exchange with Pastor, she let me know that she met the family in 1996 as part of a five-day photojournalism workshop. The family became the subject of her class. Pastor remarked that she was so captivated by the family that she kept in touch with them throughout the years.

29. This sling covers her arm in six of the twenty pictures in the collection.

30. In chapter 4, I discuss at length fathers with intellectual disabilities. There is a dearth of narratives or research that examine the experiences of fathers with intellectual disabilities.

31. Garland-Thomson, "Misfits," 592.

32. Ibid., 594.

33. Ibid., 601.

34. Ibid., 593.

35. Ibid.

36. She writes, "Misfitting, I would argue, ignites a vivid recognition of our fleshliness, and the contingencies of human embodiment" (ibid., 597–98). While intellectual disability is most often an embodied experience, the mind/body dualist split seems to mark intellectual disability as a condition of the mind, read through intelligence and inability to adapt, not necessarily by managing inaccessible physical spaces. This ableist interpretation of intellectual disability can further isolate individuals from larger disability communities.

37. Ibid., 597.

38. Michel Foucault et al., *Society Must Be Defended: Lectures at the Collège de France, 1975–76* (New York: Picador, 2003), 7. Foucault uses psychiatry as an example of a system that subjugates knowledge of those labeled "ill" and in need of treatment. He later connects this subjugation of the "mad" and control of childhood masturbation as expressions of the bourgeois system of power and repression (ibid., 23–40). In a subsequent lecture he questions, "What happens at the moment of, at the level of the procedure of subjugation, or in the continuous and uninterrupted processes that subjugate bodies, direct gestures, and regulate forms of behavior?" (ibid., 28).

39. In chapter 2 I discuss how notions of competence are limiting in constructing individuals with intellectual disabilities as supposedly unable to lead self-determining lives.

40. Foucault et al., *Society Must Be Defended*, 10.

41. In their introduction to *Strange Affinities*, Grace Kyungwon Hong and Roderick Ferguson write, "Women of color feminism and queer of color critique profoundly question nationalist and identitarian modes of political or-

ganization and craft alternative understandings of subjectivity, collectivity, and power . . . Women of color feminism and queer of color critique reveal the ways in which racialized communities are not homogeneous but instead have always policed and preserved the difference between those who are able to conform to categories of normativity, respectability, and value, and those who are forcibly excluded from such categories. As we argue, such a comparative method is immensely important in the current moment, as neoliberal modes of power rely on such valuations to subject the racialized poor to brutal violence *through* rhetorics of individual freedom and responsibility." Hong and Ferguson, *Strange Affinities: The Gender and Sexual Politics of Comparative Racialization* (Durham: Duke University Press, 2011), 2. While they seem to overlook an embodied analysis or even an explicit disability lens, Hong and Ferguson challenge me to think about the need to construct a comparative analysis not to foster a uniform narrative but rather to question the need to make experiences legible through the exclusion or distancing of another. The alternative understandings of subjectivity, power, and collectivity remain a position of great potential and charged power.

42. I appreciate Alexis Boylan helping me think through these issues and interpretations.

43. Alyson Cole raised this point at the 2013 American Studies Association Conference where I presented a shorter version of this chapter. I appreciate her assistance in placing this image in context with others of mother and child at rest.

44. Robert McRuer, "Critical Investments: AIDS, Christopher Reeve, and Queer/Disability Studies," *Journal of Medical Humanities* 23, no. 3 (2002): 236. McRuer is quite compelling in his analysis of the erasure of queerness and disability, and I find his coalitional thinking essential. He writes, "I seek to theorize critical practices, that is, that refuse methodological distancing in order to further systemic critique and coalition-building" (ibid., 226).

45. Carrie Sandahl, "Queering the Crip or Cripping the Queer? Intersections of Queer and Crip Identities in Solo Autobiographical Performance," *GLQ* 9, nos. 1–2 (2003): 36.

46. The organization Forward Together, formally known as Asian Communities for Reproductive Justice, defines reproductive justice as follows: "When all people have the social, political and economic power and resources to make healthy decisions about our gender, bodies and sexuality for ourselves, our families and our communities. Reproductive justice aims to transform power inequities and create long-term systemic change, and therefore relies on the leadership of communities most impacted by reproductive oppression. The reproductive justice framework recognizes that all individuals are part of communities and that our strategies must lift up entire

communities to support individuals." This definition is widely available on the website for Forward Together or on the website for their project, Strong Families. I accessed this definition in their publication "Three Applications of the Reproductive Justice Lens," available at http://strongfamiliesmovement .org/assets/docs/ACRJ-Three-Applications-of-the-RJ-Lens.pdf.

47. Both organizations point to the history of sterilization abuse of women with disabilities. While at times disability may seem like an afterthought in their analysis, I want to acknowledge that their efforts to include a disability analysis are essential in fostering more coalitional work between different communities addressing reproductive intrusions and oppressions. With more coalitional work, disability analyses can move from a mere footnote to become more centrally incorporated.

48. For example see, Gwynnyth Llewellyn, "People with Intellectual Disability as Parents: Perspectives from the Professional Literature," *Journal of Intellectual and Developmental Disability* 16, no. 4 (1990): 369–80; Tim Booth and Wendy Booth, *Parenting under Pressure: Mothers and Fathers with Learning Difficulties* (Philadelphia: Open University Press, 1994); Tim Booth and Wendy Booth, "Men in the Lives of Mothers with Intellectual Disabilities," *Journal of Applied Research in Intellectual Disabilities* 15, no. 3 (2002): 187–99; Tim Booth and Wendy Booth, "Parents with Learning Difficulties in the Child Protection System," *Journal of Intellectual Disabilities* 9, no. 2 (2005): 109–29; Susan Collings and Gwynnyth Llewellyn, "Children of Parents with Intellectual Disability: Facing Poor Outcomes or Faring Okay?" *Journal of Intellectual and Developmental Disability* 37, no. 1 (2012): 65–82; Rachel Mayes and Gwynnyth Llewellyn, "Mothering Differently: Narratives of Mothers with Intellectual Disability Whose Children Have Been Compulsorily Removed," *Journal of Intellectual and Developmental Disability* 37, no. 2 (2012): 121–30; David McConnell and Gwynnyth Llewellyn, "Social Inequality, 'the Deviant Parent,' and Child Protection Practice," *Australian Journal of Social Issues* 40, no. 4 (2005): 553–66.

49. Llewellyn, "People with Intellectual Disability as Parents," 373.

50. Booth and Booth, *Parenting under Pressure*; David May and Murray K. Simpson, "The Parent Trap: Marriage, Parenthood, and Adulthood for People with Intellectual Disabilities," *Critical Social Policy* 23, no. 1 (2003): 25–43; David McConnell and Gwynnyth Llewellyn, "Stereotypes, Parents with Intellectual Disability, and Child Protection," *Journal of Social Welfare and Family Law* 24, no. 3 (2002): 297–317; Catherine Wade, Gwynnyth Llewellyn, and Jan Matthews, "Review of Parent Training Interventions for Parents with Intellectual Disability," *Journal of Applied Research in Intellectual Disabilities* 21, no. 4 (2008): 351–66.

51. Gwynnyth Llewellyn, "Talking with Parents with Intellectual Disability," in *Does This Child Need Help? Identification and Early Intervention*, ed.

Christine Johnson (Sydney: Australian Early Intervention Association, 1993), 162–69.

52. Ibid., 167.

53. Llewellyn, "People with Intellectual Disability as Parents," 337

54. Solinger, "Beggars and Choosers," 413.

55. This statement is no longer available. It was last accessed on November 6, 2010. When thinking about reproduction and parenting, often very public cases of women with intellectual disabilities dominate our attention. The "Ashley X" or "pillow angel" case in Seattle involved physicians, at the request of her parents, performing a hysterectomy and procedure to remove breast buds on their seven-year-old daughter. The parents not only wanted to prevent future menstruation and reproductive ability, but also wanted their daughter to remain smaller in stature so they could provide personal care assistance easily. Additionally, the parents considered that because their daughter's secondary sexual characteristics were removed, she would be less likely to experience sexual assault in the future. Putting aside the faulty logic that removing their daughter's breasts will somehow protect her from future abuse, the procedure has been debated and suggested, by some, as a solution to prevent unwanted pregnancy and maintain a childlike stature. The contemporary focus on controlling the reproductive capabilities of women with intellectual disabilities potentially continues the eugenic legacy of considering some women as inappropriate to reproduce.

56. This conflict of mental age provides much of the tension in the fictional movie *I Am Sam* (New Line Home Entertainment, 2001).

57. Margrit Shildrick, *Dangerous Discourses of Disability, Subjectivity, and Sexuality* (New York: Palgrave Macmillan, 2009), 64.

58. Ibid.

59. Solinger, "Beggars and Choosers," 413–14.

60. María Lugones, "Playfulness, 'World'-Traveling, and Loving Perception," *Hypatia* 2, no. 2 (1987): 4. Lugones remarks that failing to identify is a learned practice; see pp. 4–9 for an in-depth discussion of her upbringing and failure to identify.

61. See Marilyn Frye, *The Politics of Reality: Essays in Feminist Theory* (Trumansburg, N.Y.: Crossing Press, 1983), for a discussion of arrogant perception. Frye uses problematic disability metaphors of seeing and sight. Similarly, Lugones uses "schizophrenia" in her article to metaphorize the experience of women of color in the United States. Both examples point to the need for further coalitional work between disability studies, feminism, and feminist disability studies.

62. Eunjung Kim, "'Heaven for Disabled People': Nationalism and International Human Rights Imagery," *Disability and Society* 26, no. 1 (2011): 103.

63. Lugones, "Playfulness, 'World'-Traveling, and Loving Perception," 18.

6. Screening Sexuality

1. James W. Trent, *Inventing the Feeble Mind: A History of Mental Retardation in the United States* (Berkeley: University of California Press, 1994), 6.

2. Martin Halliwell, *Images of Idiocy: The Idiot Figure in Modern Fiction and Film* (Burlington, Vt.: Ashgate, 2004). According to Halliwell, "Idiocy cannot be easily defined as a specific 'condition' . . . scientific attempts to do so have usually floundered. Idiocy can more accurately be said to refer to a range of human experiences and traits that are difficult to classify, ultimately deriving from neurological impairment, but often reflected in forms of asocial behavior that can be visually mimicked" (ibid., 1). Often the result is that what is represented capitalizes on visual markers of stereotypical behaviors and demeanors. Characters with idiocy or intellectual disability are represented with external signifiers that supposedly reflect inner intellect.

3. Ibid., 216.

4. Ibid., 221.

5. Stuart Murray, *Representing Autism: Culture, Narrative, Fascination* (Liverpool: Liverpool University Press, 2008), 8.

6. Ibid., 106.

7. Margaret Price, *Mad at School: Rhetorics of Mental Disability and Academic Life* (Ann Arbor: University of Michigan Press, 2011).

8. Ibid., 1–4.

9. Sharon L. Snyder and David T. Mitchell, *Cultural Locations of Disability* (Chicago: University of Chicago Press, 2006), 19–20.

10. Julie Elman offers an excellent analysis of the intersections between disability and HIV/AIDS activism through the series *Life Goes On*. See Elman, "Cripping Safe Sex," *Journal of Bioethical Inquiry* 9, no. 3 (2012): 317–26. Elman writes, "As *Life* negotiates the thin line between resistance to and reconsolidation of cultural norms of sexuality and ability, I argue that it offered a crip politics of sexuality by engaging questions of sexual justice and pleasure for youth, disabled people, and people with HIV/AIDS—populations whose sexualities generally have been regarded as problematic, pathological, or nonexistent" (ibid., 318).

11. Tobin Siebers, "Disability as Masquerade," *Literature and Medicine* 23, no. 1 (2004): 17.

12. Philippa Gates, "Always a Partner in Crime: Black Masculinity in the Hollywood Detective Film," *Journal of Popular Film and Television* 32, no. 1 (2004): 20–29.

13. Cynthia Fuchs, "The Buddy Politic," in *Screening the Male: Exploring Masculinities in Hollywood Cinema*, ed. Steven Cohan and Ina Rae Hark (New York: Routledge, 1993), 194.

14. Trent, *Inventing the Feeble Mind*.

15. Mel Stuart et al., *Bill* (BCI Eclipse Co., 2007).

16. Morrow also wrote the story and cowrote the screenplay for *Rain Man*.

17. Anthony Page et al., *Bill: On His Own* (Brentwood Home Video, 2007).

18. Lennard J. Davis, *Enforcing Normalcy: Disability, Deafness, and the Body* (New York: Verso, 1995); Snyder and Mitchell, *Cultural Locations of Disability.*

19. I discuss sex education materials in chapter 2.

20. Barry and his wife, Bev (Largo Woodruff), call Bill, "Wild Bill of Borneo." The story of Bill Sackter is well documented. The real Bill Sackter ran a coffee shop on the campus of the University of Iowa until his death in 1983. He received the Handicapped Iowan of the Year award in 1976 and was later celebrated by President Jimmy Carter. A recent documentary, *A Friend Indeed: The Bill Sackter Story* tells Bill's story using photographs and footage shot by Barry Morrow. See Lane Wyrick, Xap Interactive, and the Extend the Dream Foundation, *A Friend Indeed: The Bill Sackter Story* (Xap Interactive, 2008).

21. Robert M. Young et al., *Dominick and Eugene* (MGM Home Entertainment, 2001).

22. Jessie Nelson et al., *I Am Sam* (New Line Home Entertainment, 2001).

23. Halliwell, *Images of Idiocy*, 225.

24. Intellectually disabled actors play the characters of Joe and Brad. Ifty and Robert participate in intellectual disability drag.

25. Valerie Lehr, *Queer Family Values: Debunking the Myth of the Nuclear Family* (Philadelphia: Temple University Press, 1999).

26. Martha Fineman, *The Autonomy Myth: A Theory of Dependency* (New York: New Press, 2004), xv.

27. Ibid., 20–21.

28. I appreciate Robert McRuer's help in thinking through the extrajudicial implications of this arrangement.

29. Robert McRuer, *Crip Theory: Cultural Signs of Queerness and Disability* (New York: New York University Press, 2006), 31.

30. David T. Mitchell and Sharon L. Snyder, *Narrative Prosthesis: Disability and the Dependencies of Discourse* (Ann Arbor: University of Michigan Press, 2000).

31. The screenplay for the film contains the following direction when Sam and Rita confess their pain and vulnerability to each other: "He looks her straight in the eye—she's undone by the intimacy of the moment, by the strength of his purity. And staring into his eyes, she begins to sob, walls crumbling. He kisses her elbow, her shoulder, her forehead, her eyes, her tears. And something ignites between them—something confused and scary and deep and filled with a passionate ache." See http://www.imsdb.com/scripts/I-am-Sam.html.

It is telling that the film ambivalently renders this moment (and its implication). What would it mean for Rita and Sam to be sexual partners?

32. James Belushi et al., *Homer and Eddie* (HBO Video, 1989).

33. Another feature common to characters with intellectual disabilities is the lack of biological family connections. Bill Sackter lived in an institution and although he has a sister, she dies before they can be reunited. Sam lived in an institution prior to living independently. Billy Bob Thornton's character in *Sling Blade* (1996) also lived in an institution because he murdered his mother and her lover. Dominick seems to be the exception to this trend.

34. Paul Longmore, "Screening Stereotypes: Images of Disabled People in Television and Motion Pictures," in *Why I Burned My Book, and Other Essays on Disability* (Philadelphia: Temple University Press, 2003); Tom Shakespeare, "Cultural Representation of Disabled People: Dustbins for Disavowal?" *Disability and Society* 9, no. 3 (1994): 283–99.

35. Juliette Lewis et al., *The Other Sister* (Buena Vista Home Entertainment, 1999); Elisabeth Shue et al., *Molly* (MGM Home Entertainment, 2000).

36. The sex education examined in chapter 2, especially the CIRCLES® curriculum, also largely reinforces that "appropriate" sexuality occurs between married heterosexual couples where reproduction is not an issue.

37. At the beginning of chapter 2, I discuss a scene from the film *Yolk* that uses the same text to provide impromptu sex education. See Stephen Lance, *Yolk* (Head Pictures, 2007).

38. Similarly, the show *Life Goes On* presents two characters with intellectual disabilities marrying and entering into a sexual relationship. For a discussion of the crip/queer potential of this television drama see Elman, "Cripping Safe Sex."

39. Pamela Block, "Sexuality, Fertility, and Danger: Twentieth-Century Images of Women with Cognitive Disabilities," *Sexuality and Disability* 18, no. 4 (2000): 250.

40. Mark Sherry discusses how there is a class-based hierarchy to intellectual disability. Often those who are of lower-class backgrounds or are poor receive diagnoses of intellectual disability at rates higher than those of upper-middle-class and wealthier backgrounds. See Sherry, *Disability and Diversity: A Sociological Perspective* (New York: Nova Science, 2008).

41. The documentary film *Monica and David* provides a contemporary example of the struggles of marriage and reproduction for individuals with intellectual disabilities. See Alexandra Codina et al., *Monica and David* (Docurama Films, 2011).

42. Often in films featuring characters with intellectual disabilities, medical professionals talk about the "mental age" of the individual as if the "mind of a three-year-old" speaks to the limitations a particular character embod-

ies. The implication is that viewers know why a particular character acts the way they do because of the age of their mind.

43. Ralph Nelson et al., *Charly* (MGM Home Entertainment, 2004); Daniel Keyes, *Flowers for Algernon* (New York: Harcourt, Brace, and World, 1966).

44. The film *Pumpkin* (Albert Berger, MGM Home Entertainment, 2002) provides a satirical look into a relationship between a man with cerebral palsy and a sorority sister. The film pokes fun at the expectation that men with disabilities are sexually unattractive to nondisabled women who embody typical standards of beauty.

45. The website d2000.com/gary.htm sold Gary T-shirts. The shirts have a picture of Gary's face with a banner above his face reading "Gary the Retard" in red block letters. Below his face is the phrase "I like boobies." Through sales of the T-shirts, the company claims to support Gary's Internet porn habit, while also allowing the wearer to "have Gary all over your chest without all that annoying drool," and that "you can have Gary's lovely face staring off your chest rather than at it." This particular site, which I last accessed on October 10, 2005, is no longer available; however, there are other fan sites that offer video clips, merchandise, or other related information.

46. Mark Sherry, *Disability Hate Crimes: Does Anyone Really Hate Disabled People?* (Burlington, Vt.: Ashgate, 2010), 30.

47. Ibid., 33.

48. Ibid., 38, 48.

49. Dan Goodley and Katherine Runswick-Cole, "The Violence of Disablism," *Sociology of Health and Illness* 33, no. 4 (2011): 614.

50. The website http://www.myspace.com/thegarytheretard is no longer active. I last accessed it on October 10, 2005. There are multiple YouTube clips of archived segments of Gary on *The Howard Stern Show*.

51. Jackson Katz, *The Macho Paradox: Why Some Men Hurt Women and How All Men Can Help* (Naperville, Ill.: Sourcebooks, 2006); Michael S. Kimmel, *The Gender of Desire: Essays on Male Sexuality* (Albany: State University of New York Press, 2005).

52. Kimmel, *The Gender of Desire*, 35.

53. C. J. Pascoe, *Dude, You're a Fag: Masculinity and Sexuality in High School* (Berkeley: University of California Press, 2007), 53.

54. Ibid., 52–83.

55. Ibid., 175.

56. Lars von Trier et al., *The Idiots* (Zentropa, 1998).

57. Anne Jerslev, "Dogma 95, Lars von Trier's *The Idiots* and the 'Idiot Project,'" in *Realism and "Reality" in Film and Media*, ed. Anne Jerslev (Copenhagen: Museum Tusculanum Press, 2002), 49.

58. Tobin Siebers, *Disability Theory* (Ann Arbor: University of Michigan

Press, 2008), 207n12. Siebers's footnote is the only disability studies engagement I was able to locate on *The Idiots*. The film is ripe for a disability studies analysis for its representation of intellectual disability and sexuality.

59. Another controversial scene occurs when one character, Stoffer, an adult man who is "spassing," is taken into a women's shower room at a local swimming pool. While in the shower, his penis becomes erect. The controversy arises because Stoffer, faking intellectual disability, uses his temporary disability status to gain access to an all-female space, which facilitates his erection. Additionally, cinematic representations of male genitalia are quite rare.

60. Jerslev, "Dogma 95, Lars von Trier's *The Idiots* and the 'Idiot Project,'" 56.

61. von Trier wanted Stoffer to "have a real erection" partially to coincide with the requirements of Dogme 95 and additionally because it would "simply be the best" if Stoffer's penis was erect (ibid., 57). For von Trier a "real" erection would perfectly highlight the apparently inappropriateness of sexual arousal in that space.

62. Two recent films, *Girlfriend* (Justin Lerner, Wayne/Lauren Film Company, 2010) and *Me, Too* (Antonio Nahrro and Álvaro Pastor, Alicia Produce, 2009, *Yo, También*), complicate the static trajectory. In both films, men with intellectual disabilities actively court women without disabilities. These films are also great texts for a disability studies analysis.

7. Smashing Disability

1. Shibani Mahtani, "'Friends Meets Skins' with a Difference," *The Guardian*, September 2, 2009.

2. *The Specials* won the 2010 Webby Award for best reality series as well as the People's Voice Award for the same category. This recognition partially demonstrates the success of the first season of the show.

3. In discussing the reality television shows *The Real World* and *Road Rules*, Mark Andrejevic points out that "the premise of the show is that the cast members live in a panopticon—not everything they are doing is taped and watched, but they have to live with the knowledge that their words and actions could, at any time, be recorded for broadcast." Andrejevic, *Reality TV: The Work of Being Watched* (Lanham, Md.: Rowman and Littlefield, 2004), 103. The housemates in *The Specials* are also subject to this panopticon and surveillance in order to share their lives and experiences. As this book was entering production, the creator, Katy Lock, announced on Facebook that the cable television station Oprah Winfrey Network would be broadcasting *The Specials* as part of a one-day marathon in September 2014 in the United States and Canada. The thirteen-episode marathon will include the first season with six reedited and expanded episodes as well as seven new episodes from the second season. Oprah Winfrey, Rosie O'Donnell, Carolyn Strauss, and

D. B. Weiss are executive producers of the second season of the show. Katy Lock and Daniel May, of KADA Media Limited, are producers of the second season. *The Specials* will also air on television in Mexico, Spain, and Sweden.

4. Ibid., 2.

5. Ibid., 5. There is an active Facebook group for *The Specials* that facilitates conversations between viewers, the producer, and cast members. There is also a hosted forum on the website for the show.

6. Margrit Shildrick, *Dangerous Discourses of Disability, Subjectivity, and Sexuality* (New York: Palgrave Macmillan, 2009), 6.

7. Examples include Paul Cambridge and Bryan Mellan, "Reconstructing the Sexuality of Men with Learning Disabilities: Empirical Evidence and Theoretical Interpretations of Need," *Disability and Society* 15, no. 2 (2000): 293–311; Monica Cuskelly and Rachel Bryde, "Attitudes towards the Sexuality of Adults with an Intellectual Disability: Parents, Support Staff, and a Community Sample," *Journal of Intellectual and Developmental Disability* 29, no. 3 (2004): 255–64; Winifred Kempton and Emily Kahn, "Sexuality and People with Intellectual Disabilities: A Historical Perspective," *Sexuality and Disability* 9, no. 2 (1991): 93–111; David Thompson, "Profiling the Sexually Abusive Behaviour of Men with Intellectual Disabilities," *Journal of Applied Research in Intellectual Disabilities* 10, no. 2 (1997): 125–39.

8. C. J. Pascoe, *Dude, You're a Fag: Masculinity and Sexuality in High School* (Berkeley: University of California Press, 2007), 13.

9. Edward W. Said, *Orientalism* (New York: Vintage Books, 1979), 5.

10. Anne McClintock, *Imperial Leather: Race, Gender, and Sexuality in the Colonial Contest* (New York: Routledge, 1995), 4–5, 14. McClintock writes in *Imperial Leather*, "I argue that race, gender and class are not distinct realms of experience, existing in splendid isolation from each other; nor can they simply be yoked together retrospectively like armatures of Lego. Rather they come into existence *in* and *through* relation to each other—if in contradictory and conflictual ways. In this sense, gender, race and class can be articulated categories" (ibid., 4–5). The encounter between the Lady Boys of Bangkok and the audience in Brighton, including Sam and his housemates, I argue, is best understood by careful attention to the contradictory and conflictual relations between race, class, gender, sexuality, *and disability.*

11. Peter A. Jackson, "Capitalism and Global Queering: National Markets, Parallels among Sexual Cultures, Multiple Queer Modernities," *GLQ* 15, no. 3 (2009): 357–95.

12. Leila J. Rupp and Verta A. Taylor, *Drag Queens at the 801 Cabaret* (Chicago: University of Chicago Press, 2003), 5.

13. Ibid., 116.

14. Raewyn Connell, *Masculinities* (Berkeley: University of California Press, 2005).

15. Jackson, "Capitalism and Global Queering," 360. MTF refers to male-to-female.

16. Lady Boys of Bangkok, "Fantasy and Feather," http://www.ladyboysof bangkok.co.uk/.

17. McClintock, *Imperial Leather*, 4–6.

18. Richard Totman comments that "there are many institutions and traditions amongst the countries of south-east Asia that are incommensurable with those of the Western world, and kathoey represent one of them. It is quite inappropriate to describe them using Western terms such as 'crossdresser,' 'transvestite' or 'gay.'" See Totman, *The Third Sex: Kathoey: Thailand's Ladyboys* (London: Souvenir Press, 2003), 10.

19. Han ten Brummelhuis, "Transformations of Transgender: The Case of the Thai *Kathoey*," in *Lady Boys, Tom Boys, Rent Boys: Male and Female Homosexualities in Contemporary Thailand*, ed. Peter Jackson and Gerard Sullivan (New York: Harrington Park Press, 1999), 124. Brummelhuis stresses in his article that for *kathoey* gender identity as opposed to sexual orientation is the central feature in their identity formulation.

20. Hannah Beech, "Where the 'Ladyboys' Are," *Time*, July 7, 2008.

21. In a 2008 article in *Time* magazine titled "Where the 'Ladyboys' Are," author Hannah Beech repeats the narrative of non-Western progress in accepting individuals who transgress gender dichotomies by glossing over any discrimination that *kathoey* face in Thailand. The trope of progress complements the Western fascination with difference and its romanticization of non-Western cultures.

22. Jackson, "Capitalism and Global Queering," 360.

23. Ibid., 359. Jackson argues that it is imperative to understand how capitalism "produces both new local forms of sexual difference and transnational commonalities" (361).

24. "Lady Boys of Bangkok Keep Edinburgh Fringe Party Going," http://www.bbc.co.uk/news/uk-scotland-edinburgh-east-fife-10918621.

25. David L. Eng, *The Feeling of Kinship: Queer Liberalism and the Racialization of Intimacy* (Durham: Duke University Press, 2010), 4.

26. Jackson, "Capitalism and Global Queering," 387.

27. Eng, *The Feeling of Kinship*, 15.

28. Rupp and Taylor remark that drag "opens a window to multiple and confusing genders and sexualities. By portraying ambiguity and inbetweenness, drag successfully invites audience members to consider what it means to be a man or woman, what it means to desire someone of a particular sex, as more complicated than they would ordinarily think." Rupp and Taylor, *Drag Queens at the 801 Cabaret*, 212.

29. Judith Butler, *Bodies That Matter: On the Discursive Limits of "Sex"* (New York: Routledge, 1993), 129.

30. Brummelhuis, "Transformations of Transgender," 130.

31. Ibid., 133.

32. Anne Fausto-Sterling discusses how bodies that do not live up to a dichotomous sex/gender system because of the appearance of a non-average phallus have to be controlled, often through violent and unnecessary corrective surgery, in order to maintain gender divisions that do not "blur the borders" of gender. Fausto-Sterling, *Sexing the Body: Gender Politics and the Construction of Sexuality* (New York: Basic Books, 2000), 5.

33. Butler, *Bodies That Matter*, 139.

34. Suzanne Kessler and Wendy McKenna, "Toward a Theory of Gender," in *The Transgender Studies Reader*, ed. Susan Stryker and Stephen Whittle (New York: Routledge, 2006), 171–72.

35. Ibid., 172, 173.

36. Ibid., 173.

37. According to José Esteban Muñoz, "Disidentification is about recycling and rethinking encoded meaning. The process of disidentification scrambles and reconstructs the encoded message of a cultural text in a fashion that both exposes the encoded message's universalizing and exclusionary machinations and recircuits its working to account for, include, and empower minority identities and identifications." José Esteban Muñoz, *Disidentifications: Queers of Color and the Performance of Politics* (Minneapolis: University of Minnesota Press, 1999), 31.

38. David L. Eng, *Racial Castration: Managing Masculinity in Asian America* (Durham: Duke University Press, 2001), 13–14.

39. "The Brains Behind: *The Specials*," http://www.netmag.co.uk/zine/discover-interview/the-brains-behind-the-specials.

40. Muñoz, *Disidentifications*, 31.

41. Anne Anlin Cheng, *The Melancholy of Race* (New York: Oxford University Press, 2001), 12.

42. M. Jacqui Alexander, *Pedagogies of Crossing: Meditations on Feminism, Sexual Politics, Memory, and the Sacred* (Durham: Duke University Press, 2005), 69.

43. Ibid., 70.

44. Eng, *The Feeling of Kinship*, 16.

45. Andrejevic, *Reality TV*, 103.

46. Richard Jenkins, *Questions of Competence: Culture, Classification, and Intellectual Disability* (New York: Cambridge University Press, 1998); Mark Rapley, *The Social Construction of Intellectual Disability* (New York: Cambridge University Press, 2004).

47. Shildrick, *Dangerous Discourses of Disability, Subjectivity, and Sexuality*, 84.

48. Sam's reading of the Lady Boys' sex/gender is presented as "wrong"

because of Robbie's insistence on informing him of the "truth." The scenes of "gender/sex misinformation" mirror another scene in which Sam finally "gets it," though that scene does not appear in the web broadcast.

49. Butler, *Bodies That Matter*, 139. Butler writes of drag performances in the film *Paris Is Burning*, "The performance is thus a kind of talking back, one that remains largely constrained by the terms of the original assailment: If a white homophobic hegemony considers the black drag queen to be a woman, that woman, constituted already by that hegemony, will become the occasion for the rearticulation of its terms; embodying the excess of that production, the queen will out-woman women, and in the process confuse and seduce an audience whose gaze must to some degree be structured through those hegemonies, an audience who, through the hyperbolic staging of the scene, will be drawn into the abjection it wants to both resist and overcome" (ibid., 132).

50. Alexander, *Pedagogies of Crossing*, 79.

51. Cheng, *The Melancholy of Race*, 10.

52. Shildrick, *Dangerous Discourses of Disability, Subjectivity, and Sexuality*, 126–27.

53. Lewis and Megan's relationship appears to be largely constructed not by visible expressions of affection (e.g., kissing, holding hands) but by claiming the labels of boyfriend and girlfriend. In the second episode, Megan discloses to the camera that they have not had their first kiss yet, despite having dated for awhile. Megan and Lewis's apparent sexual innocence is in direct contrast to Sam's vocal sexual expression of desire in this episode and later in the series. After Lewis and Megan end their relationship, Sam actively flirts with Megan. This flirting places strain on Sam and Lewis's friendship and causes some overall unease between the housemates.

54. Sam and his housemate Hilly are also shown wrestling in the kitchen. The producer asks if Sam and Hilly are secretly attracted to each other. They loudly deny the questioning, although Lucy seems to think it might be true. The wrestling scene and Lewis and Megan's date night show examples of "innocent" interactions between individuals with intellectual disabilities of the opposite sex.

55. Shildrick, *Dangerous Discourses of Disability, Subjectivity, and Sexuality*, 143.

56. Leila J. Rupp, Verta Taylor, and Eve Ilana Shapiro, "Drag Queens and Drag Kings: The Difference Gender Makes," *Sexualities* 13, no. 3 (2010): 286–87. Andrejevic remarks that "reality programming highlights the increasing importance not just of surveillance but of interactive technologies that rearrange the conventional distinctions between work and play and between consumption and production." Andrejevic, *Reality TV*, 17. Sam's productive labor as a reality star and gender theorist is seen through his interactions with his housemates, support staff, and the camera in this episode.

Index

person-first language: and self-
advocacy, 12
pity, xi, 24, 30, 40, 42, 43, 44, 210n93;
relationship to respect, 40, 45
politics of wonder, 121–22, 123, 124
Price, Margaret, 148
privacy: lack of privacy in residential settings, 6, 86, 90, 103, 122;
and masturbation, 86, 89, 96, 103;
reproduction, 122; white racialized standards, 123

queer liberalism, 123, 178–79
queer of color critique, 4
queer theory, 127–28, 193; coalitions,
234n13; and futurity, 127–28,
233–34n10

Rain Man, 149
Rapley, Mark, 10, 37, 40
Razack, Sherene, 23, 26
reality television. *See Specials, The*
Reefer Madness, 88
representations of intellectual disability: connected to professional
assessments / management, 147,
150, 160, 163; cure, 163–64; disability drag, 149, 169–70; obscure
eugenic history, 161; paternalistic,
171; sexually ableist, 157, 160, 164;
sex work, 157, 160; stereotypical,
149, 156, 170, 171, 240n2. *See also*
independence; narrative prosthesis; sexual ableism
reproductive justice, 125, 127, 128,
130, 139, 144, 193, 194; coalitions,
127, 139, 144, 193, 234n13, 238n47;
definition, 237–38n46. *See also*
reproductive rights; sexual
ableism
reproductive rights, 105, 110, 114, 115,
118, 122, 124, 126, 141–43; ableist

assumptions, 126; autonomy,
110, birth control, 106, 122, 130;
and the state, 105, 129, 192; UN
conventions, 112, 114–15
risk. *See* sex education
Roberts, Dorothy, 129, 131
Robinson, Beatrice, 96
Rockefeller, Jennette, 54, 55
Rosen, Raymond, 86
Rubin, Gayle, 56
Rupp, Leila, 176

Sackter, Bill, 150, 241n20. *See also*
Bill; *Bill: On His Own*; Morrow,
Barry
Said, Edward, 175
Sandahl, Carrie, 42, 43, 139
Schiavo, Terri, 106
Sedgwick, Eve, 84, 87
sex education: abstinence only, 49,
59, 78; assumptions of risk, 51,
61, 73, 76, 218–19n117; educator
unease, 59; heteronormativity,
66–67, 72, 75–76, 79; morality,
49, 51, 55–56, 97–98, 213n30; political views, 73; stranger danger
or harm reduction, 7, 53, 60, 71,
72, 73, 100, 160, 161, 194; "street
language" and sex education,
62–65, 68, 78, 215–16n56, 216n60;
use of dolls and drawings,
65–68, 78–79. *See also* sexual
pleasure
Sex Information and Education
Council of the United States, 49
sexual ableism: assessments of
competence, 35–36, 40; assumptions of risk, 52; challenges to,
102, 171, 174, 181, 189, 190; definition, 3, 106; harm reduction, 60;
interlocking systems of oppression, 45, 97, 106, 114, 123, 168, 175,

Michael Gill has a PhD in disability studies from the University of Illinois at Chicago. He teaches in Gender, Women's, and Sexuality Studies at Grinnell College. He is coeditor (with Cathy Schlund-Vials) of *Disability, Human Rights, and the Limits of Humanitarianism.*